1995

RADICAL SURGERY

RADICAL SURGERY

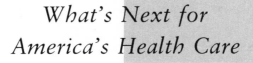

What's Next for
America's Health Care

JOSEPH A. CALIFANO, JR.

TIMES 𝕿 BOOKS

RANDOM HOUSE

Library of Congress Cataloging-in-Publication Data

Califano, Joseph A., Jr.
Radical surgery : what's next for America's health care / Joseph
A. Califano, Jr.—1st ed.
p.   cm.
Includes bibliographical references and index.
ISBN 0-8129-2413-4
1. Health care reform—United States.   2. Medical policy—United
States.   3. Medical economics—United States.   I. Title.
RA395.A3C318   1994
362.1'0973—dc20   94-19974

Manufactured in the United States of America
9 8 7 6 5 4 3 2
First Edition

For Hilary
Each day, thanks to her love, I am reborn.
And
For Joe III, my son the doctor, and
his wife, Beth, my daughter-in-law the nurse

The author is donating all royalties
from this book to the
Center on Addiction and Substance Abuse
at Columbia University.

This book is about why our politicians and physicians have re-peatedly failed to make affordable health care available to all Americans and why, if we are to succeed, we—you and I—must take the matter of reform into our own hands.

Never has the best of American health care been in such peril. The next decade will be vexing, exciting, and unpredictable, with thrills and threats for each of us, and lots of bare-knuckled street fights among doctors, hospitals, insurers, big and small businesses, pharmaceutical companies, nurses, unions, ethicists, managed care organizations, Republicans and Democrats, liberals and con-servatives, presidents and Congresses. As patients and citizens, you and I have too much at stake to leave driving the health care reform bus to them.

For more than thirty years I've been wrestling with America's health care system and, like most who've gotten into this match, I've been matted more than I've pinned. This book draws on all my experience—as an aide to Secretary of Defense Robert McNamara trying to squeeze cost savings out of military health care systems, as President Lyndon Johnson's top assistant for domestic affairs in the 1960s when he cobbled together Medicare, Medicaid, and more than two dozen other federal health programs, as an attorney in private practice representing pharmaceutical companies and other health care providers, as secretary of Health, Education, and Welfare under President Jimmy Carter, as chair of the health care committee of Chrysler Corporation's board of directors, as adviser to several large purchasers and purveyors of care, as special counsel to the governor of New York State to examine alcohol and drug abuse in the early 1980s, and as a member of the boards of a health insurer, a hospital, and a university medical affairs committee overseeing a major research and teaching complex.

Perhaps most important have been my personal experiences, particularly those of recent years: living through the deaths of my mother and father at home in their beds and watching my law partner Edward Bennett Williams and my father-in-law, Bill Paley, use every ounce of their formidable energy, their unlimited resources, and every available medical miracle in their struggles to stay alive; witnessing my stepdaughter's battle with anorexia; undergoing my own heavy-duty stomach surgery; putting a son through Harvard Medical School and watching him learn to become an otolaryngologist at Johns Hopkins Medical Center.

My earlier book *America's Health Care Revolution: Who Lives? Who Dies? Who Pays?* concentrated on financing and delivery of health care services, and (unfortunately) most of what it predicted ten years ago has come to pass because of our failure to take timely action. This book deals with more fundamental, closer-to-the-heart-mind-and-soul matters, the promise and pitfalls ahead, the corruption of Congress, and the medical miracles and emotional mayhem that our scientific genius and self-indulgence hold in store for each of us. Some bits of history and themes from my earlier book are recounted where necessary to give the reader historical perspective and reveal the evolution of my own thinking.

Over the course of my experience with our health care system, I have been increasingly struck by the limits of legislative fixes, the infinite capacity of our scientific genius, and the dimly appreciated impact of the aging of America. But nothing has impressed me more than the ravages of substance abuse—alcohol, tobacco, legal and illegal drugs—on our society. At HEW every doctor I consulted told me that I could not hope to have an effective health promotion and disease prevention program unless I mounted a massive attack on tobacco and cigarette smoking. I did just that—and it cost me my job.

In May of 1979, as I became more aware of the damage alcoholism and alcohol abuse inflict on our families and our society, I pressed for a comprehensive program to attack the problem. There, as well as in the investigation for the governor of New York, I learned of the pernicious power of alcohol and drug abuse to fill hospital beds, prison cells, welfare rolls, and emergency rooms and to scatter the homeless on our city streets. While Chrysler's health care costs have been rising at half the rate of increase for business generally, the cost of treating substance abuse continues its double-digit climb in the auto industry as it does in most large industries. At Kmart, when individuals who applied for a job in the early 1990s were asked to take a preemployment drug test, 30 percent dropped out; and of those remaining, 7 to 9 percent tested positive. That 7 to 9 percent, I have learned, is about the average portion of job seekers who come up positive in preemployment drug testing by large companies, even when they are warned in advance that they'll be tested.

As I began to talk to friends about this, Jim Burke, the former chairman of Johnson & Johnson and current chair of the Partnership for a Drug-Free America, said, "*You* ought to do something about it." As anyone who knows Jim Burke will appreciate, he didn't just say it once. He repeated it every time he talked to me.

I began discussing the problem of substance abuse with individuals around the country—doctors, businessmen, lawyers, film and television artists and producers, news editors and reporters, government officials and frontline experts in voluntary agencies, recovering alcoholics and drug addicts. I discovered that no institution in America gathered together all the skills needed to deal with all substance abuse in all aspects of society. And none was dedicated to informing the American people of the impact of all substance abuse on their lives, to finding out what works in prevention and treatment, and to encouraging every individual and institution to take responsibility to combat substance abuse. I decided to build such an organization.

I talked to several universities and concluded that an affiliation with Columbia made the most sense. Mike Sovern, then president of Columbia, and Herb Pardes, the university's vice president for medical affairs, were enthusiastic from the moment I broached the idea. On its campus, Columbia has graduate schools in business, social work, law, architecture, medicine, public health, nursing, and dentistry, as well as the renowned Teachers College; nearby are Barnard, the John Jay College of Criminal Justice, and Union and Jewish Theological Seminaries—a unique concentration of professional disciplines needed to attack the problem of substance abuse in America.

In 1991 I went to see Steve Schroeder, the physician who had recently become president of the Robert Wood Johnson Foundation in Princeton, New Jersey. He and the foundation's board had just decided to place substance abuse among their top three priorities. I had similar conversations with David Hamburg of the

Carnegie Corporation, Margaret Mahoney of the Commonwealth Fund, David Mahoney of the Dana Foundation, Franklin Thomas of the Ford Foundation, and Drew Altman of the Kaiser Family Foundation. They all agreed to support the new organization, with the Robert Wood Johnson Foundation picking up the lion's share of the initial costs.

In remarkably short order, I was able to recruit an extraordinary board of directors: Jim Burke, Betty Ford, Doug Fraser, Barbara Jordan, Don Keough, LaSalle Leffall, Manuel Pacheco, Linda Johnson Rice, John Rosenwald, Mike Sovern (who gave his seat to Columbia's new president, George Rupp), and Frank Wells (who since his untimely death has been succeeded by Mickey Schulhof).

Initially, I had planned to devote about half my time to this enterprise and half to practicing law at Dewey Ballantine. But the more I came to understand how substance abuse was implicated in just about every problem of American society—health care, homelessness, crime, violence, worker productivity, product quality, the civility of city life—the more committed I became. In 1992, I decided to devote the rest of my life to this enterprise and became the full-time chairman and president of the Center on Addiction and Substance Abuse at Columbia University—CASA.

That's how CASA—the Italian and Spanish word for house, to symbolize bringing under one roof all the skills needed to attack all substance abuse in all corners of society—was born. And that's why all the royalties I receive from this book about what it will take to succeed in making care available to all our citizens, and what lies ahead for you—whether patient, provider, or payer—in the frenetic arena of American health care, will be donated to this Center.

CONTENTS

RADICAL SURGERY

CHAPTER ONE

RADICAL SURGERY

As Jesus went along, the people were crowding him from every side. Among them was a woman who had suffered from severe bleeding for twelve years; she had spent all she had on doctors, but no one had been able to cure her. She came up in the crowd behind Jesus and touched the edge of his cloak, and her bleeding stopped at once.
     —*The Gospel according to Luke, ch. 8, also reported in Mark, ch. 5, demonstrating that running out of money as a result of medical bills and hoping for miracle cures are at least as old as the Bible*

Now comes the hard part for the American way of health.

As never before, Americans are aware of the high cost of treating illness and injury and the injustice of leaving millions of citizens out in the cold. But 85 percent of our people enjoy access to the best medical care in the world, and many of them are scared that the Congress and the president will screw it up in any effort, however well-intentioned, to contain costs and let the other 15 percent in the door.

In 1994, President and Mrs. Clinton shoved health reform to the top of Capitol Hill's agenda with a zest the nation hadn't seen since Lyndon Johnson struck up the band for Medicare and Medicaid in the 1960s. But political money tied the Congress and the president in a knot, as special interests in feeding frenzy circled several thousand pages of fine print in bills no member of Congress had read, much less understood, and political action committees lined the pockets of key committee members to protect their pieces of the trillion-dollar health industry. Nevertheless, Washington's thrust at reorganizing health care and redistributing its riches hit an industry already near chaos with the force of an earthquake, and the aftershocks will shake its foundations for the rest of the decade.

The good news is the political consensus that all Americans should have timely access to care. The bad news is that the self-centered nation's capital has lost sight of the rapidly shifting health care landscape beyond the Beltway. Washington remains mired in a single-minded struggle over how the federal government should manipulate the way sick care is paid for and delivered—when thirty years of experience demonstrate that simply doing that will not get the jobs of containing costs and expanding access done. Such manipulation will have little impact on the demographic, social, scientific, cultural, moral, and legal forces that potently influence the American way of health and fuel its high costs.

If affordable, quality care is to become part of the everyday lives of individual Americans, radical surgery will be required in the way we approach and think about health, life, and death in America.

Performing this surgery is a delicate and dicey undertaking. It will require the president to put away his veto pen, Hillary Rodham Clinton to cool her charged rhetoric, and Republican and

Democratic Senate and House leaders to get out of their partisan playpens. It will require the politicians, planners, and policy wonks to learn the lesson of 1994—that no one is smart enough to write a single law to revamp the entire health care system. And it will require all of us to recognize that reforming a swiftly evolving health care system is a perpetual process and achieving universal coverage is a long-term proposition certain to be chockful of surprises and course changes along the way.

Those who wield the scalpels must act with the painstaking attention to detail and meticulous care that neurosurgeons and cardiologists reserve for life-threatening brain tumors and heart transplants, for we are operating on the world's most sophisticated health care system; nearly one-sixth of the nation's economy; and the aches, pains, broken bones, vital organs, and lives of America's children, parents, and grandparents.

This surgery must be performed under especially difficult conditions. There is a portentous turbulence about American health care. The providers—doctors, hospitals, health maintenance organizations (HMOs), pharmaceutical giants—are reshaping health care, scrambling into mergers and networks, cooking up new delivery systems, and mounting aggressive marketing campaigns.

Doctors, some demoralized to the point of retiring early, and hospital administrators despair as bureaucratic hassling and pressures to trim costs intrude on their medical practices. The financial strain on top medical centers threatens the nation's leadership in research. Urban public hospitals are being crushed under the load of AIDS (Acquired Immune Deficiency Syndrome), tuberculosis, and substance abuse cases. Physicians press their concerns and opinions not only with their colleagues, but also with their patients.

Drug companies fear that reduced margins will cut their ability to maintain their international lead in new discoveries and to investigate long-shot treatments for diseases that cripple and kill millions of Americans. High technology fires up health costs. Medical miracles outpace our ability to conceive wise emotional, ethical, and legal frameworks to help us confront the vexing choices these new inventions present patients and physicians. The aging of America, a nation at the dawn of the world's first four-generation society, is filling our nursing homes and emptying our wallets. Our scientific genius is losing touch with our people.

Sweeping reconstruction of the American health care system is under way and will continue well into the next century. All the payers, providers, and politicians want to get their hands on the scalpel but leave fingerprints only if the operation succeeds. Senators and representatives, governors and mayors jockey for position to take the credit for any benefits of reform—and to avoid the blame for any failures and higher costs. What many of them know, but few admit, is that the hard part of reform is about to begin.

A HOUSE OF SURPRISES

Before the Congress is a medicare bill that cries out for enactment. The cost of personal health care has taken off on a straight line upward. In 1950 the annual cost of personal health care was $10.6 billion. Today it is $28.6 billion. . . . Unless we can enact an adequate medicare program, a large segment of our population will be denuded financially by severe illness.

Is it too much to ask the national community to agree to a simple, low-cost program in which an American worker puts in $1 a month

of his own money, and his employer puts in $1 a month of his com-
pany's money that is tax deductible, and the Government puts up
nothing, so that the worker can solve his medical cost problems with
dignity and not disaster? I hope that we will be able to pass a medicare
program before this Congress adjourns.
—*President Lyndon B. Johnson, December 4, 1963,*
urging members of the AFL-CIO to support
the enactment of Medicare, which cost the
taxpayers $160 billion in 1994

A half century of promises, proposals, and political parries
provides a hands-on lesson on how treacherous it can be to operate on the health care system and how the best of intentions can
produce the worst of unintended consequences when the goal is
reinventing health care in America.

The first surprise from a benevolent act of government can be
traced to World War II. The war sparked research that produced
wonder drugs, such as penicillin, and dramatic advances in surgery. People no longer went to the hospital just to ease the pain of
dying; they went to get cured. Dazzled by the powers of modern
medicine, patients wanted access to it. As wartime employers tried
to attract scarce workers, the War Labor Board administering
wage and price controls held the line on pay hikes, but permitted
increases in fringe benefits. Health insurance became the premier
fringe, and employers doled it out with a generous ladle.

Congress came along in 1947 with the Taft-Hartley Act, a rule
book for labor management relations designed to curb the power
of big unions. Unexpectedly the Supreme Court decided that the
act gave unions the right to negotiate fringe benefits, notably
health care. And negotiate they did—so well that, in six years, the
number of workers and dependents with hefty health insurance
packages rocketed from three million to thirty million.

In 1959, Big Steel ended a 116-day strike by setting a pattern to pay the entire health insurance premium for workers, thus handing every steelworker a health care credit card on which they'd never see a bill. Powerful unions in other industries, such as autos, aluminum, and communications, demanded the same deal and got it from employers who paid scant attention because health care cost so little. As a result, the employers became hostage to a health care industry that had no incentive to contain costs.

The hand of government grew strong during the 1960s. To get health care to poor rural Americans, Congress passed the Kerr-Mills Act in 1960, with the sponsorship of the powerful Oklahoma senator and the Arkansas congressman who chaired the House Ways and Means Committee. The package covered everything from hospital, surgical, and physician care to drugs and false teeth, then a special need of the poor elderly in the South. But to the dismay of Senator Robert Kerr and Representative Wilbur Mills, by 1963 five large industrial states with only 32 percent of the elderly population (California, New York, Massachusetts, Michigan, and Pennsylvania) had grabbed 90 percent of the federal money in their bill.

Seizing upon Mills's frustration, during the negotiations over Medicare, Lyndon Johnson cooked up the idea that Kerr-Mills could be changed to cover welfare recipients and other "medically indigent" individuals without regard to age. That, Johnson told Mills, would get funds to "poor mamas and babies" in rural and southern states. To enhance the appeal of his program and offer a hand to the rural elderly who would otherwise live alone in isolated areas, Johnson added coverage of nursing home care.

Thus was Medicaid born, with little appreciation of the imminent aging of America (prolonged by the health care provided by Medicare and Medicaid) or the separation of family generations that a mobile society and rising divorce rate would encourage. Johnson and Mills would turn in their graves to learn that in 1994 Medicaid spent a quarter of its $150 billion budget on nursing homes, having created an $85 billion industry, up from $2 billion in 1965. And they would chortle to learn that Medicaid is busting the budgets of the big industrial states.

The ripple of unexpected consequences did not end there. To pry Medicare and Medicaid out of the Senate Finance Committee, Johnson had to agree to pay hospitals their costs plus a guaranteed percentage, and to pay doctors fees that were "reasonable," "customary," and "prevailing" in their communities, a reimbursement scheme commercial insurers had rejected for years because it gave physicians the power to raise their own fees.

Johnson went along because he was anxious to ensure access to care for poor and older Americans. In early 1965, sitting in his small green hideaway next to the Oval Office, Johnson pressed White House lobbyist Larry O'Brien and Health, Education, and Welfare legislative aide Wilbur Cohen (who later became HEW secretary) to get the Medicare/Medicaid bill out of the Congress and onto his desk for signing.

"It'll cost a half-billion dollars to make the changes in reimbursement standards to get the bill out of the Senate Finance Committee," Cohen explained.

"Five hundred million! Is that all?" Johnson exclaimed with a wave of his big hand. "Do it. Move that damn bill out now before we lose it."

With his single-minded focus on access for the poor and elderly, Johnson grossly underestimated the price of turning over keys for the federal treasury to doctors, hospitals, nursing homes, and insurers. When he tried to change the locks three years later, Congress refused to give him authority to establish new, sensible payment systems to encourage efficient health care delivery and restrain costs.

The next unpleasant surprise came from our well-intentioned effort to increase the number of doctors. I was then on the White House staff as President Johnson's top domestic aide. We feared that with too few doctors to handle the increased demand from new federal programs, the price of their scarce services would rise. Over the strenuous objections of the American Medical Association, we rammed through legislation to provide funds to double the number of doctors graduating from medical school each year from eight thousand to sixteen thousand.

We have since discovered that more doctors mean more care and higher health care costs. Even our efforts to democratize access to the best medicine by financing the training of more specialists bit back, as more specialists encouraged more referrals to specialists and consequent spiraling medical bills.

In 1965, Johnson got Congress to pass the Heart Disease, Cancer and Stroke bill to create great medical centers in every part of the nation. "You shouldn't have to travel to New York or Boston to get the best medical care," he would complain. "That kind of care should be available in Houston, Cleveland, Dallas, Seattle, and St. Louis—in every major city." By creating these centers, providing funds for them to conduct sophisticated research, and paying medical schools to train specialists to serve them, this Great Society effort did indeed democratize high-tech treatment— but it also poured high-octane gasoline on the fires of health care inflation.

LBJ and every president since have sought to stem booming health care costs, trying everything from price controls to promoting HMOs and managed care. To hold down doctors' fees, Medicare established a list of procedures for reimbursement, capping the amount it would pay for each. That effort created gigantic insurance company bureaucracies to play catch-up with doctors who simply created additional procedures and performed them more frequently. In the late 1960s, there were two thousand medical procedure payment codes. Today, there are more than seven thousand, most with subcategories.

Stunned by the explosion in high-ticket technology and the expansion of hospitals well beyond necessary capacity (prompted by the Hill-Burton Act of 1946, which financed hospital construction, and by Medicare, which reimbursed capital costs), in 1974 Congress passed the Health Planning and Resources Development Act, which required hospitals to obtain certificates of need before they could increase the number of beds, build new wings, or buy expensive equipment.

Surprised again! When as secretary of Health, Education, and Welfare in the late 1970s I tried to eliminate more than 130,000 unnecessary hospital beds, the cumbersome certificate-of-need program gave hospitals an incentive to resist. They feared that if circumstances changed (say, because of an epidemic of some new disease or the return of an old one such as tuberculosis), they would never get permission to expand.

Next came the attempt to hold down hospital costs by creating Diagnosis Related Groups (DRGs) to limit lengths of stay and intensity of care for Medicare hospitalizations by creating a fixed payment based on a patient's diagnosis, age, overall health status, and other criteria. The results? The population of Medicare patients promptly got "sicker" as doctors jacked up diagnoses to the highest-paying DRGs possible. And commercial insurance premiums rose as hospitals hiked charges to private plans that didn't have DRG limits, in order to compensate for the shortfall from Medicare and Medicaid.

The fashion in the 1990s is managed care, which strives to curb unnecessary hospitalization, surgery, and tests by scrutinizing physicians' decisions and financially penalizing doctors and patients for unnecessary care. Managed care has helped contain some costs, but its process of reviewing every physician, procedure, prescription, and provider has helped make America's health care system the world's most expensive to administer at an annual cost approaching $200 billion, and it has angered doctors and patients seeking reimbursement from penurious insurers.

As public and private bureaucrats, trying to foist the burden of health care costs onto someone else's shoulders, continue to play "gotcha!" with doctors and hospitals, patients are left to wonder whether they can afford the care they need and whether their bills will be bankrolled by their insurer or bankrupt their personal finances. In moments of candor, some bureaucrats even confess a little guilt that cutting costs—not improving quality of care—has become the pacesetter for health policymakers in the 1990s.

I make this recital not to show that policymakers have been playing "Abbott and Costello Go to the Doctor" for the past fifty years and not simply to confess my own miscalculations in tinkering with American health care, but to demonstrate that the principle of *caveat emptor* applies to reinventions of the system devised by policy wonks. The radical surgery that lies ahead is too important to be left to the best and brightest politicians, physicians, and policy gurus. Each of us must be prepared to take a scalpel in hand.

WHAT'S WRONG?

We, the richest, most technologically and economically advanced nation in the world's history, haven't got it together to provide timely, affordable, high-quality care to all our people.

Why not?

Because we're obsessed with the financing and delivery of sick care.

To have a system that will provide each of us all the care we need—and no more—we must change fundamentally the way we think about health.

First, we must look at all three dimensions of health: research, health promotion and disease prevention, and treatment. Trying to fix the nation's health care system by focusing solely on how we pay for and provide sick care is like trying to cure leukemia by treating only one part of the bone marrow.

Second, we must acknowledge the impact of powerful forces in modern society that affect health and drive up the costs of care. What do seat belts, divorce, gun laws, beer, chewing tobacco, food, poverty, air pollution, violence, discrimination, education, sex, sunshine, toys, stress, speed limits, icy sidewalks, lead paint, lousy parents, butter, and bungee jumping have in common? In ways big and small, they all affect our health care system.

Third, we must recognize how the pandemic of substance abuse and addiction, the aging of our population, and the rush of technological innovation present a formidable triple threat that any serious attempt to restrain health care costs must address front and center.

Fourth, we must understand how our inventive and scientific genius, which has pushed the envelope of life, self-preservation, and death, inevitably invites religion and ethics into the inner sanctum of society's health care system, inciting tense conflicts among a people that constitute the most pluralistic civilization under one flag since God scrambled the tongues at the Tower of Babel. We must devise ways to accommodate deeply held, often conflicting beliefs about when life begins and ends—and who has the right to begin and end it.

Fifth, governments, businesses, insurers, and doctors must accept the limits of their ability to fool with human nature. One rule will always hold: Cutting costs is fine for government bureaucrats and corporate financial officers, but spare no expense when it comes to me or my family.

Sixth, we must understand how cultural attitudes that influence individual behavior offer greater opportunities to curb costs and increase access than all the laws, regulations, financing gimmicks, and theories of the policy wonks sitting in Washington, state capitols, city halls, and corporate suites, and all the Monday morning quarterbacks perched before their computer terminals at insurance and managed-care companies.

Seventh, we must accept the reality of our own mortality, understand the essence of human dignity, and accept responsibility for our own health. That means a vast change in the way we live and die.

Eighth, we must accept the fact that health care is a one-on-one, personal service experience, and touching will always be a key part of healing.

Ninth, we must free federal and state elected officials from dependence on private money for their political campaigns. Health industry lobbyists dig into their deep pockets to press for more sick care at the expense of health promotion and disease prevention.

Tenth, we must learn from our successes (there have been many) and failures (there have been at least as many) that unintended effects are the rule, not the exception, in the history of tinkering with the health care industry. Murphy's Law was written for America's health care reformers.

Eleventh, we must be careful to preserve the best of American medicine, for at its best, America's system of treating the sick has no peer. That means heeding the African Basuto tribe's proverb "If a man does away with his traditional way of living and throws away his good customs, he had better first make certain that he has something of value to replace them."

The stakes are high. At risk is not only whether our children and grandchildren will have to be wealthy enough to fly to Geneva, Munich, or Tokyo to get the best health care, instead of driving to New York, Chicago, or Houston, but also whether we can mend the seams of the social fabric that binds the generations, with children caring for their parents as their parents cared for them; whether we can fulfill our commitment to social justice for every citizen, whatever the hue of his skin or the depth of his pockets; and whether we can distribute resources fairly and honor the dignity to which each individual is entitled. At risk is not simply much of our national wealth, but much of our individual and national self-esteem and our claim to moral integrity.

WHAT NEXT?

As we examine all the dimensions of our distinctly American system, look over the horizon to see how other forces affect our health, and accept the demographic, psychological, and scientific realities of our nation as it enters the twenty-first century, we will see that only radical surgery, performed with exacting care, can save the best of American medicine, enhance its genius and greatness, and democratize its miracle cures.

But before we can determine how and where to perform that surgery, we must diagnose America's health care system, which is on the cusp of chaos.

CHAPTER TWO

THE CUSP OF CHAOS

Never have such sound and fury attended American health care. Never have the system and the industry been in such turmoil.

Once upon a time in America, modern medicine was a doctor carrying a little black bag filled with a thermometer; stethoscope; cotton balls; throat swabs; a magnifying glass to concentrate light for peering into the ears, noses, and eyes of patients; sticks to hold down your tongue when you said "ahhh"; aspirin to relieve aches and pains; and perhaps small bottles of medicinal potions or Smith Brothers cherry-flavored cough drops to soothe the sore throats of children.

These were about the contents of the little black bag carried by the doctor who in 1939 visited my grandfather at 1335 Bergen Street in Brooklyn, New York, when he wasn't feeling too well. The doctor talked to Grandpa Califano, a short man with a full mustache and weak kidneys. He took his temperature, poked around, peered down his throat, and pressed the stethoscope against his chest and back. He then told my Aunt Rosalie Scotto (in whose house my grandfather was living) that her eighty-year-old father was fine and departed for his next house call.

Before the doctor got to the corner of Bergen Street and Kingston Avenue, less than half a block away, my grandfather died of a heart attack. Grandpa Califano could just as easily have lived for another five years for all the doctor knew.

Doctors don't make many house calls anymore, but technological miracles, pharmaceutical wonders, and rigorous training in medical schools and hospitals have given them the ability to find out, with more accuracy than hunch, and sooner rather than later, what's wrong with us and how to relieve our ills and aches.

God still keeps plenty of surprises to Himself, but the offices of today's doctors and hospitals bulge with high-tech scanners that can reveal the body's inner secrets without breaking the skin; intricate tools that can remove gallbladders and repair knee cartilage through tiny incisions; hulking machines that can stand in for hearts, lungs, and kidneys that have stopped working; and prescription pads that can open the door to a world of powerful drugs to remedy everything from influenza and high blood pressure to diabetes and depression.

Training and hiring the medicine men and women of the 1990s demand a lot more money than it cost to prepare Grandpa Califano's doctor, and their sophisticated tools, machines, and wonder drugs are far more expensive than the contents of his small black bag. This potent combination of the best minds and technology that money can buy has the power to hold off the angel of death, heal the sick, sooth the anxious, and bankrupt the nation, all at the same time.

Needled by anxious constituents who demand access to this world of medical miracles and "damn the cost!" and by a deep-pockets industry that makes its money treating ailments, Congress has concentrated obsessively on providing sick care to its constituents. This one-dimensional focus is not enough to assure every

American access to affordable, quality care, however numerous the laws, tight the regulations, and loud the trumpeters of political promises. To understand why, we must survey the varied and swiftly changing topography of the health care system—its disparate quality, monumental achievements, tragic failures, and mind-boggling complexity.

THE TRILLION-DOLLAR POT

As America approaches the twenty-first century, doctors administer, if they don't always control, the world's most spectacularly advanced and expensive medical care. Health care in America has grown from a genteel profession of neighborhood doctors who in 1940 oversaw a $4 billion system, to a trillion-dollar-a-year enterprise in 1994 that exceeds all the goods and services produced by half the states in the country.

Health is the nation's biggest business. It accounts for almost a sixth of the entire economy, heading toward a fifth at the turn of the century. Health care spending has been climbing many times faster than the population, which has generally been increasing about one percent a year since the early 1960s. In 1994, we spent nearly $4,000 for every man, woman, child, and fetus in America. At the top of the twenty-first century, that bill will exceed $6,000.

The health industry directly employs almost eleven million Americans, ranging from highly trained and skilled brain surgeons to poorly educated, sometimes illiterate bedpan attendants in hospitals. Public and private hospitals have more than five million workers. Doctors' offices engage one and a half million. More than two million work in nursing care facilities or help patients at home. Dentists' offices employ more than half a million, as do laboratories and offices of other health practitioners, such as chiropractors, dieticians, and physical therapists. The medical instruments and supplies business, health insurers, and the pharmaceutical industry each put roughly three hundred thousand individuals to work.

Over the decade ending in 1993, the health industry produced one of every seven new jobs in the economy. Even during the months of deep recession (from July 1990 to March 1991) when the rest of the economy lost two million jobs, health care added 224,000 men and women to its payroll. In the sluggish two years after the recession, it accounted for two-thirds of the 850,000 jobs created. In 1994, the health industry employed more people than construction and transportation combined.

Despite its spectacular size and successes, the American health care system is a source of national embarrassment as well as pride. Millions of Americans get care that is too little or too late, leaving preventable and treatable ailments to fester, spread, and kill. Hospitals struggle to make ends meet as the quality of their care and surrounding amenities deteriorates. Doctors are demoralized as patients and plaintiffs' lawyers second-guess their judgment, while administrators and auditors by the thousands stick their fingers into every nook and cranny of the system, with the ironic promise of improving efficiency.

America—the place to go if you've got an undiagnosed ailment or life-threatening disease and the money to pay the bills—has a health care system in unprecedented turmoil. To understand this, it is first necessary to know where all the money goes and just what we—the employers, workers, and taxpayers who foot the bills—receive for the trillion dollars we ante into the health industry.

TEMPLES OF THE MEDICINE MEN AND WOMEN:
39 CENTS OF EVERY DOLLAR

Here is what Connecticut's Stamford Hospital is up against this morning:

A twenty-year-old Guatemalan woman lies unconscious in the critical care ward. Her new daughter, four months premature, is in neonatal. Since she is an illegal immigrant, Medicaid won't pay her bill, mounting at $2,000 a day. No one will.

In the oncology unit, an old woman with breast cancer grows weaker. "I don't think she's leaving the hospital," says her doctor, who hopes she will refuse the chemotherapy that would painfully prolong her life. There is another pressure, says nurse Susan Worland: "The insurance company keeps calling me, saying: 'When can she go home? When can she go home?' "

—Business Week, *January 17, 1994*

America's 6,500 hospitals, which house 1.2 million beds, are the high-tech temples of America's medicine men and women. They collect almost 40 percent of the trillion dollars spent on health care a year; yet many are in serious trouble. Most (5,292) are community, short-stay institutions that we think of if we have to go to the hospital.

Half of all hospitals, with 674,000 beds, are private, nonprofit institutions. Federal, state, and local governments run another third, with 370,000 beds, including 171 Veterans Administration and 125 military hospitals. The rest, with 133,000 beds, operate for a profit; many are publicly held companies whose stockholders demand dividends and rising equity value, just like the owners of any other corporation. Of the 790 psychiatric hospitals, half are for-profit enterprises.

Hospitals are changing faster than our perception of them.

Getting into a hospital bed is much harder in 1994 than it was in the early 1980s. Despite a 10 percent increase in the general population from 1982 to 1992, the number of admissions to community hospitals dropped almost 15 percent, from 36.4 million to 31 million. Once you're in the hospital, however, getting out is a lot easier than it was in the early 1980s. Pressured by Medicare and private insurers to cut costs, community hospitals have reduced the average length of stay by 7 percent over the same period, and the average stay for elderly patients, who are most likely to linger, dropped 18 percent.

In comparison, health care systems in other countries look languorous. If you have a baby in America, you'll almost certainly be out of the hospital within forty-eight hours. In Canada, your stay would last about four days, and in Switzerland, you'd be treated to a week of pampering. It's rare for patients with cataracts to be in an American hospital more than a few hours; in English and German hospitals, they stay more than a week. In America, heart attack victims usually leave the hospital within nine days; German, Canadian, and Spanish hospitals keep them for two weeks. A bout with bronchitis? Expect a six-day stay in America, twelve in England, and seventeen if you catch the bug in Germany.

The result of fewer admissions and briefer stays in American hospitals is that even after eliminating 182,000 beds from 1982 to 1992, only two-thirds of those remaining were occupied on a typical day in 1994. In many hospitals more than half the beds are empty. Any ordinary business operating at less than 50 percent of capacity would go into bankruptcy. But the nonprofits still keep their doors open and the for-profits still manage to turn a buck for their investors.

How can this be?

For most hospitals, the price a patient pays to spend the night has become a loss leader, much like selling a can of tennis balls for $1.75 at a sports store in the hope that consumers will get hooked on the sport and buy piles of high-profit tennis gear. Medicaid and Medicare pay less than what it costs a hospital to host a patient overnight; private insurers are demanding the same low price. However, once the bed is filled, the cash register starts ringing for insurers that reimburse for each service hospitals provide. Money comes from charges for everything from high-priced diagnostic and treatment technology to aspirins, sleeping pills, and disposable thermometers.

"Technology is where the money is," a hospital lobbyist admitted. Nine of ten community hospitals have an ultrasound machine ($200 an exam). Three of four have a CAT (computerized axial tomography) scanner ($500 a scan). One in four has an MRI (magnetic resonance imaging) machine ($1,000 an image). One in ten has a PET (positron emission tomography) scanner ($1,500 a scan).

These beeping and blinking diagnostic machines are just the tip of the technology iceberg. One in five community hospitals offers open heart surgery (at least $30,000). Many can shoot shock waves at your torso to pulverize kidney stones ($2,000 a lithotripsy), or transplant organs ($100,000 to $300,000 for a new heart, kidney, liver, or lung).

Hospitals also pile on charges for low-tech, small-change extras that add up to big profits: $26 for eye patches (cost: 90 cents), $45 for a bag of saline solution (cost: 81 cents), $104 for crutches (cost: $8), $118 for heating pads (cost: $6), and $278 for thigh-bone slings (cost: $38).

No wonder when the Conference Board, a respected business research organization in New York City, asked individuals to rank fifty products and services (from poultry to lawyers' fees) according to value received for price paid, hospital charges came in dead last. The experience of Bob Solomon, a Princeton, New Jersey, resident, helps explain why. Solomon didn't worry about the expense of his heart surgery in 1993 because he had excellent private insurance. But when curiosity prompted a look at his hospital bills, Solomon was astounded by a $47,783.57 charge, accompanied by the concise explanation: "MISCELLANEOUS."

As government and business health care purchasers pressed to trim inpatient costs, hospitals scratched around for other places to make money. They found one in outpatient treatment. While inpatient admissions fell during the 1980s, outpatient visits to community hospitals rose 41 percent. In 1982, hospitals performed one in five surgical procedures on an outpatient basis. By 1992, more than half of all hospital-based surgery was done without an overnight stay. Many hospitals also added rehabilitation, home health care, nutrition counseling, and alcohol and drug treatment to their catalogue of outpatient services.

With little scrutiny of outpatient procedures in the mid-1980s, many hospitals and ophthalmologists billed more for a cataract operation performed on an outpatient basis than for one performed in the hospital. Some unbundled charges that would normally have appeared on a single bill, dividing them into several charges to trigger additional reimbursement. Hospitals began billing preadmission testing as a separate outpatient procedure, rather than as a part of the inpatient treatment for which the tests were a prerequisite.

Private insurers and government regulators responded by tightening the bureaucratic screws. To put a lid on cataract surgery, Congress passed a law limiting payments for outpatient, as well as inpatient, cataract surgery. To curb the practice of unbundling, Medicare extended the preadmission period considered as inpatient care from one to three days.

With each parry and thrust, insurance auditors loomed more heavily over the shoulders of hospitals and doctors, piling on paperwork and forcing them to hire help. On an average day in 1968, American hospitals employed 435,100 managers and clerks to oversee care for 1,378,000 patients. By 1990, the number of hospital administrators had tripled to 1,221,600 even though the number of patients had fallen 38 percent to 853,000. By 1994, hospital administrative costs had climbed to $100 billion.

This prickly administrative hair shirt, combined with the demands of technologically sophisticated treatment, have hiked the number of employees in American hospitals far above those in Western Europe. There are almost four hospital workers for each hospital bed in the United States, compared to two or fewer in most European countries. Even so, in a 1992 survey of ten thousand nurses, 70 percent said they didn't have enough time to spend with patients.

THE DECLINE IN QUALITY

A mildly retarded, diabetic woman, feeling lethargic and having difficulty breathing, entered North Central Bronx Hospital of New York City. After diagnosing the patient's ailment as acute pulmonary edema (lungs filled with fluid), the hospital rushed her to the intensive care unit. Despite her condition, the staff gave her fluids intravenously, overloading her body. In a frenzy, she removed a tube that had been inserted to help her breathe. A broken elevator caused a 15-minute delay before an anesthetist arrived to replace the tube. The patient didn't respond to treatment and died in five days. When a routine state health department investigation uncovered the facts, hospital officials promised to repair the building's elevators.
—New York State Health Department documents, 1993

Many city hospitals, particularly public ones, are understaffed, underfinanced, and overwhelmed with AIDS, tuberculosis, accidents, and ailments related to poverty. Institutions of last resort for urban America's social problems, their emergency rooms are wall to wall with drug and alcohol abusers, victims of violence, and uninsured patients with minor health concerns but without regular doctors.

Some hospitals can be as dangerous as city streets. Stanley Brezenoff, who headed New York City's Health and Hospitals Corporation in the 1980s, told me that among his primary concerns were assault, rape, and even murder of employees by drug-crazed patients, especially in emergency rooms. In 1993, Damascio Ibarra Torres, age forty, walked into the emergency room of the University of Southern California Hospital in Los Angeles and opened fire on three doctors, seriously wounding them, because he'd been required to wait at the hospital while in pain.

Even the finest medical centers are threatened by the rapid boil of social and financial pressures that are transforming health care during the 1990s. Teaching hospitals are being forced to adapt to stiff price competition that employers and insurers have imposed on the business of health. Traditionally such hospitals attracted patients by offering the most advanced and complete services with little concern for the price, a rivalry well suited to cutting-edge medical providers. If some patients couldn't afford to pay their bills, teaching hospitals dipped into their endowments or charged more to the fully insured. Such payments and Medicare reimbursement helped cover the expense of educating medical students and conducting research to push the limits of medical care. In the early 1990s, as endowments shrank, big corporate purchasers demanded lower prices, and Medicare capped payments below cost, teaching hospitals accumulated a growing pile of unpaid bills. This brave new world of price competition threatens the greatness of American medicine.

The competition comes at hospitals from all sides. Insurance companies are assembling their own networks of health care providers. Doctors are gussying up their offices with equipment every bit as high-tech as that available in many hospitals. More than 1,500 outpatient surgical centers throughout the country offer everything from cataract extractions to hernia repairs.

Many rural and some urban hospitals have been reduced to marginal health care providers; some have even become dangerous. From 1981 to 1992, admissions fell 39 percent at rural hospitals and 8 percent at urban hospitals. Three-fourths of the surviving 2,300 rural community hospitals had fewer than a hundred beds, and on a typical day not even half were occupied. Bowing to financial pressures to cut corners as misguided local pride keeps these hospitals open, many are falling below acceptable standards of quality.

THE MEDICINE MEN AND WOMEN: 19 CENTS OF EVERY DOLLAR

The nation's six hundred thousand doctors take almost $200 billion a year of the money Americans spend on health care. More important, physicians control 75 percent of all health care expenditures. That means you can't change the health care system without their cooperation, and how physicians practice medicine will be decisive in the success or failure of any reform efforts. Beating up the image of doctors may help politicians ram through legislative reforms, but it does little to maintain, much less enhance, the quality of care. More influential than all the laws and auditors are how doctors are trained and motivated, how they view their responsibility to patients, how they react to the lures and prods of governments and employers who pay for their services and to the demands of patients who seek them.

With their power to prescribe drugs, order up every manner of diagnostic test, perform surgical procedures, and place patients in hospital beds and intensive care units, the most expensive weapon in the medical arsenal is not a $7 million PET scanner, a $2,000-a-month course of therapy for a chronic disease, a $3,000-a-day intensive care unit, or a billion-dollar tertiary care hospital. The most expensive weapon is the doctor's pen, which can launch juggernauts of health care spending.

After years as underpaid and overworked residents, medical students expect to enter a lucrative profession. Surgeons, whose average income is $260,000 a year, earn more than twice as much as general and family practitioners, whose average income is $115,000 a year. Some surgeons make millions. You won't find millionaires among general and family practitioners; a quarter of them make less than $75,000.*

So doctors stampede to specialties such as heart surgery (average 1993 income: $630,000), cardiology ($400,000), orthopedic surgery ($375,000), diagnostic radiology ($340,000), and anesthesiology ($260,000). The conventional wisdom of most planners favors a mix of one specialist to each primary care doctor in general and family medicine, internal medicine, and pediatrics. But the current ratio is a top-heavy two to one which, coupled with limits on the practice of medicine by nurses, results in acute shortages of

---

*Interestingly, the pay of a congressional member, many of whom want to cap physician fees, comes to at least $208,000 annually, nearly double the average family physician's net income of $115,000. The base pay of a senator or representative is $133,600 (majority and minority leaders receive $148,400; the Speaker of the House, $171,500). The value of a typical pension is $60,000 a year; family health insurance coverage, roughly $10,000; benefits, such as airport parking and a tax deduction for maintaining D.C. and home-state residences, $5,000. The $208,000 does not include the value of "franked" mail, free long-distance telephone service, subsidized gyms and haircuts, and other perks.

primary care in some areas, and in others forces specialists, whose services are much costlier, to fill the void.

In September 1989, when my son Joe III entered Harvard Medical School, the overwhelming majority of his class professed an intention to go into primary care. By graduation in June 1993, more than 75 percent of the class had opted for specialties, prompted not only by monetary rewards and the need to pay off education debts, but also by an interest in research; the role models of talented, subspecialized professors; the excitement and satisfaction of pushing the envelope of medical discovery; and the hope of having more control over their working hours. My son chose otolaryngology for several of those reasons.

If recent trends (in 1993, fewer than one in five medical school graduates chose primary care) and Harvard's class of 1993 are any indication, as America enters the twenty-first century the likes of Dr. James Kildare and Marcus Welby, M.D., family doctors devoted to delivering basic care with patience and a human touch, are an endangered species.

THE MYSTERY OF MEDICINE

In the old days, patients would go to church and pray to God when they wanted a miracle. Now they go to the hospital and demand it of physicians. We have to re-establish a common sense notion that doctors can only do what nature allows them to do. We are not God.
—*Larry Schneiderman, an internist at the University of California–San Diego School of Medicine*

Physicians used to quip that the difference between a doctor and God was that God did not think he was a doctor. Today few doctors claim divine wisdom. Even with an armada of advanced pharmaceutical and medical tools, physicians are painfully aware of how little they know about what makes people sick or healthy and how at variance their sense of mystery is with the demanding expectations of patients who seek a quick cure for every ill.

A graduating student at Harvard Medical School's 1993 commencement captured the limits of modern medicine when he remarked that, in their first year, new students answered most questions by saying, "I don't know." But after four years in the nation's top medical school, learning from world-class experts and Nobel winners, the new graduate's answer to most questions was "*We* don't know."

Sometimes it takes a tragedy to expose the guesswork and limits of medical care. After collapsing during a basketball game on April 29, 1993, Reggie Lewis, captain of the Boston Celtics, sought the best medical care that money could buy. A "dream team" of twelve specialists convened by the New England Baptist Hospital warned that the superstar suffered from a career-ending, life-threatening heart condition. But a second team of specialists at Brigham and Women's Hospital concluded that Lewis had a benign neurological problem that should not curtail his career. Confused, Lewis sought a third opinion from another group of preeminent specialists, but they couldn't resolve the dispute.

On July 27, 1993, Lewis died of a heart attack during a low-key workout on the basketball court.

RUNNING IN PLACE: BUREAUCRATIC TRAPS AND LAWYERS' LAIRS

Get the insurance companies out of my hair. I did not go to medical school to spend 40 percent of my time talking to nonphysicians on the phone about trivial details that have nothing to do with patient care. I went to medical school to meet patients and take care of patients.
—Gilbert Mudge, Jr., cardiologist, on "Who Shall Be Healed?"
Public Broadcasting System, January 1993

After preparing for ten years or so to hang out their shingles, doctors resent the time they must spend on the phone reviewing every procedure and prescription with government bureaucrats and insurance company clerks who sit poised before computer profiles of patients and beneath the banner of managed care. Often, high school graduates without medical training are at the other end of the line, deciding whether to reject or approve a doctor's bill. Reginald Harris, an internist in Shelby, North Carolina, complained, "It makes us a little suspicious when we provide a diagnosis and the reviewer says, 'Spell it.' "

By 1992, virtually all insurers required approval before admission to a hospital (except in emergencies), conducted ongoing reviews of a patient's treatment, and managed individual cases almost daily to hold down costs on large claims. Most insurers now monitor mental health care, require a second opinion for elective surgery, offer incentives to choose ambulatory over inpatient surgery, and penalize patients who seek nonurgent care in emergency rooms. These managed-care strategies make insurers the bad guys in the eyes of the patients, doctors, and hospitals and fat targets for political potshots.

Yet, in the new world of costly medical procedures and with doctors' bills rising an average of 11 percent a year from 1980 to 1994, insurers are not likely to back off. On a typical day, Dr. Stephen Boren, a medical director of CNA Insurance Company, handled numerous requests involving millions of dollars, including: three for high-dose chemotherapy with bone marrow transplants to treat breast cancer, one for a liver transplant to treat alcoholic cirrhosis, one for treatment of an infant with a hypoplastic heart (who died—$700,000 in medical bills and a heart transplant later), and two for kidney transplants in patients with renal failure.

In 1993 I had an operation to remove about a foot of my

intestine. It was performed at New York Hospital by one of the nation's top abdominal surgeons. My health insurance paid for the surgery ($5,000), but refused to pay the $150 that the surgeon charged to remove the staples a few weeks later. The reason: Insisting that it was unnecessary to use staples, the reviewer thought that dissolving sutures would have been sufficient. My doctor's response: Any surgeon who would make a foot-long incision in someone's stomach in 1993 and not use staples as well as sutures would be irresponsible.

A few years ago, Peter Goldberg, then president of the Prudential Foundation, was rushed to the hospital with severe chest pain and shortness of breath. Doctors concluded he needed an immediate coronary bypass. But Goldberg had to wait on a gurney while one of the physicians called his managed-care plan to convince its administrators of the need in advance of the surgery so that Goldberg would receive maximum reimbursement. Fortunately Goldberg survived the half-hour and the operation was a success, but his story shows that no one can escape the bureaucratic traps that threaten the quality of American health care.

At the same time, the medical malpractice system puts pressure on doctors to run batteries of unnecessary tests. As doctors see it, they're pinched between the malpractice lawyers' rock and the managed-care hard place. The onslaught of litigation, with its premium on flamboyant advocacy before impressionable juries, pushes them to subject patients to the risk and expense of procedures and tests that they consider unnecessary or inappropriate, and tight-fisted insurance and government bureaucrats press them not to perform procedures that they believe are necessary and appropriate.

In 1989, my stepdaughter Brooke had a painful earache. Our family doctor prescribed an antibiotic. The ache persisted and

Brooke experienced occasional balance difficulties. She went to Dr. Patrick Coyne, one of the top otolaryngologists in Washington, D.C. He ordered similar therapy and told her that it took time to kill the kind of infection from which she was suffering. Feeling no improvement two days later, at her mother's suggestion Brooke called Dr. Coyne and asked whether she might have a brain tumor and should get a CAT scan.

Dr. Coyne called me. He knew my views about unnecessary care, but with Brooke's request, he felt he had no choice but to refer her to a neurologist. I asked him what the odds were of Brooke having any tumor. "She's no more likely to have a tumor than you or me. Near zero. But with her asking for it, I have to refer her to a neurologist and let him make the decision."

When Brooke went to the neurologist, he called and told me that it was "almost inconceivable" that she had a tumor, but she expressed such concern that he had to give her a brain scan. "Why, if you're so sure she's okay?" I asked. Without hesitation, he responded, "If she's the one in a million that has a tumor and I don't scan her, neither you nor I would ever forgive ourselves." And he added pointedly, "Both you and your daughter are lawyers." Brooke's brain scan was negative and in short order the antibiotics resolved the infection.

The practice of medicine has become suspect, with legions of insurers and lawyers shoving one another to second-guess doctors' decisions and quick to see greed or incompetence. Once set on a pedestal of service, caring, and curing, physicians are now mired in a bureaucratic sewer that is hell-bent on flushing out waste, however sharply it curtails a doctor's discretion in treating a patient.

MERGER MANIA

Attracted by the promise of a steady income and someone else to negotiate the bureaucratic maze, many doctors are selling their practices to corporations that manage the business of health for a profit. Dr. Ben Shwachman of Los Angeles explains, "You can't just hang up a shingle, open the door, and get patients anymore. You have to get contracts, and contracts go through huge conglomerates formed by hospitals, physicians, or insurance companies."

The sale of medical practices by physicians to health care networks, including for-profit insurers entering the managed-care business, is reminiscent of investment bankers moving from one Wall Street firm to another, selling their contacts with clients to the highest bidder. To help doctors become masters of the universe of financial manipulation as well as masters of the universe of increasingly complex medicine, the American Medical Association publishes a book called *Enhancing the Value of Your Medical Practice,* which it advertises as "practical and clearly written advice on marketing, start-up, expansion, mergers, acquisitions, financing, joint ventures and retirement plans."

Trying to keep for-profit enterprises out of the trillion-dollar business of health is like trying to keep ants away from a picnic. Yet having a majority of doctors working for managed-care companies, devoted to cutting costs and, in many cases, to making profits, poses a threat to the tradition of patient-oriented medicine, which may not always suit the short-term, lean-and-mean goals of investors. Dr. Fred Mansfield, an orthopedic surgeon in Boston, complains, "It's harder and harder to make the personal connection with patients when you don't have the power to make a little room in the system. You can't be the benevolent father-figure anymore. You're just a provider."

The University of Pennsylvania, Duke, and Georgetown University hospitals have set aside big bucks to buy medical practices of physicians to secure a flow of patients from primary care doctors. In the early 1990s, Manhattan-based New York Hospital, a teaching institution of which I am a governor, began an aggressive strategy to affiliate with hospitals and doctors in the city's outer boroughs and in neighboring New Jersey, Westchester County, and Connecticut, in order to enhance its market share in the new price-competitive, volume-conscious world of medicine. Merger mania gripped even the staid streets of Boston in 1993, as two old medical dowagers, Massachusetts General and Brigham and Women's hospitals, inked a deal to combine.

For many doctors and hospitals, the business of medicine is more business than medicine. For me, its gets harder each year to tell the difference between sitting on the board of Chrysler or Kmart and sitting on the board of New York Hospital or Georgetown University's medical affairs committee.

HEADING FOR THE EXITS

James Cleveland, a family practitioner in Englewood, New Jersey, says he wouldn't become a doctor again because of insurance hassles, high costs and the fact that he doesn't get time to build the relationships he wants with the 50 to 60 patients he sees daily. Even the newest physicians are having doubts. Dr. Suzanne El-Attar, who just graduated from the University of Pittsburgh owing $96,000, explains, "I've heard from physicians, 'Don't choose this career. Do something else,' and that's discouraging because I haven't even really started yet."
—USA Today, *October 2, 1993*

Revulsion to this bottom-line fixation is leading some doctors to retire early, others to reconsider their choice of profession, and some of the most talented candidates for a life in medicine to stay away from the field.

If he could choose again, James Weaver, a vascular surgeon in Durham, North Carolina, wouldn't be a doctor. "I am totally at the mercy of bureaucrats," he said. In 1991, Dr. Weaver treated a sixty-eight-year-old patient with a blood clot in his lung. When the clot went to his leg, Weaver amputated. The patient suffered respiratory failure and needed intensive care. When the patient developed an ulcer that required surgery, he told Dr. Weaver, "I want to live." Despite aggressive treatment, the patient died eight weeks later. Medicare picked up only $15,000 of the $115,000 bill, refusing to pay for treatments and costs it considered excessive.

"What the hell do you want me to do?" asked Weaver. "I would do the same thing for the next patient, but I can't help but think about dollars, and none of us wants our own doctor to be thinking about costs."

In 1993, I met with a group of medical students at Columbia University to discuss the history of health care in America. The first question came from a second-year student, who asked: "When did doctors become the bad guys?" The cost of demonizing doctors does not show up in government or corporate budgets, but over time it poses a lethal threat to the quality of medical care, one of the few remaining fields in which we are justifiably xenophobic. The medical profession brought much of the "bad guys" image on itself, particularly by its tenacious lobbying to preserve the economic status of physicians. Indeed, the current situation smacks more of Greek tragedy than murder mystery. Yet, however the blame is distributed, making doctors the villains is sure to make patients the victims in the brave new world of American health care.

NURSING HOMES AND HOME HEALTH CARE:
10 CENTS OF EVERY DOLLAR

"A 76-year-old patient of mine died the other day," said Joanne Lynn, a geriatrician in Washington, D.C. "The real tragedy was that he'd been taking care of his 95-year-old mother at home, and now she has no one."

"An elderly friend of mine was in a nursing home for eight years," reported Ethel Shanas, a gerontologist at the University of Illinois. "Her son was putting his own son and daughter through college—and at the same time, having to pay her nursing home bills."

James Birren, a gerontologist at the University of Southern California, told of a friend who on the same day visited her grandmother in a nursing home and then baby-sat for her infant granddaughter.

—The Wall Street Journal, July 30, 1984

Nursing homes are the Jack's beanstalk of American health care. A $2-billion-a-year, mostly mom-and-pop enterprise before Medicaid was passed in 1965, nursing homes grew into an $85 billion industry by 1994, grabbing more than eight cents of every health care dollar.

Roughly sixteen thousand nursing homes provide long-term care to 1.5 million elderly and disabled residents, three out of four of them women. The Catholic Church, other religious denominations, and nonprofit organizations operate three thousand homes, and governments run about eight hundred, but the vast majority are for-profit enterprises.

The industry is marked by large organizations that rival great hotel chains like Marriott, Hilton, and Sheraton, although nursing homes enjoy 90 percent occupancy rates and waiting lists that hotels and hospitals envy. Beverly Enterprises, Inc., has 838 homes with an 88 percent occupancy rate; Hillhaven Corporation, 301 homes and a 94 percent occupancy rate; Manor HealthCare Corp., 162 homes and an 88 percent occupancy rate.

The budding branch of nursing care is the $20-billion-a-year home health care industry: thirteen thousand provider organizations that offer part-time or intermittent nursing, physical and speech therapy, and other assistance at home. Growing at a 35 percent annual rate, home care is the most rapidly expanding segment of the health business.

Almost half of the three million Americans who turn sixty-five each year can expect to live for some time in a nursing home. In 1994, thirty-three million Americans were sixty-five or older; that number will double in a generation. By then the over-sixty-five crowd will constitute one-fifth of all Americans. No society, not even one as rich as the United States, can support the nursing and home health care industries on their present trajectory.

BUFFERIN, BETA-BLOCKERS, BAND-AIDS, AND BREAKTHROUGHS: 9 CENTS OF EVERY DOLLAR

Dr. Carolyn Westhoff looked forward to the arrival in the U.S. of the long-acting contraceptive Norplant as the first good news for family planning in years. But then Wyeth-Ayerst Laboratories launched Norplant, packaged with an insertion kit, at a price of $350. In other countries, Norplant (without the kit) cost as little as $23. "I was stunned," says Dr. Westhoff. "After all the stresses on budgets of the last decade, this seemed like a bad joke." While acknowledging that public funds financed the development of Norplant, Wyeth pointed to market research that indicated it could have charged an even higher price. "We think it's very fairly priced," says Marc Deitch, Wyeth's medical director.
                                    —The Wall Street Journal, *August 30, 1993*

Drugs and other over-the-counter medical products, the researchers who discover them, and the 200,000 pharmacists who distribute them take nine cents of every health dollar, but it's the $60 billion worth of prescription pharmaceuticals, with their high profits and miraculous powers, that attracts all the attention—and antipathy.

The United States harbors the world's most sophisticated and successful pharmaceutical industry. Its discoveries have provided some of the nation's and the world's most cost-effective medical miracles—from vaccines for childhood diseases to hypertension, cholesterol, and ulcer pills that have eliminated the need for billions of dollars of risky medical procedures.

These research investments have also produced some of the world's most expensive drugs, such as Genzyme Corp.'s Ceredase for Gaucher's disease, which can cost $300,000 a year. Genentech's Pulmozyme, a drug for cystic fibrosis victims, costs $10,000 a year. Dr. David Wolf, one of the nation's top hematologists, points out that the drug levamisole is used to treat dogs for worm infestation. When research found it effective in treating colon cancer in humans, he prescribed it for his patients. But they had to pay one hundred times more than the veterinary price when the cost was jacked up to $1,200 a year for human consumption. Most prescription pharmaceuticals cost more in the United States than in any other nation on earth.

Politicians are quick to see the potential for citizen outrage: Americans pay more than half the cost of drugs from their own pockets, and the elderly, who vote in larger proportion than any other segment of the population, use three times as many prescriptions as those under age sixty-five. Arkansas Democrat David Pryor became the U.S. Senate's attack dog, nipping at the industry's profits, reminding anyone who would listen that the United

States is the only industrialized country that does not control prescription drug prices.

Pharmaceutical company executives argue that pot-of-gold profits from patent monopolies give them the motivation and guts to be the high rollers of risky medical research and development. But they admit spending even more on promotion and marketing to create demand and educate providers and patients, sometimes developing "me-too" drugs that do not add therapeutic value to a pharmacist's existing inventory.

While scavenging government officials swarm around fat drug company profits, private market forces pose an even more clear and present threat as employers and managed-care providers squeeze deep discounts from pharmaceutical companies and limit reimbursement for off-patent drugs to the lowest generic price. Competition from generic drugs, which account for some 50 percent of all prescriptions, can promptly drive down the price of brand-name products as much as 80 percent after a patent expires. By the end of the century, pharmaceuticals with combined 1994 sales in excess of $15 billion will come off patent.

Adding to this stew of price pressures, America's lust to litigate makes executives reluctant to release new products unless they are certain the price will cover the cost of inevitable lawsuits. But victims of killers such as AIDS, cancer, and Alzheimer's disease want aggressive research and quick access—at an affordable price—to promising discoveries, regardless of their side effects. When the alternative is death, they argue, riskier policies make sense.

Still haunted by the nightmares of deformed Thalidomide babies in the 1960s and fearful of media and congressional second-guessing, the Food and Drug Administration lacks the will, despite additional resources from user fees, to assess rapidly the safety and effectiveness of new drugs. The entire approval process takes nine years on average; the same drugs are commonly available in other countries in three years. Stung by a number of missteps, the FDA's medical-device approval process has ground almost to a halt. In 1994, its backlog of applications for new devices approached one thousand.

In all, pharmaceutical, medical-device, and other health care companies spend $15 billion on research to develop profitable products to treat everything from cardiovascular disease and cancer to cataracts and corns, and to find new diagnostic techniques, prostheses, and anything else for what ails the population. The National Institutes of Health and private funders, notably foundations and medical center endowments, spend another $15 billion, much of it on basic research.

Despite these investments, America's long-standing supremacy in biomedical research is in peril. Funding for basic research at NIH has not kept pace with demand and opportunity over the past eight years. Cost-conscious insurers and employers are squeezing budgets of teaching hospitals, which conduct the bulk of cutting-edge applied research. At the same time, the research funding process has become highly politicized, as Congress has taken to overriding scientific judgments to placate pressure groups and large campaign contributors.

THE MONEY CHANGERS AND CHERRY PICKERS: 6 CENTS OF EVERY DOLLAR

Dr. Mary Ann Duke, an opthalmologist in Potomac, Maryland, knows firsthand how difficult it is to practice medicine in the world of managed care. Dr. Duke has been turned down by insurance compa-

nies who run networks that she sought to join. "I never dreamed when I took the Hippocratic Oath that I'd be denied my right to practice medicine by an insurance company. The bottom line is, the insurance companies rule medicine. It's not the doctors. It's not the hospitals. It's not Hillary Clinton or anyone else. It's the insurance companies because they have the deep pockets."
—The Washington Post, *December 14, 1993*

Some 1,500 private insurers are the money changers in the temples of American health care, keeping for themselves about $50 billion of the $300 billion in premiums that pass through their hands each year. As the administrators of private health policies and Medicare, they spin the wheel of health care fortune and decide who gets paid what for tending to Americans' ills. Government insurance administrators take another $10 billion.

Until the 1980s, health insurers acted as shills for doctors and hospitals, letting them dominate their boards and representing their interests with beneficiaries. Nonprofit Blue Cross and Blue Shield organizations and commercial insurers pushed up premiums with abandon to pass on increased charges from providers of health care and, in the case of commercial insurers, to retain a comfortable profit. Then some large corporations, unions, and governments got smart. They demanded that insurers hold down administrative expenses and negotiate with doctors and hospitals to lower the cost of care for employees.

To stay financially viable in the newly competitive world, many Blue Cross and Blue Shield plans adopted the practice of "experience rating." Long used by commercial insurers, this practice puts the emphasis not on offering the best health care at the lowest prices, but on seeking out the healthiest, lowest-cost patients. Denying insurance to individuals with expensive preexisting conditions, such as AIDS, alcoholism, and diabetes, became common business practice among the nation's insurers and the companies that paid their premiums. This leaves the sickest to scratch for very expensive coverage and elbows many of them into the ranks of uninsured.

A single year's increase in health insurance premiums can equal a decade's increase in the general cost-of-living index. On average, premiums rose about 15 percent annually during the early 1980s, slowing in the late 1980s and early 1990s, but still running well above the rate of increase in the consumer price index. As a result, many employers, providers, and legislators want to drive insurers from the lucrative temples of the health care industry.

To this end, most large corporations self-insure by setting aside their own reserves of money to cover employee health benefits and paying insurers only to administer and screen claims, a trend that has accelerated in recent years as smaller businesses have followed the lead of large employers.

Trying to salvage their place and profits in the transformation of American health care, insurers are assembling their own networks by signing up hospitals and doctors as they remake themselves into for-profit providers of health care. Hospitals, doctors, HMOs, and long-term care facilities are organizing themselves into networks that bypass the money changers by dealing directly with big corporate purchasers of health care. Hundreds of insurance companies, too small to play in the new high-stakes game, are going out of business.

PREVENTION: 3 CENTS OF EVERY DOLLAR

Government efforts to keep the public healthy, such as arresting the spread of tuberculosis bacilli or flu viruses, providing vaccines for diseases such as measles, and educating us about the dangers of AIDS or smoking, consume only about $33 billion a year, three measly cents of every health care dollar.

No better example of the cost of failing to use an ounce of prevention exists than the tuberculosis epidemic that has afflicted most large cities in the 1990s. In the late 1980s, Dr. James Mason, then director of the Centers for Disease Control and Prevention (and later assistant secretary for health in the Department of Health and Human Services), spotted a handful of TB cases in a few American cities. Fearing a major resurgence of this highly contagious disease, in 1989 he urged his superiors at HHS and members of Congress to provide $36 million to stamp it out before it spread. His request was denied. After all, he was told, TB was a disease of the past that we had virtually eliminated from the American scene, and besides, we had other, more immediate health care priorities.

In 1994, America spent close to half a billion dollars to treat TB victims crowding urban hospitals throughout the nation. The disease has complicated the treatment of AIDS victims and substance abusers and has moved into the countryside, attacking individuals in every state and most every community of fifty thousand or more people. We knew how to prevent the spread of TB, but we chose to be penny-unwise instead.

OTHER HEALTH PROFESSIONALS, SATELLITES, AND A FEW PARASITES: 14 CENTS OF EVERY DOLLAR—AND MORE

Dentists, who pick off five cents of every dollar, are the physicians' financial and professional horror film come true. Advances in preventive care and the greater use of dental hygienists have held down dentists' income. The number of dentistry degrees awarded each year peaked at 5,585 in 1983, falling to about 3,500 in 1993.

Other professionals, such as chiropractors, podiatrists, optometrists, occupational therapists, psychologists, and nurses not paid by doctors, hospitals, and other institutions, collect five cents of each health care dollar. Health services provided at factories, offices, and schools take two cents. The construction industry collects one cent. Retail purchases of durable medical equipment, such as wheelchairs, eyeglasses, crutches, and hearing aids, account for another cent.

Beyond these recipients of the nation's health care dollar, entrepreneurs, ready to profit handsomely from the business of health, abound. An army of lawyers puts tassels on their loafers and gold links in their french cuffs by representing plaintiffs and defendants in malpractice litigation. Investment bankers advise hospitals, HMOs, pharmaceutical companies, and insurers that seek to raise money or merge into larger enterprises. Advertisers benefit from the marketing boom set off by insurers and providers ranging from teaching hospitals to cosmetic surgeons, all hawking remedies for what ails Americans. Union officials put bread on the table by representing hospital workers.

And thousands of lobbyists in Washington, D.C., and state capitals bill millions of dollars every year to protect profitable slivers of a trillion-dollar industry.

WHO ANTES THIS TRILLION-DOLLAR POT?

Kazimer Patelski, age 62, never thought he would have to worry about health care during his retirement. After all, he had worked for McDon-

nell Douglas for 28 years, and had been the company's managing director of Houston Mission Control for the Apollo program. In October 1992, the company announced the suspension of nonunion retiree health benefits beginning in 1993. Instead, the company would give employees a one-time payment of $18,000. Patelski, who had polio as a child, is confined to a wheelchair. "After all these years and all these promises," he said, "I feel I've been cheated out of my health insurance."

—The Washington Post, *March 3, 1993*

Who picks up the one-trillion-dollar tab for health care?

No matter how much we try to avoid it, we all do.

The feds want to dump more of the bill on states and private employers. The states and large corporations want to pass more of the burden to the federal government. Small business, retailers, and hotels try to shift the bill to big corporations, the manufacturing industry, the feds and the states. Large and small businesses, the feds, and the states want patients to pay more for their health care. Individual patients and American taxpayers, on perpetual prowl for a free lunch, want to dump costs back onto their employers and governments. Each is trying to get field position to take on the smallest burden possible in America's rapidly changing health care system.

Despite all this frenzied tossing, health care costs have been dumped on pretty much the same doorsteps over the last decade. In the early 1990s, the government covered about 35 percent of all personal health expenditures, compared to 32 percent in 1980. Business picked up 28 percent of the tab, compared to 27 percent. And individuals paid 34 percent (through premiums, coinsurance, deductibles, Medicare taxes, and payments for services not covered by insurance), down from 38 percent. (Philanthropies and nonpatient revenues such as those from hospital gift shops and parking fees cover 3 percent of costs.)

WHAT ARE THE BIG BUCKS BUYING?

The trillion dollars that Americans spend on health care should be more than enough to provide all our people all the care they need. An equal amount would be enough to provide care for 750 million Britons, 620 million Japanese, or 500 million Germans. But in the American way of health, a trillion dollars isn't sufficient to treat 260 million Americans.

Instead, we waste some $250 billion.

We are buying billions in bureaucratic waste. America spends some $200 billion on administrative costs borne by private insurers, Medicare, and Medicaid, as well as the doctors, nurses, hospitals and nursing homes—their secretaries, assistants, and accountants—who handle the paperwork created by four billion insurance claims each year.

We are buying billions in fraud and abuse. Health industry officials and government watchdogs agree that as much as $100 billion a year is lost through fraud and abuse, including padded bills, charges for tests and procedures never performed, and double billing.

We are buying kaleidoscopic care. The treatment that Americans receive varies not so much with their medical needs as with the thickness of their wallet, the location of their doctor, the generosity of their employer, the power of their union, the regulations of bureaucrats, and the whims of politicians.

• If you're a man who retires in Florida rather than in Maine, you're four times as likely to have your prostate surgically removed. If you're a woman with localized breast cancer, your chances of a radical mastectomy are a third higher if you live in Iowa rather than Seattle, Washington.

• If you're a United Auto Workers retiree in Michigan, you'll trigger far more Medicare spending than a non-UAW beneficiary—even though you're almost certain to be in better health—because years of first-dollar insurance coverage have encouraged you to use the system profligately.

• If you're a privately insured pregnant woman, your chances of delivering your baby by cesarean section are 25 percent higher than they would be if you were covered by Medicaid or some other public program, regardless of age, ethnicity, prior history—even regardless of any complications with your pregnancy.

• If you're a poor woman, you're far more likely to have a hysterectomy (the second most common major operation on women behind cesarean sections) than if your income tops $35,000, in good measure because you're less likely to have regular gynecological checkups which detect cervical cancer, benign fibroid tumors, or slippage of the uterus in time to prevent surgery.

The reasons for these variations in care are many. The more surgeons in an area, the more surgery; the more specialists, the more referrals to specialists. Good doctors often agree to disagree on the best treatment for complex problems, and as long as a patient has generous insurance, every incentive in the system—from fee-for-service plans that pay only when doctors unsheathe their scalpels and needles, to patient demands and medical malpractice awards—encourages them to do something.

Dr. Robert Brook at the Rand Corporation, who believes that a fourth to a third of the nation's treatment dollars are spent on needless or even harmful procedures and pills, warns, "The number of machines, procedures, and drugs now exceeds the ability of most physicians to remember their proper use, complication rate, or efficacy." As a result, doctors hang on to obsolete practices and don't—or can't—keep up with the latest medical research. Often they add new procedures and pills to old regimens, rather than substituting one for the other.

For the well-insured and affluent, early detection followed by timely, high-quality surgical and pharmaceutical remedies is the rule. For those who lack adequate insurance and can't afford to buy access to primary care, damage control in emergency rooms is the norm.

Dr. Beverly Morgan, a California doctor, posed as three different patients—one with private insurance, one with Medicaid coverage, and one without insurance—all seeking an MRI scan at the seventeen freestanding centers in Orange County. The MRI centers offered next-day service to the privately insured patient, who complained of a minor orthopedic problem. Most would not accept the Medicaid patient, who said she had been diagnosed with a possible brain tumor, although six offered to see her within three weeks if her doctor would first complete extensive paperwork. Nearly every center turned away the uninsured patient with a brain tumor diagnosis, although one center offered a deal: $500 in cash up front and another $700 after the scan.

For the well-insured, there's no better place to be than America if you have a life-threatening disease. Among industrial nations, we have the highest cure rates for cervical, stomach, and uterine cancer and the second highest cure rate for breast cancer. We have the world's finest cardiologists and medical centers to treat heart disease. For the well-to-do in the United States, there is no waiting in line as there often is in other countries, and success rates on the operating table—and the quality of life thereafter—are unsurpassed.

Even so, the towering sum the United States spends on health care has not made Americans any healthier than citizens of other nations. In 1993, the U.S. spent $3,400 per capita; Canada, $2,100; Germany and France, $1,900; Italy, $1,600; Japan, $1,500; and the United Kingdom, $1,200. Yet the life expectancy of Americans was seventy-five years, compared to seventy-seven in Canada, France, and Germany, seventy-eight in Italy, seventy-nine in Japan, and seventy-six in the United Kingdom.

Other nations are also much better at keeping their children healthy. The United States ranks twentieth among twenty-four economically developed countries in its ability to prevent infant deaths, with 8.9 infant deaths per thousand live births compared to the top nation, Japan, at 4.6 per thousand. Most industrialized countries fully immunize their children within a year of birth; we don't come close—with one of the lowest rates among industrialized nations of preschool immunizations against diseases such as measles, mumps, and polio.

THE CUSP OF CHAOS

It's finger-pointing time in the blame game of American health care. Some 85 percent of corporate executive officers say doctors are responsible for rising costs. Employees, the consumers of health care, accuse doctors and insurers. Doctors, on the other hand, lay the fault on patients, insurers, government, and malpractice lawyers. President Bill Clinton and First Lady Hillary Rodham Clinton attack insurance and pharmaceutical companies. The Democrats and Republicans, the feds and the states, the doctors and the nurses fire away at each other. Patients shirk responsibility for their own health, then complain about doctors if they can't fix every ailment.

The stench of mistrust fouls the air between doctors and patients, insurers, nurses, and hospital administrators. Health care reform has degenerated into wealth care reform, a clash of well-heeled financial interests, fighting over that trillion-dollar pot, as beholden politicians collect their campaign contributions and dole out the goodies. Meanwhile, the divide between care of the affluent and the disadvantaged widens, even as Medicare and the federal share of Medicaid remain the fastest-growing programs bankrolled by Washington, covering more than sixty million Americans at a cost of some $300 billion in 1994, more than four times what the federal government spends on education, job training, employment, and social services combined.

The battle between greedy geezers who want it all in their twilight years and selfish young turks who recoil at paying the bill grows nastier. Substance abuse and addiction, poverty and violence—all degrade the physical and spiritual integrity of our society and strain the resources of the health care system, while attracting too little attention in the context of health care. Americans are getting angry as costs go up, lines get longer, quality declines, and taxes rise.

Lost in the tumult are the human needs of the patients—to hold a hand, say a prayer, talk to a relative, nurse, or doctor, be comforted after treatment, and die in dignity. These very real needs of body and soul have become obscured in the cacophonic symphony of beeping monitors, churning machines, brutal radiation and chemotherapy, imagers that swallow bodies, doctors exhausted from bureaucratic hassles during the day and sore-eyed from reading the fine print of medical journals at night.

No wonder former secretary of Health and Human Services Louis Sullivan, a physician and medical educator, warns, "The system must change. It's going to be painful, but if we don't do it now, it's simply going to be more painful later when our system collapses." There's lots of churning, but none of it—not managed competition or managed care, not pushes for universal coverage or national health insurance, not more government control or tighter-fisted corporate CEOs—can do the job alone. What is needed now is a top-to-bottom overhaul of the way we think and act about health care in America.

CHAPTER THREE

RECONCEIVING HEALTH: FROM TOP TO BOTTOM

The time has come for each of us—provider, payer, and patient— to transform our concept of health care in America.

The essence of this transformation is not a new government program or business plan, but a cultural sea change among our people and the nation's powerful elites. We must acknowledge both the limits of medicalization and the breadth of factors that affect health. We must recognize that our quixotic desire to drink from the fountain of immortality and the well of cosmetic perfection can demean the dignity of human existence and trample on the basic health needs of the less powerful. And we must temper our insistence upon absolute individual autonomy while we accept more responsibility for our own health.

It's time to scrap the myopic idea that health care means mending the ill and the injured and the conventional nostrum that equates twisting and turning the finance and delivery of sick care with health care reform. Our vision should encompass the full spectrum of health in our nation and be exciting enough to enlist the formidable energy, will, and resources required to attack all dimensions of the system.

THE FEDERAL FETISH

From the moment in 1965 when President Lyndon Johnson but-tonholed Congress to enact Medicare and Medicaid, the federal government has suffered from a fetish that the key to health care reform is to manipulate the financing and delivery of treatment for illness and injury. In fact, bankrolling medical services only un-locks the door to more sick care, for experience has taught that medical treatment follows reimbursement the way an avaricious prospector answers the cry of the gold rush.

In 1968, as spending took off in the wake of the Great Society health care programs, Johnson asked Congress for authority to use "new methods of payment as they prove effective in providing high quality medical care more efficiently and at lower cost" in order to correct three major deficiencies: the tilt of insurance plans that "encourage doctors and patients to choose hospitalization even when other, less costly forms of care would be equally effec-tive"; the fee-for-service system, which has "no strong economic incentives to encourage [doctors] to avoid providing care that is unnecessary"; and the fact that "hospitals charge on a cost basis, which places no penalty on inefficient operations."

Congress refused to act and, for the next twenty-five years, whether the president was Richard Nixon, Gerald Ford, Jimmy Carter, Ronald Reagan, George Bush, or Bill Clinton and whether the political tilt of the White House or Congress was conservative or liberal, Democrat or Republican, the federal fetish has been that altering how we pay for and deliver sick care could remedy the accumulating symptoms of chaos in American health care.

In my first months as secretary of Health, Education, and Wel-fare in 1977, I created the Health Care Financing Administration—HCFA, which is commonly pronounced HICKFA—to manage Medicare and Medicaid. I should have named it the Sick Care Financing Administration—SICKFA—to capture its true mission: to provide funds to cure and relieve the pain of older and poor Americans after they've fallen ill.

Just about every reform proposal since has beaten loudly on the same drum. Congress after Congress has produced elaborate attempts to calibrate the payment and delivery system, having it run by the same guys, largely insurers, that for a generation have exhibited such single-minded devotion to financing and delivering sick care.

Defying this federal fixation—and often because of it—health care spending has persistently climbed two, three, and, on occasion, four times the rate of increase in the overall cost of living and many times more rapidly than increases in the population. Despite the slower pace of medical care inflation in 1993, the $100 billion jump over 1992 was the largest rise in a single year.

The institutional framework in which the nation's capital shapes health care policy feeds this federal fetish. Two congressional committees, Senate Finance and House Ways and Means, dominate health care legislation. Because they are responsible for taxation and Social Security—the hooks they used to snare control over Medicare and most of Medicaid in the 1960s—their financial orientation tints the glasses through which they see health care. More important, legalized political bribery in the form of donations to members of Congress from the moneyed interests they oversee (HMOs, insurers, pharmaceutical companies, doctors, and hospitals) keeps the eyes of these committee members locked on the financial aspects of health care.

The deficit reduction deals and one-year federal budget cycle also color the view inside the Beltway. Congress and presidents have slashed funds for programs such as childhood immunization, prenatal care for poor women, and early treatment for tuberculosis in order to reduce the immediate year's budget, even though they know such actions will increase costs in future years. They can worry about those years when they are upon them—if they're still in office. For the moment, incumbents have more pressing personal priorities: raising campaign funds and reelection.

The focus on short-run savings can produce absurd results. On February 20, 1993, doctors gave Secretary of Defense Les Aspin a typhoid shot known to cause nausea and fever. The shot, which cost thirty-five cents, aggravated Aspin's congenital heart condition. Having difficulty breathing, Aspin entered Georgetown University's intensive care unit at a cost of more than $2,000 a day. An oral vaccine that would have avoided such adverse side effects cost $1.90. But a Defense Department spokesman said, "It's my understanding that the injection vaccine was used because it's cheaper."

BUSINESS PLAYS FOLLOW THE FEDERAL LEADER

Though slow to realize that health care costs were eating their lunch, large corporate employers, once aroused, put their eggs in the same basket as the feds: manipulating the financing and delivery of care for acute illness and injury.

They started by reminding their insurance companies who buttered the bread and demanding better, lower-cost deals with hospitals and other providers. They introduced copayments and deductibles for medical treatment and pushed their employees into HMOs and preferred provider organizations (PPOs), which promised to care for the sick at a lower price. Some companies dropped their health care coverage altogether, obliging the employee to buy his own insurance. Corporate executives, confident that they could handle health costs in the same macho way they deal with any other profit-squeezing expense, sought to manage care just as they manage their business: with tightfisted financial controls.

This bottom-line focus is not surprising from those who get paid to compete successfully in markets, hold down costs, and produce dividends and higher stock prices for shareholders. Their concentration on short-term profits, combined with high rates of employee turnover in our mobile society, gives executives little incentive to invest in their employees' long-term health. They are motivated to keep employees out of the sick-care system during their shift with the company and to pay as little as possible for such care when it's needed. Unlike governments, the legal duty of corporate executives is not to serve all people fairly, but to serve up profits to investors.

The corporate move toward managed care has met with some temporary success. Free from political constraints that Congress imposes to protect special interests and that prevent the federal executive from wringing inefficiencies out of health care delivery, many large corporations have trimmed the rate of increase in their health costs from double to single digits. In 1993, Chrysler's health care costs rose only 4.2 percent.

Yet with all its huffing and puffing, the $256 billion that business spent on health care in 1993 still rivaled the $275 billion it picked up in after-tax profits. While imposing copayments and deductibles on workers may discourage some needless resort by employees to doctors and hospitals, such measures chiefly shift costs to workers, rather than reduce them, and often encourage immediate savings at the expense of long-term costs.

The rush to managed care has also helped make the nation's system costly to administer. Dr. Stephen Kelly, a family practitioner in Dobbs Ferry, New York, has joined forty managed-care networks in order to keep the patients he has served for years. But each network has different rules about how much he can charge and what procedures he can perform, and each has driven down his fees, forcing him to see more patients, spend less time with each, and make fewer house calls.

Managed care is likely to produce diminishing savings as administrative costs pile up and onetime reductions, such as those related to hospitalization, are realized. Managed-care organizations tend to attract the healthiest patients (even among Medicare beneficiaries) and have not demonstrated an ability to constrain costs related to the aging population, technology explosion, or substance abuse much better than their fee-for-service competitors. The bottom-line mentality of many managed-care providers often discourages them from serving the very sick, Medicaid recipients, and the uninsured.

Whether its customers are poor or affluent, managed care leaves doctors and nurses little time to counsel patients and sit with them when they are suffering. The two-fisted impact of high-tech care and bottom-line managed care puts powerful dehumanizing forces at the front of American medicine and threatens to ignore the needs of ailing individuals to be talked to, as well as to be cut, injected, and medicated, as the doctor hurries to the next patient.

THE WHOLE TRINITY OF HEALTH

The first move toward a broader vision is to train our sights on the whole trinity of health care: research, health promotion and disease prevention, and treatment.

RESEARCH

Americans tend to look upon the nation's research effort as a hunt for miracle cures and silver bullets that will license them to abuse their bodies and minds without worry about the unhealthy consequences. We are infatuated with pills and procedures to soothe our hangovers, ease our indigestion, quiet our hemorrhoids, relieve our stress, suck away excess fat, and, when the piper finally calls, to remove our cancerous tissues, reopen our clogged arteries, or replace our organs. With such medical marvels, we can drink and eat whatever we want, smoke and chew tobacco, work and play under tremendous pressures, stay up late at night, pursue sexual whims, and sleep rather than exercise in the morning.

There's no dispute over the value of the medical research that discovered childhood vaccines, which have saved billions of dollars in health care costs and made possible the elimination of smallpox. But modern medical researchers have turned much of their awesome genius to more exotic pursuits. The technological wizardry of their products—the respirators, artificial hearts, and organ transplants that grab our headlines and imaginations—have blurred the line between life and death, extending for days, weeks, sometimes even months, the breath and heartbeats of patients who would have been pronounced or left for dead just a few years ago.

Should we continue to invest billions of limited research dollars to extend the life of the terminally ill when so many millions of individuals are being maimed and killed because they do not understand the dangers of sun and smoking or the importance of low-fat, high-fiber diets, regular exercise, and prenatal care, or because they are just not motivated to act on these health truths? Which is more valuable to society: a machine that adds a few days of life to the terminally ill or a technique that persuades thousands to pursue healthy life-styles?

In the absence of careful judgment, unrestrained medical innovation and the rivalry among hospitals to offer big-ticket technology tend to stymie efforts to contain health spending. We have four times the number of mammogram machines we need, an excess that produces the bizarre combination of overcapacity and rising prices, as hospitals and imaging centers raise prices to recover the fixed costs of their underutilized machinery. "Only in America," as Paul Starr of Princeton University noted, "are poor women denied a mammogram because there is too much equipment."

There is an irresistable impulse in American medicine to use innovations simply because they exist. Even when a new procedure might be expected to save money, it can increase costs. Why? Because doctors and patients, like children infatuated by a new toy, become quicker to use it.

New techniques of questionable benefit also proliferate, pumped up by heavy marketing. In the name of early detection and protection against the gunslingers of malpractice litigation, the indiscriminate use of diagnostic and screening technologies has become a common, costly mark of American medicine. Imaging centers advertise, some with musical jingles, on radio stations in the New York City area, urging listeners to come by for an MRI.

Today's research portends tomorrow's health costs or savings. The pursuit of knowledge is essential, but we need a major shift in the way America invests its research dollars and the kind of clinical and demonstration programs that federal and state governments support. We should look at what could be achieved for the public's health, if the genius we have funded to invent ways to forestall death for brief periods of time were committed to developing techniques to promote health, prevent disease, and attend to matters like substance abuse, eliminating disability and dependence among the elderly, and a healthy start for our children from the moment of conception.

HEALTH PROMOTION AND DISEASE PREVENTION

While we sweat and strain to assure that everybody can get into the trillion-dollar sick-care system, we commit only $33 billion to keeping them out of it by promoting the health of our citizens and preventing disease. Yet that's the only sure way to keep individuals healthy longer and contain health care costs.

Universal health insurance is an imperative of social justice because no one has complete control over whether or when illness will strike. Individuals who don't smoke get lung cancer, and people who gobble down fiber and never touch steak or butter get colon cancer. Life is sprinkled with unpreventable tragedies and ailments that, without insurance, can be financially devastating. But the overarching fact is that most of us do not take steps that will greatly reduce our vulnerability to disease.

The power of prevention is enormous and much of its source is outside the world of medicine. At the start of the twentieth century, tuberculosis, diphtheria, influenza, pneumonia, cholera, and gastrointestinal infections were the top causes of death and disability in America. Three major prevention initiatives virtually eliminated these diseases in the United States, and two of them had nothing to do with doctors and medicine: The introduction of sewer and sanitation systems was a tribute to engineering genius, and America's incredibly efficient distribution system combined with Louis Pasteur's genius to put pasteurized milk at every doorstep. Only the third, the discovery of vaccines and mass immunization programs, falls within a traditional definition of medical research, and it is notable that even here the discovery was not a cure for the afflicted, but a way to prevent the illness.

These initiatives refashioned the terrain of America's sick-care system. In 1900, 580 out of every 100,000 Americans died from infectious diseases, such as pneumonia and influenza; by 1990 they killed only 30 of every 100,000. Today, cancer, cardiovascular disease, and stroke are the nation's big killers and cripplers, with AIDS and violence rising in the ranks—and substance abuse lurking in all their dark shadows. The road to reducing these modern-day killers is paved not with high-tech medicine, but with sensible diets and exercise, sexual abstinence or monogamy, avoidance of stress and sun, safe housing and neighborhoods, alleviation of poverty, gun control, and a comprehensive and intelligent attack on substance abuse.

The resurgence of tuberculosis in our cities and its sinister creep into the countryside and workplaces of the nation, from California to Maine, puts in stark relief the limits of sick care and the importance of prevention. We have the capacity to prevent TB, but the role of doctors is marginal. The fertile soil in which TB spreads, and the logical focus of attacks on the problem, is decrepit housing and homelessness, unsanitary living conditions, drug and alcohol abuse, and AIDS.

TREATMENT

The one inexorable rule of the health care system in America is that we get what we pay for, and we are paying too much for treatments to prolong life for a few medicated moments.

We spend billions to keep people alive, however fragile their life and however extraordinary the expense of mechanical or other medical support systems. Almost a third of Medicare's $160 billion annual bill goes to individuals who have less than a year to live. Nearly half of that is spent during the last month of life. Most every elderly hospital patient whom doctors resuscitate when his heart stops beating spends the rest of his days in the hospital, often on advanced life-support systems such as mechanical ventilators.

More than a third of Medicaid's $150 billion annual bill is for long-term care, mostly to warehouse elderly women, and billions more in private money goes to nursing homes for our ailing parents and grandparents. Yet we invest little on research and prevention to help the elderly maintain their independence and avoid disabling ailments and injuries.

We spend millions to treat diseases that are preventable with vaccines. Though we were on the verge of eradicating measles in the United States, between 1989 and 1991 the disease infected 55,000 people, causing 11,000 hospitalizations and 132 deaths. In Milwaukee alone, a 1989 measles outbreak infected 1,100 people, killed three, and cost $3 million in medical and hospital bills. For one-tenth the eventual cost, the outbreak could have been averted by immunizing high-risk individuals.

We spend $100,000 to bring a premature and underweight baby to full term in a hypertech neonatal hospital wing, despite evidence that the child is likely to suffer severe mental and physical disabilities throughout his life. Yet each year, we fail to ensure that one million pregnant women get early, quality prenatal care that could, at far lower cost, curb the low birthweight that triggers so much intensive and expensive neonatal care.

Such a lopsided tilt to treatment is a declaration of self-defeat in the campaign to make Americans healthy. Creating a culture of health care will require a massive shift in our habits and values that begins with a recognition that our health depends on far more than the doctors who treat us, the hospitals that admit us, and the pills in our medicine cabinets.

CASTING A WIDE NET

By training and inclination, Dr. Robert Mackersie is more concerned with how to sew up an aorta than how to identify the roots of urban violence, but the epidemic of death and injury from guns has moved the surgeon, who runs the trauma unit at San Francisco General Hospital, to advocacy. Doctors are reaching the limits of their craft, he says, and must now turn to gun control and violence prevention. "For surgeons to make the jump from hard science to this morass that most of us view as social sciences is a big leap," said Dr. Mackersie. "But we've run out of ways to decrease mortality, and what we're left with is prevention."
—The New York Times, *November 16, 1993*

Effective measures, big and small, that seize opportunities to address the many threats to America's health and nourish a culture of health care can be found in every stream of American life. But to discern them in all their variety we must cast a wide net.

RECKLESS DRIVING

Buckling up and enforcing fifty-five-miles-per-hour speed limits and drunk-driving laws not only save lives; they reduce health care costs. The chances of death or serious injury in an automobile accident double with every ten-miles-per-hour increase in driving speed and jump if you take off your seat belt. Each year speed-related crashes incapacitate 80,000 individuals and kill more than 15,000. The National Safety Council set the medical costs of all traffic accidents at $20 billion in 1992. That is the equivalent of a $2,500 rebate on every new car purchased that year.

Something as simple as wearing seat belts started as a nuisance for most drivers. But by the early 1990s, three out of five drivers were wearing seat belts, compared to about one in ten in 1980.

Why the change from ignored nuisance to driver's habit? One reason is the wave of mandatory seat belt laws. By 1991, forty-two states had them and all fifty required the use of child safety seats. During the 1980s, the feds mandated that new cars contain automatic protection, such as motorized seat belts or air bags.

But of far more significance was the decision of most television entertainment producers to have their characters put on a seat belt whenever they got in a car to drive (even if the character then proceeded to drive like a madman and kill several people with an automatic weapon as he tore through city streets, smashing fruit-and-vegetable carts). Sensing the change in attitude, car manufacturers bet that safety could sell cars, which triggered heavy advertising of seat belts and air bags. Between 1983 and 1993, thanks to this combination of public and private initiatives, the use of seat belts has saved more than thirty thousand lives and prevented hundreds of thousands of injuries.

AIR, WATER, AND PAINT

Despite decades of discussion, air and water pollutants continue to pad America's health care bill. Air pollution causes or aggravates diseases such as chronic bronchitis, pulmonary emphysema, lung cancer, and bronchial asthma, and delivers a $50 billion health care bill. Roughly two-thirds of us live in areas that do not meet Environmental Protection Agency standards for air quality.

Asthma alone triggers a half-million hospitalizations and two million emergency room visits a year. Ozone and other air pollutants, including indoor emissions from fireplaces and wood-burning stoves and secondhand cigarette smoke, aggravate asthma. Children are particularly susceptible; the prevalence of asthma is a third higher among them than among senior citizens.

Thanks to pollution, water safety has become a major issue in many American cities. In New York and the Washington, D.C., area, the dangers of unsafe water precipitated major public health threats requiring urgent action in 1993. Because of unsafe water supplies, some cities may see revivals of diseases, like dysentery and cholera, once thought to have been banished from the American health care scene.

Lead poisoning from peeling paint qualifies as the number one environmental threat to the health of America's children. High levels of lead in a child's bloodstream can cause convulsion, coma, retardation, seizure, and even death. Lower levels can impair the central nervous system, delay cognitive development, hamper hearing, and starve bones of needed calcium. Some two million children under the age of six in America have lead blood levels high enough to stunt intellectual and physical development.

VIOLENCE, GUNS

Curbing America's lust for violence and its romance with guns is key to restraining health care costs. Violence lays a $20 billion health care bill on the American people each year. Almost half the men, women, and children who enter hospital emergency rooms display symptoms of violence. Harried doctors and nurses treat the trauma, but rarely recognize the cause, and have little or no incentive to address it. Instead, they rush to the next emergency, leaving the victim to return after the next beating.

Violence wears many ugly masks: child and spouse abuse, assault and battery, rape, homicide, and suicide. Contrary to popular belief that the best way to avoid being assaulted or killed is to avoid strangers and stay home, most mayhem occurs there, among people who know each other, who are drinking or using drugs, and who argue with a gun or knife close at hand.

Some seven million violent crimes were committed in 1993. From 1973 to 1993, the number of violent crimes rose 24 percent. Homicide and suicide now claim sixty thousand lives annually; in two years, that's enough to wipe out a city the size of Albany, Ann Arbor, or Abilene. As Secretary of Health and Human Services Donna Shalala remarked, "In this country, domestic violence is just about as common as giving birth—about four million instances [annually] of each."

Guns are the weapons of choice; two-thirds of all murders involve firearms. Gunshot wounds triggered close to $2 billion in health care spending during 1994. There are thirty-seven homicides for each one hundred thousand fifteen-to-twenty-four-year-old men in the United States; the next highest industrial nation is Italy with four. In Greece, it's 1.3; in Japan and Britain, less than one. Pollster George Gallup suggests, "If violence were a disease, we would be searching frantically for a solution."

Violence is a public health pandemic in America, and Americans are starting to take note. A 1993 survey found that the public, dismayed by indirect or direct experience with gun violence, has begun to view gun control as a health care concern as well as an issue of crime and constitutional rights. For the first time since Lyndon Johnson convinced Congress to pass gun control legislation in 1968, the House and Senate in 1993 and 1994 acted to set a waiting period for gun purchasers and ban assault weapons. The American Medical Association has urged physicians to sharpen their skills at detecting the signs of violent abuse and providing prompt counseling and appropriate referrals to victims.

But too many victims and physicians regard the ravages of violence as just another ailment to be patched up with modern medicine. As Laurence Purdy, a California doctor, put it:

> Shootings and knifings happen every day, and the bloody, torn, and ripped bodies come and go through our emergency room as regularly as patients with any natural affliction. . . . [Violence] has become just another common ailment we can suture together and make right with the phenomenal and ever-ready technomagic in the hospital. . . . Through our equanimity in regarding homicide as just another disease, we have allowed it to share that uneasy pedestal, with cancer and heart disease, as one of America's leading killers.

Substance Abuse and Addiction

Substance abuse and addiction is the bloodthirsty buddy of violence and crime. Alcohol and drugs play a leading role in most violent tragedies: turf wars among drug dealers, crimes to get money to support drug habits, domestic fights, car crashes, and newborn babies scarred for life by alcohol-, drug-, and cigarette-abusing mothers. Even when substance abuse is not the sole cause, through intoxication, withdrawal, loss of inhibitions, drug-induced mental disorders, and short- and long-term psychotic states, drug and alcohol use can intensify or prolong a violent situation.

Drugs and alcohol are implicated in most domestic violence. Add the muggings and robberies by drug-crazed perpetrators, the date rape by high school and college students high on beer, pot, or cocaine, and it's easy to understand why our nation is drowning in a flood of violent crime that brings with it a wave of health care spending.

How can any member of Congress or state legislator think that tinkering with the financing and delivery of sick care will stop this carnage?

POVERTY AND POOR EDUCATION

Poverty is the most persistent and pernicious companion of poor health. Individuals with family incomes under $9,000 a year have a death rate more than triple that of those with incomes above $25,000. The less educated the individual, the greater the likelihood of premature death and disease.

The poor need lots more than universal health insurance to alter this sorry state. For evidence, we need only look to England, where similar disparities in death rates and health status between affluent and poor exist despite fifty years of national health insurance. Individuals living in poverty need jobs, education, safe housing, safe recreation, sewage systems, adequate police protection, and substance abuse programs—just for starters. Some doctors strive to address these problems when they see poor patients. But those doctors are the exception that proves it can be done.

At the Child Health Services clinic in Manchester, New Hampshire, doctors, nurse practitioners, social service workers, and nutritionists address the full range of problems that almost a thousand poor children and their parents suffer each year. "We spend more than half our time just trying to help a family stabilize its household," said Selma Deitch, the pediatrician who founded the clinic in 1980.

For the staff, this means: helping families find subsidized

housing free of lead paint; finding mental health care for parents and counseling for children of alcoholics; helping families qualify for Medicaid and food stamps; getting adults into high-school-equivalency-diploma programs and job training; finding warm clothes for the winter and cool clothes for the summer; and seeing that nursing bottles are filled with milk—because some mothers fill them with Cremora, a cheap and nonnutritious milk substitute, when milk and money run out.

Many children come from school with notes from the teacher to "put this child on Ritalin," a drug for attention-deficit disorders. "Some children truly have neurological attention deficits," says Deitch, but most are simply "going to school after fights in the morning at home, without breakfast, without socks. That's why they're distracted and disruptive in school."

Managed care may offer efficiencies to corporate executives and politicians, but as usually practiced it is not likely to help poor families. When pediatricians at a local HMO see poor children in Manchester, they routinely see fifty kids a day for a ten-minute visit per child. There's no way doctors can get a sense of what's happening at home practicing that kind of assembly-line medicine. Absent such knowledge, doctors are not likely to be of much help to the long-term health of the children. Without allowance for the need to spend more time with poor children and their parents, reform of the health care system is unlikely to benefit them.

DISCRIMINATION

When the National Commission on AIDS recommended in 1993 that more resources be directed at minority populations since they are under greatest siege from the disease, Yale Law School professor Harlon Dalton agreed, but warned, "Once it is learned that the face of AIDS is darkening, broad public support may fade."

The severe health problems of minority Americans, who constitute only a quarter of the population but half of the individuals in poverty, go well beyond AIDS. The mortality rate for African-American infants is 17.6 deaths per thousand—more than double the 7.3 death rate for white infants. Immunization rates for African-American children are far below those for white children. More than two-thirds of the 350,000 African-American children living in urban neighborhoods with family incomes below $6,000 a year suffer from lead poisoning.

Even when blacks have the same insurance coverage as whites, they receiver lower-quality health care. Research has found that seriously ill African-American Medicare patients receive worse care than other equally sick Medicare patients whatever the hospital—rural or urban, community or teaching. Black heart attack victims at Veterans Administration hospitals receive less aggressive treatment than whites with the same ailment. Pregnant black women are about 20 percent more likely not to be advised by their doctors to quit smoking and 30 percent more likely not to be told to give up alcohol. Blacks, who are disproportionately represented on waiting lists for kidney transplants, are less likely to get them than are whites.

An average African-American man pays Social Security taxes all his life, but he's lucky to enjoy the benefits for a year. Life expectancy for black males is sixty-five years; white men can expect to live to age seventy-three. The death rate from asthma among blacks is three times higher than among whites. Homicide is the leading cause of death among African-American men and women between fourteen and twenty-five.

If whites constituted the entire population, the nation would rank tenth internationally in infant mortality (still not good enough, but better than twentieth), thirteenth in life expectancy for men (instead of eighteenth), and eleventh for women (instead of fifteenth). And we would at least be in the same ballpark with other industrialized nations in immunizing children.

As secretary of Health, Education, and Welfare in the late 1970s, when pressing to enforce the rights of women, Hispanics, or the disabled, I had little trouble moving aggressively to integrate hospitals, schools, or other facilities, or to make them more accessible to all. But when we moved to open institutions to African Americans, I faced intense resistance. Sadly, the ghost of discrimination still haunts the corridors of American health care.

THE REAL KILLERS AND CRIPPLERS

In a 1993 study, the federal government reported the leading causes of death as heart disease (720,000 deaths), cancer (505,000), stroke (144,000), accidents (92,000), emphysema (87,000), pneumonia and influenza (80,000), diabetes (48,000), suicide (31,000), chronic liver disease and cirrhosis (26,000), and AIDS (25,000).

But a study of the *root* causes of these leading killers produces a different deadly pantheon: tobacco (more than 400,000 deaths), diet and sedentary habits (300,000), alcohol (100,000), infections (many preventable by vaccines) (90,000), environmental hazards (60,000), guns (35,000), sexual behavior (30,000), motor vehicles (25,000), and illicit drug use (20,000).

We are fooling ourselves if we think we can provide affordable health care for all without snaring our careless habits on the road, in the bar, and at home; the pollutants that not only sully our environment but poison our people; our reckless romance with guns and violence; the tenacious scourge of poverty and discrimination; and the pandemic of substance abuse and addiction.

PATIENT, HEAL THYSELF

The dominant objective of private and public concerns with health care should be to motivate people to stay out of the hospital and keep their fingers out of the pill bottle. It is a matter of social justice, in the Catholic religion a corporal work of mercy, to care for the sick. But unless we turn our heads to staying healthy, even the cleverest financial jugglers and managers will have trouble finding the resources to provide all the sick care needed.

Rich or poor, black or white, young or old, individual responsibility for health is the key to any just system of care and a healthy America. Each of us can do more for our own health than any distinguished doctor, dazzling drug, marvelous machine or high-tech hospital. And each of us can assume a fair share of our health care bills.

Instead, we are quick to point the finger at somebody else. In 1993, when the *Los Angeles Times* asked fifteen hundred adults who or what is responsible for rising health costs, the respondents had a hard time choosing among doctors (35 percent), insurers (19 percent), malpractice suits (14 percent), and government (14 percent). Notably absent from the list were themselves—the patients who neglect their health.

The thorny politics of health care reform have inspired more than one politician to promise that somebody else will pick up the tab for unencumbered access to sick care—employers, doctors, hospitals, insurers, government. Too many leaders play on the public's endless quest for something for nothing. By combining the cliché that health care is a right with the hoax that reform is a free lunch, politicians pander to the hedonistic—and wholly unrealistic—temptation that we can do whatever we want to our minds and bodies and a fully funded bag of medical miracles will be there to restore us.

What we eat, drink, and breathe, how we sleep, how we handle stress, how we exercise, how we value life and view death—in short, how we live—can eliminate more health care bills than the most sophisticated medical ministrations. Managing care is damage control after we've fallen into the sick-care system. It is we—you and I—who have the most to say about whether we enter that system.

THE WINDMILL OF IMMORTALITY

Syndicated satirist Art Buchwald diagnosed the American sick-care system at the first benefit awards dinner of the Center on Addiction and Substance Abuse at Columbia University, held at the Pierre Hotel in New York: "I have been asked many times, 'Why is health care so expensive?' The answer is simple. People are refusing to die. Everyone wants to stay alive so they can appear on the Willard Scott show. Twenty-five years ago, people died at 65 when Social Security said they should. Now, if you read The New York Times, *they are passing away at 90 and 97. Unless we can persuade people that it is not in their best interest to stay alive, we will never bring down the cost of medicine."*
—June 1, 1993

Perhaps because of our frontier heritage, Americans refuse to believe there are limits—even to life itself. Consider the struggle in America to define terms such as "death with dignity," which really means death without dying, and "growing old gracefully," a related term that, on closer analysis, means living a long time without aging. Dying in one's sleep at 92 after having won three sets of tennis from one's 40-year-old

grandson that afternoon and having made love to one's wife twice that same evening—this is about the only scenario I have found most American men will accept as fulfilling their idea of death with dignity and growing old gracefully.
    —*Dr. Willard Gaylin,* Harper's Magazine, *October 1993*

However astonishing the modern miracles of medicine men and women, the death rate has remained the same from time immemorial: one per person. Unfortunately, the American way of health care is creating an illusion that by putting that ineluctable reality out of mind, we can put it out of sight. As one wit put it, Americans are the only people who think death may be optional.

Ponce de León's pursuit of the fountain of youth, like the quest for the Holy Grail, was a quixotic journey—but the fantasy is alive and well in the current American insistence on immortality. That hope is understandable for any human being, but particularly for one living in a decidedly materialistic, secular society that worships at the altar of here and now.

What most religions and other civilizations consider the immortality of the soul—life forever after death on earth—is not sufficient for a people skeptical about the existence of a Supreme Being and everlasting soul. For such a people, the promise of forestalling death becomes a consuming drive. Many Americans pursue their daily lives in the belief that the future is now, "for me it's all or nothing" here on earth, and they certainly plan to have it all while they're here.

Faith in a false icon who can bestow medical miracles to fend off death lets us readily accept spending almost a third of Medicare's dollars on patients with less than a year to live. We revere the ability of $3,000-a-day intensive care units to keep crowds of elderly, chronically ill patients with little chance of survival alive for a few more hours, days, or weeks. We marvel at the survival of individuals suspended in a vegetative state by artificial hydration, nutrition, and breathing.

We applaud the government's decision in 1972 to bankroll end-stage kidney dialysis for all patients who need it, at an annual bill of $8 billion. We support the daily decisions by doctors and patients to spend billions more on artificial hearts, organ transplants, and brutal, long-shot chemotherapy to maintain individuals in fragile states. We root for neonatal units that keep newborns alive, however limited their chance of survival or marginal their lives will be after they leave their $2,000-a-day incubators.

The lopsided financing of the research and delivery of such exotic and expensive technology, the promotion of mechanical miracles by medical equipment companies, and the nostrums of America's medicine men and women have sired the most expensive campaign of deceptive advertising in the world's history, attracting billions of dollars a year for the snake oil of a promise to sustain life, no matter how tortured, for a little while longer. The successful peddling of a shot at the futile hope of near-immortality has begot a grotesque distortion of our medical and human values.

Wanting to stay alive is as natural as taking a breath, and it is in our national interest to nourish the scientific genius that pushes the margins of knowledge. Those desperate enemies of technology, the Luddites, who smashed machines in textile mills in England more than a century ago, solved nothing in their day, and their modern-day descendants will solve nothing in ours. But the American medical machine is toying unfairly with our natural instinct to stay alive for just a few more days or weeks. However unintentionally, it has seduced us to accept, applaud, and grasp for its extraordinary ability to keep individuals breathing and their blood flowing with tubes, wires, machines, and medicines that damn near kill them.

Doctors, the essential partners in this hunt for a few more hours in a hospital bed, get early indoctrination in this culture. Medical schools train physicians to extend life, to attend to managing and curing illness rather than preventing it, to give the burgeoning elderly population (from which a third of their income derives) plenty of pills, tubes, surgery, and tests, rather than compassionate care. What we need from our doctors is less of this new T.L.C.—technology, lasers, and CAT scans—and more of the old T.L.C.—tender loving care—grounded in a basic respect for human dignity.

Medical students get lots of lessons in how to extend life, but they are undertrained in understanding human suffering. As a result, America's modern medicine men and women lack what ethicist Daniel Callahan, director of the Hastings Center, calls "a capacity to acknowledge our own mortality and our common vulnerability, as well as to understand the privacy and hiddenness of much pain and suffering in others."

The most well-intentioned country doctor can lose sight of this core value. In January 1986, my eighty-six-year-old father called me in Washington from his home in Spring Lake, New Jersey. He was crying. "They want to send your mother to the hospital. You told us you'd never let them send us to the hospital," he said through his sobs.

"What's wrong with Mom?" I asked.

"I don't know," my father cried. "Here, talk to the doctor."

"Your mother has kidney failure," the doctor said.

"She's going to be ninety-three this June. And she's demented. Why not leave her at home?" I asked.

"She must get kidney dialysis and other treatment in the hospital," the doctor responded. "If she stays here, she'll be dead in a matter of days."

"I'm leaving immediately for Spring Lake. Don't do anything till I get there."

When I arrived about four hours later, it was almost three in the morning. My father's eyes were raw and red from crying as he sat next to my mother's bed, holding her hand.

"Don't let them send your mother to the hospital," he pleaded. In her own way, Mother made the same plea to me.

I turned to the doctor. "My mother's going to stay here," I said.

"I can't be responsible for what happens," he responded. "You realize that your mother will be dead in a few days."

"She's ready for God," I said softly.

The doctor left. I stayed for a few days and then returned to Washington. With my father at her side, holding her hand for the better part of each day, my mother lived for almost six months, and died at peace in her own bed.

THE WINDMILL OF PERFECTION

"Radial Keratotomy Corrected My Nearsightedness . . . and Improved My Golf Game! The doctor didn't tell me that Radial Keratotomy, the surgical procedure to correct my nearsightedness, would also improve my golf game; but it did! My game improved by more than 10 strokes in three months because I can now see better and judge distance effectively. What a relief for someone like me, who had suffered from severe nearsightedness since childhood." —James Smith
—Advertisement for Northern Virginia Vision Center, Inc., in The Washington Post, *May 18, 1994*

The accompanist to the quest for eternal youth is our search for perfection. Americans want flawless beauty and the perfect child. They yearn for the ideal nose, the whitest teeth, the fully rounded female breast, eyes free of crow's feet, bags, and eyeglasses, hips free of fat, bald spots camouflaged by hair transplants, retirements full of sex and sports, sex lives free of inhibitions and punctuated by perfect orgasms every time.

As much of medicine has become more mercenary than ministering, doctors and other providers have responded by giving—as they plead in defending their actions—simply what patients demand. Physicians and therapists have brought billions of dollars of services under the rubric of health care, as an army of cosmetic surgeons, fertility clinics, and eugenics researchers caters to fashionable attitudes of what constitutes perfection and desirability during a particular season. In the process, they value individual traits—intelligence, beauty, strength, eye and hair color—more than the person and reduce the whole to a sum of desirable and undesirable parts.

Indeed, Americans happily spend their money on cosmetic surgery to fix eyelids, tighten chins, iron out facial wrinkles, and eliminate spots on the backs of hands. They buy perpetually white teeth with false caps and take long-shot medicines to stimulate hair growth where a bald spot twinkles. They undergo risky surgery for nearsightedness and laser surgery for snoring. Men and women wear contact lenses not to improve eyesight, but to change eye color, the way they change shoes to match their clothing. Women get silicone implants to enlarge their breasts. Men gulp handfuls of steroids to pump up their pecs.

Americans are more concerned about being thin than being thoughtful, and they enlist the powers of the health care system in their quest. Men and women go for all kinds of trendy binges—on protein-deprived diets, sudden bursts of back-straining exercise, pills to suppress appetite, health foods with dubious claims, animal fluid and tissue injections—all to stay young and svelte forever. They endure painful and expensive procedures to take off a few pounds, while thousands of young women become anorexics, bulimics, and analysands trying to keep from starving themselves to death. As the chorus of cosmeticians and masseurs working over aging film star Norma Desmond sings in *Sunset Boulevard:*

> Of course there's bound to be a little suffering.
> Eternal youth is worth a little suffering.

Newspapers abound with advertisements of cosmetic surgeons promising beauty. "Doctor" Ruth, who holds no medical degree, offers televised advice on how to have great sex. And those who find all their persistent imperfections a little too unsettling can call their doctors and ask for a prescription of Valium, Prozac, or any number of pills to soothe their mild anxieties. Licensed as a treatment for depression, Prozac is now commonly prescribed for "ailments" such as fear of public speaking, obesity, premenstrual syndrome, anxiety at the start of retirement, and "dysthymia," the psychological term for chronic discontent. As one physician admitted, "The patients love it."

Altering personality is the latest medical fad. Neuropsychiatrist Richard Restak tells us most of the research on how the brain functions will be aimed not so much at patients as at people who are already functioning normally "enriching [their] memory, enhancing intelligence, heightening concentration, and altering for the good people's internal moods."

Not content with limiting our quest for perfection to ourselves, many impose it on their children. Prenatal technologies that once served to alert parents to severe problems, such as Down syndrome, are now used to satisfy demands for children of a certain gender or for children free from milder deformities or disabilities.

To help answer such petitions, in the early 1980s, Robert Graham established the Repository for Germinal Choice to seek out and stockpile the sperm of "superior" individuals like Nobel winners. Since then, sperm banks have busted out all over, marketing the donor's education level, weight, height, hobbies, and even eye color.

All of this is done in the name of health care.

When these insatiable yearnings for immortality and perfection combine with the increasing demand of individual Americans for the right to do anything they wish (in the name of individual autonomy, as in "my body, myself") and anything anyone else is doing (as in "I can do anything you can do better"), then health care becomes a cover for self-indulgence and hedonism.

THE WINDMILL OF HYPERMEDICALIZATION

In our pursuit of a discomfortless society, we have medicalized all manner of treatments. Richard McCormick, the brilliant Jesuit moral theologian and health ethicist, crisply poses the question:

> Who is the patient here, who is sick—the individual, or society? . . . This broad understanding of "health" can too easily reflect a sickness of society in its judgments about the meaning of the person. In our time and in some societies, people are hospitalized because of nonconformity. That suggests that the notion of "health" is becoming increasingly nonsomatized and getting out of control.

The damage our penchant for medicalizing social problems can do is starkly apparent in the nation's failure to reduce teen pregnancy. In 1978, when I was secretary of Health, Education, and Welfare, the problem of teenage pregnancy had been dumped on

the U.S. Public Health Service. Then, as in 1994, a million teenagers—about one in nine women aged fifteen to nineteen years—got
pregnant each year.

The Public Health Service measured its success largely by count-
ing the number of individuals who were given birth control devices
by HEW-funded family planning clinics. But we were taking the
wrong measurement. Most every teenager who seeks out a family
planning clinic (almost all are female) already fears she's pregnant.
The clinic had these teenagers fill out some forms and take a test
to determine whether they were pregnant. Then a "counselor"
rushed each client through a chart that listed various birth control
techniques and helped her pick one. There was no discussion of
values or problems these teenagers might have. The clinics saw
thousands of young women, but had no impact on the rate of teen
pregnancy.

Sex education in elementary and secondary schools is most
effective in tempering promiscuous conduct and teen pregnancy
where students share the same values. Parochial schools guided by
similar religious beliefs (whether Christian, Jewish, or Muslim)
and schools in rural areas where parents share common values are
more likely to have effective programs than are large urban
schools, where concern for social and religious differences drives
school officials to medicalize sex education, and in the process,
disembowel teen sexual conduct of any human or moral values.

Sexual intercourse among teenagers creates an enormous demand for medical treatment. Many sexually active teenagers
become victims or transmitters of diseases like AIDS and gonorrhea. Of the million teenagers who become pregnant each year,
some four hundred thousand have abortions, which for some can
create or aggravate mental health problems. Of the more than five
hundred thousand who do not have an abortion or miscarriage,

thousands have pregnancies complicated by maternal smoking, drinking, and drug abuse, and by premature delivery and low-birthweight babies.

The health care system is responsible for dealing with these medical problems—and it should be. Medical science can also contribute discoveries, such as condoms and other contraceptive products, that reduce the incidence of teenage pregnancy and transmission of disease. But twenty years of medicalization has not reduced teen pregnancy in America, nor has it slowed the spread of sexually transmitted diseases among teens. Life for American teenagers is not just a bowl of condoms.

Meanwhile, the social and economic consequences continue to grow. More teens who are not married are having children. Almost 80 percent of unmarried women who have a child before finishing high school live in poverty. Teen pregnancy costs the government more than $34 billion a year in welfare payments ($13 billion), Medicaid bills ($15 billion), and food stamps ($6 billion).

The persistence of this problem is a sorry reflection of the social forces at large for thirty years: poverty and broken families that lead some teens to seek love and status by having a baby, anything-goes moral standards, the declining authority of institutions such as family, church, and school, and a mass culture that treats sex not as a serious personal responsibility—often not even as an act of love—but as a glittering consumer item to be exploited and consumed at the moment of desire. Our teens live in a society where personal self-discipline is more necessary—and less popular—than ever. And for them, popularity is everything.

What many choose to call sexual liberation has brought with it unhappy consequences for millions of teens: the pressure to experiment with adult behavior before they are ready, emotionally, morally, or economically, to shoulder adult responsibility, and the wrenching disruption of life and education caused by an unintended pregnancy and its consequences. This is not liberation. It is bondage for the child-mother and the mother's child.

The responsibility for stopping the conduct that causes teenage pregnancy—promiscuity, use of alcohol or drugs, failure to use a condom, lack of a loving family, lack of hope—rests not only with politicians and policymakers, but with parents in the first instance, as well as with teachers, social workers, clergy, and those who set the moral standards and social mores of the times. By medicalizing the teenage pregnancy problem we have relieved them all of responsibility and trivialized the complexity of the solution.

For most of us, the birth of a child is an occasion of great joy and hope, an investment in the future, a consecration of life. But for hundreds of thousands of teenagers—particularly the majority who are unmarried—the birth of a child can usher in a dismal future of unemployment, poverty, family breakdown, emotional stress, dependency on public agencies, and health problems for mother and child. Preventing such tragedy and comforting those in such pain requires a lot more than a medical degree.

Perhaps the ultimate expression of medicalization comes from the World Health Organization definition of health: "a state of complete physical, mental and social well-being, and not merely the absence of disease or infirmity." In another time, in another age, the adjective *spiritual* would have been included, and Christians and Muslims would have considered it a definition not of health, but of heaven; Buddhists, a sketch of Nirvana; Jews, a description of the time after the Messiah's arrival.

THE FORGOTTEN FINGERS OF HEALTH CARE

Just as society medicalizes all sorts of social concerns, American medicine is losing its human touch. The fetish with financing and delivering sick care and the reverence accorded new technologies are degrading the profession of medicine, pressuring doctors and nurses to master the tricks of regulatory manipulation and mechanical medicine rather than the art of compassionate healing. Dr. Arnold Relman, editor emeritus of *The New England Journal of Medicine,* who has long recognized the need for more efficiency in the health system, is quick to insist that doctors and nurses must have enough time to talk with their patients in order to understand the whys and whats of their ailments and to develop a relationship of personal trust and confidence.

The practice of medicine, the profession of providing health care, is a sacred calling, not a for-profit enterprise. This central truth is being choked in the thick underbrush of regulatory and insurance reimbursement rules and crushed in the machinery of modern hospital centers with their operating rooms and intensive care units, nuclear scanners, heaving ventilators, tubes and gadgets that can mimic just about every organ and wrestle with the will of God. Healing requires more than hooking up to the right machine or swallowing the perfect pill.

Modern medical practice leaves little time for touching. Laurence Ronan, a general practitioner in Boston, complains, "I have fifteen minutes to see you. On top of which I have to fill out a form, and there are times when I have to give a third of my time to those forms, some of them virtually impenetrable. In that fifteen minutes, what do I focus on, especially at the end of the exam, when the patient suddenly tells me that her husband beats her, or someone else tells me he's impotent? None of that fits into fifteen minutes."

Three incidents taught me more about health care than the thousands of pages of material I studied in the Department of Health, Education, and Welfare and during my years since.

In November 1978, I met with the heroic Polish prelate, Stefan Cardinal Wyszynski, at his residence in Warsaw. The cardinal's presence was powerful enough to fill the cavernous room, despite the weakness of his quiet voice. "There are too many machines and tubes and wires," he said. "Even with the best machines, people often die or remain sick because they have no human contact, because they do not touch other people. People need contact to be cured."

The cardinal asked if doctors I'd met in Poland or the United States were sensitive to "the need for one person to touch another."

"Some," I replied.

"You are the minister of health," he said. "When you go back home I hope you will urge doctors in the United States to recognize how important human contact is."

The second incident occurred on the air shuttle from New York to Washington in 1985. I was sitting in the same row with Vernon Jordan, the courageous civil rights leader with whom I had worked when he was registering southern voters in the 1960s and I was an assistant to President Lyndon Johnson. A few years earlier, Jordan had been seriously wounded by a shot in the back one evening as he entered a hotel.

"You know what kept me alive, Joe?" he asked. "It wasn't the skill of the doctor,* though he was superb. It was the fact that he

---

*LaSalle Leffall, head of the Department of Surgery at Howard University College of Medicine.

held my hand for the better part of three days in the hospital. Just holding my hand. That touching is why I survived."

The third was my own experience with heavy-duty surgery at New York Hospital to remove a foot of my intestine. John Whitsell, a surgeon as highly skilled in these matters as any in the world, performed the operation in late May 1993. I was eager to recover rapidly because I wanted to preside over the first fundraising dinner for the Center on Addiction and Substance Abuse at Columbia University, the think/action tank that I had founded several months earlier.

What speeded my recovery was the constant presence of my wife, Hilary; dedicated Irish nurses such as Marguerita McGonnell-Guerin and Anne Kelly, who held my hand through the night; Rev. Walter Modrys, the Jesuit pastor of St. Ignatius Church who visited and prayed with me; and the care of Dr. Tom Nash, my family physician, who came each day to encourage me. Without that touching, I would not have spent June 2, the evening of CASA's inaugural dinner, among the friends and generous supporters of CASA, but in room 1219 at New York Hospital.

Commercial insurers and governments don't reimburse doctors for touching and managed-care corporations don't give bonuses for it. As a result, few physicians feel they can afford the time to talk to patients at any length about their problems and how to take care of their health. Federal, state, and private payers and most HMOs limit their attention (and reimbursement) to sick care delivered cost-effectively and efficiently, which usually means quickly.

As a result, many patients are voting with their feet and pocketbooks for nontraditional health care providers willing to touch and talk as well as probe, prescribe, and pierce. More than a third of all adult patients seek unconventional forms of care, from herbal therapy to acupuncture. Most are under a traditional doctor's care at the time, but they rarely reveal their extracurricular medical sojourns.

Patients reaching for alternative treatment methods typically cite back problems, anxiety, headaches, chronic pain, or cancer as their principal health concern. In 1990, their out-of-pocket payments for such care came to $10.3 billion, nudging the $12.8 billion all Americans paid out of pocket to hospitals. Most striking, patients made 425 million visits to providers of unconventional therapies, far exceeding their 388 million visits to traditional primary care doctors. So widespread has the practice become that in 1992, the National Institutes of Health opened an Office of Alternative Medicine to evaluate unconventional healing treatments.

Dr. Dean Ornish, a member of the new office's advisory panel, employs an innovative alternative to coronary bypass surgery. His patients who suffer from coronary artery disease adopt a regimen of very-low-fat diet, exercise, and meditation to reverse their heart blockages. "If we can address the more fundamental reasons why people get sick," Ornish argues, "it is not only more medically effective, but also more cost-effective."

Proponents claim that unconventional therapies offer more humane, less invasive treatments. Dr. Joseph Jacobs, former director of the Office of Alternative Medicine, notes, "Some of these alternative therapies take a holistic view and more caring view of a patient. This is often hard to achieve in a conventional medical setting, especially if you're lying in a chair with your feet in stirrups."

Jennifer Jacobs (no relation), a family physician, agrees: "The fact that people are willing to spend so much means they think there's something missing in standard treatment." Charles Halpern, president of the Nathan Cummings Foundation, is more blunt: "Traditional medicine is failing its patients."

The increasing demand for alternative therapy should alert traditional physicians that something is lacking in the way many ply their profession, and it should give government and private insurers second thoughts about how the bureaucratic handcuffs of managed care foreclose touching by physicians pressed to spend less time with patients in order to cut costs.

WHO? ME?

The medicalization of so many of our personal problems and the abundance of surgical procedures to mend our bodies and pharmaceuticals to soothe our minds conspire with our insistence on absolute autonomy over our life-styles to push individual responsibility and ethical concerns to the back of the bus.

Torn by the daily stresses of modern life, Americans, from corporate chief executives to secretaries fresh from high school, turn to the medical system for help. Except for those with the most prudent doctors, many end up with a prescription for tranquilizers or antidepressant drugs to keep going, rather than examining how the way they work and play might be changed to ease their stress or temper their swings from high to low.

I remember talking to Carl Albert, the Oklahoma Democrat who was Speaker of the U.S. House of Representatives from 1970 to 1976, about Librium and Valium when Congress was setting restrictions on dangerous drugs and deciding how strictly to control those tranquilizers. The House Speaker stuck his hand in his pocket and pulled out a plastic container filled with Valium. "These pills aren't dangerous," he said. "They're great. I couldn't get through the day around here without them!"

A few drinks every night makes it easier to show up at the pressure-cooker office the next day. Hypertension pills ease high blood pressure, allowing us to continue with unhealthy diets or stressful jobs. Cholesterol reduction pills permit us to keep eating butter and eggs. Miracle surgery lets us smoke (the bad lung can be removed), eat fatty foods (an angioplasty or coronary bypass can clear arteries), and avoid exercise (liposuction rids us of excess fat, and silicone firms up breasts and bottoms).

An array of over-the-counter medications can relieve the discomfort of excessive eating and drinking. In the days of decline of the Roman empire, bacchanalia participants left the dinner between courses to tickle their throats with feathers till they induced vomiting so they could return to eat and drink more. In modern America, there are Tylenol and Pepto-Bismol for hangovers and heartburn, pills to suppress the appetite, drops to clear bloodshot eyes so the boss won't know about a few drinks too many the night before, and fancy spas where the affluent can go twice a year to shed excess pounds.

There are pills to keep us awake, so students can study all night and Wall Street lawyers and investment bankers can negotiate around the clock to close another deal. And there are pills to put us to sleep, so that when we are run-down, overexcited, or worried after tense days, we can bounce back for more.

The medications and the myriad procedures that aim to perfect the human condition are valuable tools. It's how we view and use them that's wrong. We see them not as palliatives when we, as fallible human beings, overindulge or get sick despite our best efforts to stay healthy. Rather, they have become a means to allow further abuse of mind and body. We use them to eat, drink, work, and play with abandon, uninhibited by a sense of individual responsibility. Indeed, if Moses were an American in the 1990s, the tablets he would bring down from the mountain would be Prozac and aspirin to ease our anxiety and the discomfort of our excesses, not a set of commandments to guide our conduct.

We are so infatuated with high-tech marvels that can breathe for us, pump our blood, and retrofit our fetuses that we have not paused to consider carefully and prayerfully the confounding ethical and moral issues that these medical miracles raise.

These questions must be moved up on the agenda. The extraordinary religious and ethnic pluralism of our society will not make it easy, but it does make it urgent that we seek ways to consider openly and fairly such highly charged matters as euthanasia, fetal manipulation, extraordinary means to extend life, neonatal care, the use of mind-altering drugs, sex-change surgery, organ transplants, and the habit of resuscitation.

These matters go to the essence of human existence. Our ability to discuss and resolve them goes to the essence of a moral and free society. These issues, like our individual health, are too important to leave to anyone except you and me.

THE NEW LOOK

If we are to achieve affordable health care for all, we must be willing to take a new look at the entire system, learn from the history of past mistakes and unintended consequences, concentrate on the real causes of illness and rising costs, and recognize how varied and subtle are both the forces that affect the health of our people and the required responses. We must resist the temptation to medicalize all our problems and stop tilting at the windmills of immortality and perfection.

Perhaps most important, we must end our infatuation with the here and now, temper our wide-eyed reverence of high technology, take responsibility for our health as individuals, remind our medicine men and women that there is a difference between Madame Curie and Dr. Frankenstein, probe the moral and ethical implications of our scientific discoveries, and remember that to touch is still to heal.

In short, we must rethink, from top to bottom, our concept of health care, recognize our human needs, and set health care in America on a realistic course to meet them.

CHAPTER FOUR

PUBLIC HEALTH ENEMY NUMBER ONE

After Harry Elphick's first heart attack in the winter of 1993, doctors told him he would need a coronary bypass. But they also told him they would not even consider performing the surgery until he gave up his 25-cigarette-a-day habit. Mr. Elphick, 47, of Manchester, England, did manage to quit smoking, but he never made it back to the hospital. He suffered a heart attack and died August 13, the day he was scheduled to return for a surgical evaluation. Dr. Colin Bray, the hospital's chief cardiologist, offered condolences, but no apology. The refusal to operate was "not a moral view, simply pragmatic," he said. A British daily, The Independent, *disagreed, "A doctor's job is to heal, not to judge."*
—The New York Times, *August 21, 1993*

Nowhere does the perfume of self-delusion so fill the air as in our individual and national denial of the carnage that substance abuse and addiction visit on our society in personal tragedies and massive health care costs. The grim reality, shrouded for too long in our self-denial, is that any effort to provide all Americans health care at affordable cost is doomed to fail unless we mount an all-fronts attack on abuse and addiction involving all substances—cigarettes, alcohol, marijuana, cocaine, crack, heroin, PCP, hallucinogens, sedatives, tranquilizers, stimulants, analgesics, inhalants, and steroids.

For the past twenty-five years, legions of health care reformers have fired their guns at doctors, hospitals, pharmaceutical companies, nursing homes, and insurance companies. They have devised bureaucratic weapons to monitor every patient and medical procedure. But their campaign, whatever its banner—managed care, managed competition, national health insurance—inevitably bogs down in the trenches of complex reimbursement formulas and red tape as special interests spin webs of self-protection. All the while, substance abuse and addiction spreads its destruction and drives up costs.

Policy wonks offer strategies to close down excess hospital beds to save $8 billion, reform medical malpractice to save $25 billion and establish quality standards to curb unnecessary procedures, such as coronary bypasses (to save $2 billion), angiograms (to save $2 billion), and cesarean sections (to save $1 billion). They devise schemes to crack down on crooks and cheaters, trim unnecessary administrative costs, encourage efficiency, increase cost sharing, competition, and regulation, and pay doctors, hospitals, pharmaceutical companies, and nursing homes less.

Some of these efforts to contain costs, such as attempts to reduce administrative waste and unnecessary procedures, are important and long overdue. Others, such as reducing payments to providers, could threaten our ability to maintain the world's most advanced pharmaceutical industry and attract the best minds to medicine and medical research. In every case, however, the promised savings are modest compared to the $200 billion in costs that substance abuse and addiction offers America's health care reformers. It's time to confront substance abuse and addiction for what it is: America's Public Health Enemy Number One.

THE EPIDEMIC OF SUBSTANCE ABUSE

We are a nation of 260 million people, diverse in our politics, professions, races, ages, religions, incomes, neighborhoods, and tastes. Yet, tragically, each one of us in inner cities and rural towns, on assembly lines and in executive suites, in Ivy League colleges and "Blackboard Jungle" city schools, has been touched by substance abuse and addiction.

• Some fifty-four million Americans are hooked on cigarettes and some ten million are hooked on smokeless tobacco.

• More than eighteen million Americans are addicted to alcohol or abuse it.

• Some eight million Americans abuse legal drugs, such as tranquilizers, amphetamines, and sleeping pills.

• Five million Americans regularly smoke marijuana, and the number of high school students puffing pot is on the rise.

• Two million Americans are addicted to or abuse cocaine, including at least half a million hooked on crack.

• Up to one million Americans are hooked on heroin, and the number is rising steadily.

• Up to one million Americans regularly use hallucinogens such as LSD and PCP.

• About one million Americans, half of them teenagers, use black-market steroids.

• Untold numbers of teens and preteens are sniffing everything from high-octane gasoline and glue to gases in hair spray cans and Reddi Whip canisters.

In 1965, when President Lyndon Johnson proposed the first federal drug rehabilitation act, he asked for $15 million to treat addicts.

We in the Johnson White House never thought the cost of treatment would exceed $50 million. In 1994, the federal government will spend more than $2 billion on drug rehabilitation and related therapy. Allowing for overlap, between 20 and 23 million Americans—10 to 11 percent of the over-twelve population—are addicted to alcohol or drugs or seriously abuse them.

With an epidemic such as this, the refusal of Harry Elphick's doctors to treat him until he kicked his cigarette addiction is understandable. Dr. Mark Jameson of Maryland refuses, except in emergencies, to treat patients who smoke. "People know when they smoke that it's adverse to their health. It's a voluntary act, but it doesn't mean I have a duty to take care of them when they suffer from their deliberate act," he argues. One doctor called Jameson's decision "the most compelling smoking cessation incentive a physician can offer," but it will take more than a few angry doctors to tackle addiction in America.

The anecdotal evidence is everywhere, even among society's most successful members: the addiction of megastars like Elizabeth Taylor and Liza Minnelli to alcohol and pills, and of Natalie Cole to alcohol and cocaine; the deaths of young movie actor River Phoenix from a mix of cocaine and heroin and of Maryland college basketball star Len Bias from a cocaine overdose; the suicide of Kurt Cobain, the popular grunge rock singer plagued by heroin and alcohol addiction; the destructive cocaine and heroin dependence of Eugene Fodor, the first American to share top honors at the Tchaikovsky violin competition in Moscow; the life-threatening alcohol and drug addiction of Robin Williams and the overdose death of Williams's friend John Belushi; the cocaine abuse by Cy Young Award winner Dwight Gooden; Mickey Mantle's alcohol abuse and the addiction-plagued careers of football stars like Washington Redskin Dexter Manley and New York

Giant Lawrence Taylor; the cocaine addiction that killed diet guru Dr. Stuart Berger at an early age.

Those who work the halls of national and state legislatures know how treacherous the lure of alcohol and pills can be in the corridors of political success. We see it in a long line of alcohol-abusing politicians, including, at the peak of their influence, two of the most powerful congressional committee chairmen in recent history, Wilbur Mills of the House Ways and Means Committee and Russell Long of the Senate Finance Committee. It takes its tragic measure among political spouses as well, including Kitty Dukakis and Betty Ford. And it strikes the innocent with sudden cruelty, as when in 1993 a drunk driver killed Senator Strom Thurmond's twenty-two-year-old daughter, Nancy.

Is there an American without a family member or friend who smoked himself or herself to premature disability and death from emphysema, lung cancer, or heart disease? When Pat Nixon died of lung cancer, few newspapers mentioned the smoking habit that this former first lady had concealed from the camera's eye for decades, sometimes even lying down on the floor of the presidential limo just to take a few drags. The celebrity morbidity and mortality hit list of tobacco includes Humphrey Bogart, Nat "King" Cole, and Babe Ruth (who chewed tobacco), and gets longer each day, claiming actress Bette Davis, pop singer and two-pack-a-day smoker Mary Wells, and poet laureate and heavy smoker Howard Nemerov, who died of cancer of the esophagus.

Who has not known of a teenager crippled or killed as a result of alcohol abuse? In March 1993, Mary Kate Kelly, an honor student at Langley High School in Virginia, jumped into a Chevy Blazer with several friends after an angry parent forced them to stop drinking beer on his front lawn. Driving on a wet and winding road, the Blazer veered and slammed into a tree. Mary Kate

Kelly was thrown from the car to her death. Only weeks before, when Langley High had suspended three softball players from athletics for drinking at a party, parents complained that it was unfair to penalize their children. After all, everybody did it. As *Washingtonian* magazine and *The Washington Post* reported in 1993, alcohol use among capital area high-schoolers was heavy and widespread and marijuana-related arrests were up 19 percent over the prior year.

Forty-two percent of college students report at least one bout of binge drinking (five or more drinks) every two weeks, and the percentage of college women who admit drinking just to get drunk shot up from 10 to 35 from 1977 to 1993. The president of one of the nation's top Jesuit colleges told me that he's never seen anything like it: "On the weekends, they just drink to get plastered, to completely obliterate their senses."

Princeton University president Harold Shapiro calls alcohol abuse "the greatest single threat to the university's fulfillment of its mission." When U.S. Health and Human Services Secretary Donna Shalala was chancellor of the University of Wisconsin, she called alcohol her greatest single concern. Michael Sovern, the retired president of Columbia University, told me that he moved the graduation ceremony from afternoon to morning in order to minimize rampant and unruly drunkenness. Surprised, I mentioned this to several other university presidents; most confessed they had done the same. Alcohol plays a pivotal role in some 90 percent of the violent crimes and rapes on college campuses, which are on the increase.

Thomas Goodale, student affairs vice president at Virginia Tech in Blacksburg, calls alcohol his "number one problem" and says "among women, the problem is worsening." Though research has shown that alcohol intoxicates women faster than men, one female William and Mary student said, "If you can't drink with the guys, people don't respect you as much." Sixty percent of college women diagnosed with a sexually transmitted disease were drunk at the time of infection. "It's sad because a woman comes in and can't talk for ten minutes because she's sobbing," said Philip Meilman, director of counseling at William and Mary. "She says, 'I woke up in bed and here was a young man, and I don't know how he got there or what happened. But we were both naked.' "

THE RODNEY KING STORY

Far from the Ivy League colleges, alcohol fueled the fires of hatred and violence that spread through Los Angeles in April 1992 and filled the city's emergency rooms after a jury acquitted four policemen of charges related to the arrest and beating of Rodney King. Indeed, the grim influence of alcohol runs throughout the story of King's arrest and trial, and the riot that followed.

Rodney King, whose father—an alcoholic—had died at age forty-two, acknowledged that he was intoxicated on the night of his arrest. When King spotted the police in his rearview mirror, he was driving to a liquor store to get more to drink. Thwarted by the police, he led them on an eighty-miles-per-hour chase that ended with his arrest.

Months later, after the policemen's acquittal, the riots began—not at the courthouse or at city hall—but at Pay-less Liquor and Deli in South Central L.A. There, around 4 P.M., five angry gang members stole some bottles of malt liquor, yelling "This is for Rodney King!" Around 6 P.M., an angry mob, pelting passing motorists, chose its first target for looting: Tom's Liquor store, from which the mob took more than a hundred cases of forty-ounce malt liquor bottles and ninety cases of sixteen-ounce malt liquor cans.

The focus of the crowd should not be a surprise. As *U.S. News & World Report* noted, 728 licensed liquor outlets smothered South Central L.A.'s crumbling landscape—an opportunity to buy booze around just about every corner.

THE HEALTH CARE CONSEQUENCES

The patient, a 75-year-old bachelor, had suffered a stroke that prevented him from swallowing. He lived alone but was taught how to manage his feeding tube. A few months after he left Greater Baltimore Medical Center, a neighbor who had agreed to monitor him told the hospital the deal was off. "When he came back to us," said Krystal Tripp, a social worker at the hospital, "he was bedridden and he had bedsores all over his body. We found he had been pouring beer into his feeding tube. He couldn't taste it anymore but still liked the feeling the alcohol gave him."
                                        —The Baltimore Sun, *August 3, 1993*

Substance abuse and addiction taxes every segment of our health care system. It contributes to or causes more than seventy conditions that require hospitalization, complicates the treatment of most illnesses, prolongs hospital stays, increases morbidity, and sharply raises costs. Heart disease, cancer, and stroke are the official leading causes of death in the U.S., but substance abuse and addiction is the chief culprit, along with poor diet and exercise patterns accounting for four of every ten deaths.

The nation's elaborate and expensive emergency rooms are largely monuments to alcohol and drug abuse. In 1992, there were more than 430,000 drug-related emergency-room episodes—and that does not include victims of heart attacks due to cigarette smoking. In the first half of 1993, record numbers of individuals with adverse reactions to heroin were rushed to hospital emergency rooms, where most were treated by busy doctors and nurses and discharged through the revolving doors of the sick-care system.

Half the nation's hospital beds hold victims of violence; auto and home accidents; cancer; heart disease; AIDS; tuberculosis; and liver, kidney, and respiratory ailments—all caused or exacerbated by the abuse of tobacco, alcohol, and drugs. A study at the Medical College of Wisconsin found that more elderly Americans are hospitalized for alcohol-related problems than for heart attacks. Many land in the most expensive domain of the hospital: the intensive care unit. Johns Hopkins University found that substance abuse accounted for more than a third of the spending in its hospital's intensive care unit, which costs more than $2,000 a day.

The Center on Addiction and Substance Abuse at Columbia University revealed that at least one of every five dollars that Medicaid spends on inpatient hospital bills can be traced to substance abuse, at a cost of some $8 billion in 1994. The center found the proportion of inpatient dollars spent by Medicare to be even higher: almost 25 percent, or $20 billion of the $80 billion Medicare spent to hospitalize the elderly and disabled in 1994. From 1994 to 2014, Medicare will spend $1 trillion on inpatient care due to substance abuse, $800 billion of that amount attributable to tobacco use.

On average, Medicaid patients with substance abuse as a secondary diagnosis are hospitalized twice as long as patients with the same primary diagnosis, but no drug or alcohol problem. On average, burn patients with a substance-abuse secondary diagnosis have 12.6-day hospital stays; those without leave the hospital in

5.6 days. Boys under age fifteen with a substance-abuse secondary diagnosis stay an average 16.4 days in the hospital, four times as long as boys with no such diagnosis; girls under fifteen with such a substance abuse diagnosis stay almost three times longer, 9.8 days.

ILLNESS

Most of us know that cigarettes are responsible for the premature death of around 435,000 people in the U.S. each year. But we do not appreciate the wide range of serious illness that smoking lays on our people. Cigarettes cause half of all coronary heart disease, are implicated in most cancers, and double the risk of stroke. Heart disease, cancer, and stroke are America's top three killers and cripplers.

At least 74 percent of all lung cancer and 50 percent of all head and neck cancer among Medicaid patients can be traced to cigarettes and alcohol. Since 1987, lung cancer has outpaced breast cancer as the leading cancer killer of women. A woman smoker has twice the risk of developing lung cancer as a man. Female smokers have up to four times more cervical cancer than non-smokers—and radiation therapy for such cancer is less effective for smokers.

In 1993, the Environmental Protection Agency designated secondhand smoke as a known human carcinogen, along with only ten other compounds. It estimated that secondhand smoke kills fifty thousand individuals a year and makes thousands more ill. The price we pay in health care costs solely for smokers comes to about $50 billion a year.

Alcohol abuse is the leading cause of chronic liver disease, including cirrhosis. It can lead to many serious gastrointestinal problems including esophageal cancer and pancreatitis, nutritional and metabolic disorders, and cardiovascular and neurological problems. Heavy drinking or smoking more than doubles the risk of oral cancer. Combined, their one-two punch jacks up the risk more than fifteen times.

Drug abuse can lead to AIDS, endocarditis, cellulitis, and hepatitis. Other diseases, including tuberculosis, can result from the weakened immune systems and debilitating life-styles of addicts. Drug abuse can also exacerbate mental illness, vascular problems, and malnutrition. And it has pushed thousands of individuals and families into poverty, where chronic health problems are endemic.

ACCIDENTS AND VIOLENCE

Alcohol and drugs are implicated in the tide of violence where America works—in the post office, fast-food restaurant, bank, or supermarket. Two-thirds of those who use illegal drugs are employed, a fact that helps explain some 666,000 incidents of workplace violence in 1992.

Some three out of four trauma *victims* test positive for drugs, to say nothing of the alcohol or drugs in the assailants of those who are attacked. Alcohol and drug abuse have been implicated in up to 80 percent of spouse-abuse cases and three-quarters of all rapes, child molestations, suicides, and homicides. The cost of related illness and therapy for the spouses, children, and parents who are left behind runs into billions of dollars. The human tragedy is incalculable.

Although drunk driving has declined since the mid-1980s, four of every ten Americans will be involved at some point during their lives in alcohol-related auto accidents that require medical care. About twenty thousand people die and another 1.2 million are injured each year in alcohol-related crashes. The annual health care costs of alcohol- and drug-related traffic accidents top $5 billion.

BABIES AND CHILDREN

Women who use tobacco, alcohol, and drugs during pregnancy put their newborn babies at savage risk.

Fetal alcohol syndrome is among the top three causes of birth defects associated with mental retardation, at health care costs of $2 billion a year. The 500,000 babies born in the U.S. each year who are exposed to illicit drugs in the womb face higher risks of stroke at birth, physical deformity, and mental deficiency. The care for such newborns costs more than $2,000 a day; in 1993, hospitalization alone for babies exposed to cocaine during pregnancy cost more than $600 million.

Most child abuse involves parental substance abuse. Thanks largely to drugs and alcohol, reports of child abuse or neglect have more than doubled from 1983 to 1993.

The price children pay for exposure to their parents' cigarette smoke is even more pervasive. Smoking retards fetal growth and doubles the danger of delivering a low-birthweight baby. It increases the risk of fetal and infant death by 25 to 50 percent. Exposure of newborns to cigarette smoke in utero or secondhand smoke after birth increases the risk of sudden infant death syndrome and leads to health problems and learning disabilities later in life.

Each year, exposure to parental smoking causes up to 300,000 cases of lower respiratory tract illness, such as bronchitis and pneumonia, in infants and young children. Secondhand smoke increases both the number of new asthma cases in children and the frequency and severity of asthma attacks in those already afflicted. No wonder former Surgeon General C. Everett Koop calls exposing children to secondhand smoke "child abuse."

AIMING FOR AMERICA'S CHILDREN

Low-alcohol cocktails, bearing such familiar brand names as Jack Daniel's and mixed with fruit juice or soda, are one of the few hot segments in the stagnant spirits industry. New drinks with syrupy-sweet taste, brightly colored labels and such cutesy names as Tahitian Tangerine and Dixie Jazzberry are flooding into grocery stores and liquor outlets. The new concoctions amount to a kind of kiddie cocktail, critics contend. Some are even sold in familiar, 12-ounce aluminum cans complete with pop-tops—just like Coke's and Pepsi's.
— The Wall Street Journal, *August 4, 1993*

Sean Marsee was shocked when, in May 1983, doctors told him he had oral cancer at age 18. He did not smoke or drink; he lifted weights and ran five miles a day. But Sean consumed a can of snuff every day and a half. Chewing tobacco was popular among high school athletes who thought it was a "safe" way to use tobacco. That spring, Sean lost part of his tongue to cancer. Before he could begin radiation, doctors found the cancer in his lymph nodes, prompting more surgery. In the fall, they found more cancer and had to remove part of his jaw. In January 1984, they found new lumps in his neck. As his condition deteriorated, Sean, still craving nicotine, confessed to his mother, "I catch myself thinking, I'll just reach over and have a dip." He died on February 25, 1984.
— Tobacco-Free Youth Reporter, *Spring 1994*

One of the most sinister aspects of our society is that those who hawk addictive substances target children and young Americans for their wares.

Virtually all Americans who are addicted to cigarettes or drugs (with the possible exception of cocaine) are hooked in their teens and early twenties. This is no secret to cigarette companies, which refuse to withdraw ads with special attraction to teens, such as the Joe Camel campaign; to beer and alcohol advertisers, which provide a big chunk of all college newspaper revenue; or to illegal drug dealers, who involve poor children in their trade and destroy their parks and recreational facilities, denying them a place to play and creating idle time to experiment with drugs.

Tobacco companies know that their long-term customers are usually people who start smoking as teenagers. So it's no surprise when they target their advertising to teens in campaigns with young, beautiful people whose social cachet is punctuated with a cigarette.

Equally predictable is their targeting young women to shore up demand. Encouraged by the success of Joe Camel, R.J. Reynolds added a female, a.k.a. "Josephine Camel," to its ads in 1994. Virginia Slims has long tried to make smoking a feminist statement, from their old cheer, "You've Come a Long Way, Baby!" to the new, sexually savvy slogan of the defiant female smoker: "Hey, if anyone tries to rein you in, just say 'Whoa!' "

Such efforts to bolster the allure of smoking among young women have been abetted by fashion moguls whose ads showcase painfully thin women smoking cigarettes *(très chic!),* and by movie actresses like Winona Ryder, who smoked incessantly (as did her costar, Ethan Hawke) in the 1994 film *Reality Bites,* which sympathetically depicted the angst of the twenty-something "Generation X."

In pushing its cigarettes, Philip Morris acts just like a street drug dealer selling cocaine or heroin. Standard operating procedure for a dealer is to give away the drugs free or at low cost to get the kids addicted. Once hooked, the dealer starts charging as much as he can. As cigarette sales of the Philip Morris flagship brand Marlboro slipped, the cigarette merchant lowered the price sharply to make a pack easier to purchase by those with fewer dollars, such as the young and the poor. Lured by the low prices, thousands got hooked on Marlboros.

Once Marlboro's market share rose from 21.5 to 26 percent, the tobacco giant began moving up the price. Michael Miles, then Philip Morris's chief executive pusher, boasted, "Our pricing strategy . . . achieved our objectives," which included "increas[ing] Philip Morris U.S.A.'s overall share of the domestic cigarette market [and] regain[ing] share for Marlboro."

For the young, getting hooked on cigarettes can open the door to illicit drug use. An analysis by the Center on Addiction and Substance Abuse at Columbia University of data derived from the NIDA (National Institute on Drug Abuse) National Household Survey on Drug Abuse reveals the link between cigarette smoking by twelve- to seventeen-year-olds and the use of hard drugs. Twelve- to seventeen-year-olds who smoke cigarettes are:

• 12 times more likely to use heroin than those who have never used cigarettes
• 51 times more likely to use cocaine
• 57 times more likely to use crack
• 23 times more likely to use marijuana
If they smoke more than a pack a day, they are:
• 51 times more likely to use heroin than those who have never used cigarettes
• 106 times more likely to use cocaine
• 111 times more likely to use crack
• 27 times more likely to use marijuana

Drinking by children can also open the door to use of illicit drugs such as marijuana and cocaine. Twelve- to seventeen-year-olds who drink alcohol are 22 times more likely to smoke pot and 50 times more likely to use cocaine than children who don't drink.

That makes all the more disturbing how beer, wine, and liquor companies have begun relying more heavily on the profitable youth market. In the late 1980s, faced with fading sales among the young, brewers decided to promote inexpensive forty-ounce bottles of malt liquor, double the potency of regular beer and more than triple the size of twelve-ounce beer bottles, in low-income neighborhoods. "It gets you pumped up," explained one teenage boy to *The New York Times.* "I feel more comfortable when I'm drinking a 40." In the early 1990s, faced with stiff competition from imports and a slowly growing market, Miller Brewing Company shot for younger drinkers with a marketing plan aimed at "making Miller Lite relevant to a new generation."

Other alcohol companies spruced up their ads for wine coolers to appeal to a younger market, and the liquor industry began a concerted effort to get young Americans to drink its products. "Jaegermeister," a seventy-proof (about 35 percent alcohol) herbal-flavored liquor, which is promoted by attractive women who roam college bars and peddle the drink, is a hot seller. "You drink them so quick, you don't realize how drunk you are," said a senior at Louisiana State University, where a student fell into a coma in November 1993 after drinking about thirty shots of Jaegermeister and other brands in an hour.

AMERICA'S CERBERUS

Substance abuse has joined with AIDS and tuberculosis to become an American version of Cerberus, a vicious, three-headed dog at the gates of the hells we have created in inner cities and running loose into every part of our nation.

Substance abuse is the fastest-growing cause of new cases of HIV infection. Intravenous drug use is implicated in a third of all AIDS cases found in teenagers and adults and more than 70 percent of all AIDS cases in women. The annual cost of treating a person infected with HIV is $10,000; for a person with full-blown AIDS, the cost jumps to $40,000.

Less widely recognized, but no less serious, is the spread of AIDS by teenagers high on beer or pot. In a random survey of sixteen- to nineteen-year-olds, as many as half admitted they were more likely to have sexual intercourse when drinking or using drugs, and less likely to use condoms, thus increasing the risk of unwanted pregnancy and of transmitting sexual diseases. As one student at Yorktown High in northern Virginia put it, "Every girl I knew who had sex in high school was wasted the first time."

Substance abuse, often abetted by immune systems weakened by AIDS, has formed a deadly alliance with tuberculosis. Alcoholics and intravenous drug users are more likely to develop the new, drug-resistant strains of this highly contagious disease. And because they often fail to take their medicine, they are more likely to spread this virulent TB to the general population.

At least a third of the homeless—some say 80 to 90 percent—are alcohol or drug abusers. Homeless shelters, with their overcrowding, poor ventilation, and concentration of drug addicts and alcoholics, are ideal breeding grounds for TB and AIDS. It takes more than $250,000 to treat an individual with drug-resistant TB, and that does not include infrastructure costs, such as isolation rooms and negative-pressure facilities.

In combination, substance abuse, AIDS, and TB pose the greatest public health crisis that urban America has faced since the plagues of typhoid and cholera in the early 1900s.

THE PEOPLE IN PRISON

The isolated community of 14,000 that Dr. Yvette Walker serves is a sinkhole of medical problems: 25 percent of her patients have syphilis, 25 percent are mentally ill and more than 75 percent are drug users. Of the women, 27 percent are HIV-positive, 30 percent have sexually transmitted diseases and 10 percent are pregnant. Dr. Walker is the medical director of health services for Rikers Island, New York City's largest jail.

—The New York Times, *January 1, 1994*

Hollywood's familiar prison scenes, filled with cigar-chomping, brass-knuckled mobsters and hoodlums—played with bravado by Humphrey Bogart, James Cagney, George Raft, and Edward G. Robinson—have long since disappeared from the American scene. Some 80 percent of 1994's more than 800,000 state prison inmates were incarcerated for violating drug laws or alcohol- and drug-related crimes such as rape, assault, child molestation, and robberies to support drug habits. Sixty percent of the more than eighty thousand federal inmates are incarcerated for drug-law violations.

In 1990, for the first time the number of individuals sent to prison for drug crimes (103,800) was higher than the number incarcerated for property crimes (102,400), and that number does not include eighty-seven thousand violent offenders, most of whose crimes were drug- or alcohol-related. Many inmates admit to regular use (often daily) of cocaine, heroin, PCP, LSD, or illicit methadone prior to committing their crime.

In 1994, the nation's prison population, triple its 1980 size, broke the one-million-inmate barrier. Federal, state, and local spending on corrections soared to more than $40 billion, a 1,000 percent rise in twenty years. The U.S. has more prisoners per capita than any other nation in the industrialized world, and keeps increasing its lead by adding more than a thousand each week.

Politicians trample one another in their stampede to build prisons, with big bucks for concrete and steel. But they fail to recognize that incarceration of drug offenders and alcohol abusers, and their high incidence of AIDS, other sexually transmitted diseases, and TB, has pushed health care to the top of the corrections agenda and budget. In 1994, federal prisons devoted some 15 percent of their resources to health services, four times what they spent in 1985. In all, federal and state prisons spend more than $2 billion on health care. State prisons employ a small army of eighteen thousand in health care units.

During 1992, the incidence of AIDS among federal and state prisoners was 362 cases per 100,000, more than twenty times the eighteen cases per 100,000 in the total U.S. population. One of five inmates at Rikers Island in New York City is HIV positive. Carol Dunn, warden at the Niantic Connecticut Correctional Institution for Women, estimates that up to 70 percent of the inmates there may be infected with HIV and 85 percent of the crimes committed by inmates are drug-related.

Often, a trip to prison only makes the traveler sicker. Overcrowding and poor ventilation create fertile environments for the spread of TB and other diseases caused by airborne bacteria and viruses. In New Jersey, state prison inmates have a TB incidence of 110 per 100,000 inmates, eleven times higher than the rate in the general population of the state. In California, the TB incidence of 80.3 per 100,000 inmates is six times the rate in the state's general population. On average, inmates who spend more than a year in jail are twice as likely to develop TB as those who leave sooner. To change the odds is costly: New York City's Rikers Island prison spent $70 million to build one hundred forty-two state-of-the-art TB cells in 1993.

During the 1980s, as state mental institutions closed, they evicted more than 30,000 Americans with serious mental illness. Many landed in jails. By 1993, some 70,000 state and federal prisoners had serious psychiatric conditions; another 175,000 needed psychiatric services. There is a high incidence of substance abuse among individuals suffering from mental illness.

Inmates are also far more likely to smoke cigarettes than are members of the general population. Some 85 percent of male prisoners are addicted smokers. In a women's prison in Illinois, 81 percent of the inmates are hooked on cigarettes.

Overwhelmed by crippling and contagious diseases, prison health care systems are severely short of doctors. Even when doctors are available, the environment discourages patient advocacy and confidentiality between doctor and patient, hallmarks of ethical, effective medical practice.

Most ominous for America's health care system is the reaction of prison officials to their health care crisis. To reduce costs, states with overcrowded prisons sometimes encourage early parole of their sickest patients, letting loose on society thousands of individuals afflicted with AIDS, TB, and other infectious and contagious diseases.

TACKLING THE PANDEMIC

By any measure for any other ailment, substance abuse and addiction is pandemic in America. Only 5 percent of the world's population, Americans provide the market for almost 50 percent of the world's cocaine. One in four Americans has a drug or alcohol disorder at some point in his life. More and more college students, our most talented young men and women, are drinking to get drunk, setting the stage for alcohol addiction in later life. Binge drinking, pot smoking, and LSD tripping are up among eighth- and tenth-graders. More high school seniors are using hallucinogens, cocaine, heroin, and pot.

The breadth and depth of this plague say something deeply troubling about our society, the way we live and work, our values, the despair of poverty in the richest nation on earth, and the aimless boredom of many affluent American youngsters. Our failure to recognize substance abuse and addiction for what it is—the most devastating health pandemic threatening our people—is a telling testament to our capacity for individual and national self-denial.

The issue was barely discussed in the 1992 presidential campaign. Why? Despite a decline in cocaine and marijuana use, with the ravages of addiction so visible on city streets across America, Republican incumbent George Bush could not support claims that he had won the war on drugs. Challenger Bill Clinton, son of an alcoholic parent and brother of a cocaine addict, did not have a program to deal convincingly with the problem.

Effective health care reform is at best a dicey and unpredictable enterprise, but it is also a hopeless one in the absence of a tenacious attack on substance abuse on all fronts: research, prevention, and treatment. There is a role for each of us. We must:

Shed our drug-of-the-month mentality and recognize that few abuse only one substance. The enemy is substance abuse and addiction—licit or illicit—not simply illegal drug addiction. For the very young, cigarettes and beer can be drugs of entry into an even more dangerous world. Many cocaine and heroin addicts started on alcohol and marijuana and continue their abuse of those substances.

Alcohol topped the list of abused substances in the early 1960s. By the end of the decade, pot was the most abused drug on college campuses, with a hefty dose of hallucinogens like LSD and PCP thrown into the mix. In the 1970s, heroin turned our city streets into alleys of terror. A report I prepared in 1980 and 1981 on drug and alcohol abuse for New York's governor Hugh Carey hardly mentioned cocaine, which became the fashion among the well-to-do and then the bane of the poor later in that decade. By 1990, crack had brought Wild West shoot-outs and the death of innocent bystanders to urban streets.

In 1994, heroin returned to the cities, as did dangerous and addictive mixtures of cocaine and heroin. The drug of choice on America's college campuses? Once again, it's alcohol, with sprinklings of LSD. And high school seniors are going back to marijuana and hallucinogens.

The enemy of public health is all substance abuse and addiction. Ricocheting from drug to drug, without recognizing the central problem of addiction, is the stuff of federal fad and political passion, not national policy.

Increase support for research into substance abuse and addiction. The wars on cancer, cardiovascular disease, and AIDS are waged with an armada of the highest-tech, costly weapons systems, while the nation battles substance abuse with cap pistols. The National

Institutes of Health invest almost $5 billion in research on the fashionable killers ($2.4 billion on cancer, $785 million on heart disease, $113 million on strokes, $1.3 billion on AIDS). It invests less than 15 percent of that amount in research on addiction and abuse of all substances—alcohol, tobacco, and drugs—the largest single cause and aggravator of all four of those killers.

If AIDS, TB, or multiple sclerosis afflicted some twenty-three million Americans as alcohol and drug addiction and abuse do, or 20 percent of the total population as nicotine addiction does, can anyone doubt that the nation would mount a research effort on the scale of World War II's Manhattan Project to develop the atomic bomb?

We need to decipher the psychological and biological causes and cures for addiction and abuse and tap into the mysteries and opportunities of genetics. We need to know why treatment works for such a small percentage of people who enter programs for the first time, how to get it to work for more, and how to make it more cost-effective. Is there an affordable system of treatment that will work for high percentages of those who enter it? Techniques to attract more addicts into treatment? Ways to identify which treatments work best for which addictions or populations? Pharmaceuticals to reach key brain cells? These and a thousand other questions about abuse and addiction must be addressed.

We also need to learn more about how to influence adolescent behavior, for an individual who negotiates his or her teens and early twenties without abusing tobacco, drugs, and (though to a somewhat lesser extent) alcohol is virtually certain never to do so.

NIH needs a National Institute on Addiction with a billion-dollar-a-year budget. A large proportion of addicts is hooked on more than one substance—cocaine snorters usually continue to abuse pot and alcohol, while many alcoholics also abuse tranquilizers, sleeping pills, and other psychoactive drugs. A National Institute on Addiction would eliminate many of the bureaucratic bouts over turf that slow and sometimes kill valuable research projects.

America's best and brightest medical and scientific minds did not just happen into cancer and cardiovascular research. Two presidents, Lyndon Johnson and Richard Nixon, declared back-to-back billion-dollar-a-year wars on each of these diseases, and Congress delivered the requested funds. As a result, talented men and women knew that if they devoted their lives to conquering these ailments, the resources would be there for their work. Until the nation makes a similar commitment to tackle substance abuse and addiction, we will not attract our top scientific minds to devote their lives to a research enterprise involving such an intractable problem.

Treatment can work to reduce drug and alcohol abuse and related health costs. Unfortunately, we do not attract enough addicts to treatment, and many who come do not stay long enough. But the need for research, basic and clinical, can hardly be overstated. Success rates of different treatment programs vary widely and solid data is hard to get. On average, of the millions of substance-abusing Americans who need treatment in a given year, fewer than 25 percent will enter programs. Of that small number, about a quarter will complete them. Of that quarter, less than half will stay free of drugs and alcohol for more than a year.

We do not know why treatment works for one and not another. Many programs have high rates of success, often related to how soon after beginning use the substance abuser seeks treatment, the length of time in treatment, aftercare, and family support. Our lack of knowledge and a deep skepticism about the efficacy of treatment programs are why, since 1990, Congress has committed less money to treatment than the administration had requested, and why in 1994 the House slashed President Clinton's request for treatment funds for hard-core addicts.

Launch a massive effort to prevent substance abuse and addiction. What little we do know about abuse and addiction begins with two propositions: It can be prevented, and the earlier we spot abuse or addiction, the greater the likelihood we can end it.

At least as many middle-class and affluent white youngsters experiment with drugs as do poor, inner-city African-American and Hispanic youths. However, the middle class and affluent are more likely to stop experimenting on their own or get early help. They have more hope in the future and more reliable support systems (families, safe housing, economic security, better schools, and counseling) and they know how to tap available resources. Poor teens, especially minorities, are more likely to stay the course of drug use long enough to get hooked.

As family, social, and legal problems increase and poverty persists, vulnerability to drug and alcohol addiction jumps and its tenacity increases. Upon hearing my complaint as secretary of Health, Education, and Welfare about the failure of our antismoking campaign to reach poor minorities, Harlem Congressman Charles Rangel snapped, "Why should it surprise you? Why should someone who has no job and doesn't know where his next meal or bed is coming from quit smoking to live five more years?"

Deeply rooted cultural shifts are necessary—and possible. Overcoming the obstacles that Rangel cites will not be easy; it requires not only government action, but initiatives by community leaders and businesses. But with public education and peer pressure, America has successfully moved from a society in which the smoker boldly asked, "Would you like a cigarette?" to one in which the smoker sheepishly whispers, "Do you mind if I smoke?"

We can have the same kind of effect on other substance abuse and addiction. The impact of the media campaign of the Partnership for a Drug-Free America demonstrates the potential of imaginative and persistent messages to spark cultural shifts. The importance of persistence in delivering the message can be seen in that a reduction in running the Partnership's ads was accompanied by the 1993 rise in marijuana users among high-schoolers. That increase followed evidence that teens perceived less risk in smoking pot, as well as in experimenting with cocaine and smoking cigarettes.

Newspapers and magazines can voluntarily drop tobacco advertising, as *Reader's Digest* and *The New Yorker* did years ago. States and cities can ban the sale of cigarettes through vending machines and enforce laws prohibiting the sale of cigarettes to minors.

Congress should increase the cigarette tax by at least two dollars a pack. That would cut the number of smokers by almost eight million people and, over time, save almost two million lives. Most important, the higher price would put cigarettes beyond the means and lunch money of most elementary and high school students.

The impact of a cigarette tax and public information campaign is clear in California, which in 1989 increased the tax on cigarettes from ten to thirty-five cents, created a new tax on smokeless tobacco of forty-two cents on the dollar, and dedicated 20 percent of the revenues to antismoking campaigns. By 1994, cigarette consumption had dropped 27 percent, three times faster than in the rest of the country. The drop in smoking saved some $386 million in direct medical costs during 1993 alone.

In 1994, the Food and Drug Administration reported that "it is our understanding that manufacturers commonly add nicotine to cigarettes" to make them more addictive. The combined impact of manufacturers spiking their cigarettes with nicotine to calibrate their addictive power and the fact that just about everyone who smokes gets hooked as a teen makes this higher tax not only a major health cost-containment measure, but an essential public health initiative to protect our children from abuse by tobacco companies.

Provide health insurance, whether funded publicly or privately, to cover treatment and aftercare. Coverage by public and private insurance programs is key to making substance abuse treatment—from intensive residential programs to outpatient care, smoking cessation classes, and nicotine patches and gum—with continuing aftercare available to all. Insurers and employers pay billions for long-shot cancer therapies that have lower success rates than many substance abuse treatment programs, but cancer is not tarred with the stigma attached to drug and alcohol abuse.

Addiction is a chronic disease, more like diabetes and high blood pressure than like a broken arm or pneumonia, which can be fixed or cured in a single round of therapy. Continuing care is as critical to treating the alcoholic or drug addict as taking insulin or hypertension pills is to the diabetic or victim of high blood pressure.

On October 28, 1975, I broke a twenty-eight-year smoking addiction that at times (particularly when I was working for President Lyndon Johnson) had reached four packs a day. To this moment, I know that if I were to smoke a single cigarette, I would be hooked again. The same is true not just for most ex-smokers, but for most alcohol, pill, cocaine, and heroin addicts. Their need for support, human as well as medical, continues—for many on a daily basis.

President Johnson quit smoking after a massive heart attack

that nearly took his life in 1954. Throughout the rest of his public career, he longed for a cigarette. When I served on his White House staff, he often said that as soon as he left office he intended to resume smoking. On January 20, 1969, after Richard Nixon's inauguration, Johnson, en route to Texas on his final flight in his *Air Force One,* lit a cigarette. He was hooked again before he landed at his ranch in Johnson City, where he died four years later, a victim of a heart attack probably brought on by smoking.

Individuals often need several tries to shed nicotine addiction. Americans understand and accept that. They must also accept the reality that it is likely to take alcoholics and drug addicts more than one attempt to break their habits. That doesn't mean we should soften up the toughness required to get them to quit, such as threat of dismissal from a job or incarceration upon repeated relapse or violation of drug laws. It does mean that we must be creative and persistent in encouraging them to get up each time they fall.

Managed-care plans must take care not to deny or limit treatment of substance abusers. One married woman with three children was drinking half a gallon of wine and a quart of vodka daily, as well as taking Xanax, a drug prescribed for anxiety. She sought treatment at a facility in Connecticut. The facility had to consult her managed-care plan, which said she would have to wait four days before it would pay any professional fees. Five hours later, the woman attempted suicide and was admitted to a hospital. Later, she tried again to kill herself and was readmitted to the hospital, where she attempted suicide for a third time. Finally her managed-care plan agreed to pay for six days of inpatient care at the facility. But the plan refused to cover outpatient care, so the Connecticut center provided no follow-up care and has no idea what happened to the woman.

Commit at least the same level of energy and financial resources to research, prevention, and treatment as we devote to interdiction, police, and pursuit. The root of America's addiction problem is not in the faraway places of Turkey's poppy fields, Southeast Asia's Golden Triangle, or South America's jungles, but within ourselves. Drugs are not invaders, but invitees, to the neighborhoods and homes of America.

Most public policies guiding the nation's various wars on drugs have failed because they have been so lopsidedly concentrated on law enforcement and interdiction. Yet one political leader after another orders up more of the same: more cops, more prisons, more tough sentences. Let's recognize these leaders, Republican and Democrat alike, for what they are: a chorus of politicians pounding the table harder and shouting louder, "If all the king's horses and all the king's men can't put Humpty Dumpty back together again, then give us more horses and more men!" Let's accept the implications of the 1994 Rand report which found that one dollar invested in treatment had a greater impact on reducing drug abuse than seven to twenty dollars spent on enforcement and interdicting supplies. And let's act on the California experience that each dollar spent on treatment for drug and alcohol abuse saves seven dollars, largely due to reductions in crime.

Take advantage of captive audiences. While children are in school, we should educate them about the dangers of substance abuse. We should make our workplaces smoke- and drug-free, and employers should encourage employees to pursue healthy life-styles. Doctors should be trained to spot the signals of substance abuse in patients and get them into appropriate treatment.

Nowhere is our failure to take advantage of captive audiences more self-defeating than in prisons. Our refusal to provide drug and alcohol treatment to every prisoner who needs it is not only a guarantee of continuing high recidivism rates and rising prison costs, it is an inexcusable breach of our obligation to protect the public health.

Resist the seductive myth of legalization, a cure worse than the disease. The seeming intractability of the drug problem has sparked occasional calls for legalization, including a gingerly foray by Surgeon General Joycelyn Elders. Such calls reveal a stunning disregard of history, experience, and human nature.

The nation has made significant progress against illegal drugs. While there remains a hard-core addicted population, vigilant education and prevention efforts have had an impact. Despite the availability of crack, cocaine use in 1992 had dropped more than 75 percent from its 1985 peak, and marijuana use among high school seniors, though rising slightly in 1993, is far below its 1979 peak.

Legalization would undermine efforts at prevention and education by removing the stigma of criminality and increasing the availability of drugs. Experience has taught us that legalization leads to wider accessibility and addiction. We have some fifty-four million nicotine addicts and more than eighteen million alcoholics and alcohol abusers, but only two million cocaine addicts. Putting the stamp of legality on snorting cocaine and smoking crack would increase the number of addicts severalfold—and light a new flame beneath health care spending.

Legalization would increase supply and decrease prices. We know from experience that when drugs are easy to get—as heroin was for U.S. soldiers in Vietnam, cocaine was at the turn of the century, and alcohol was after the repeal of Prohibition—use and addiction rise. If cocaine use were legalized, Dr. Herbert Kleber, executive vice president and medical director of the Center on

Addiction and Substance Abuse at Columbia University and one of the nation's top experts in the field, says that we "can expect the number of cocaine addicts to rise to some twenty or twenty-five million."

New social acceptability, fostered by legalization, would prompt a sharp rise in teenage drug use. Exercising their right to free speech, Madison Avenue hucksters could make it as attractive to do a few lines as to down a few beers. Tobacco provides a bitter lesson. While smoking declined among adults in the 1980s, it barely budged among teenagers, seduced by the lure of Joe Camel and other sleek cigarette ads. In contrast, marijuana use by high school seniors dropped 60 percent. Such a decline would not have occurred if marijuana had been legal.

Even if we tried to keep the distribution of drugs away from the private sector, lower prices would certainly draw in more young and poor people. A gram of cocaine that costs eighty dollars on the illegal market could cost as little as ten dollars to import legally, pushing down the price of a dose to as low as fifty cents, well within the reach of elementary or secondary school students. In the mid-1980s, when cocaine, which had been available only as an expensive powder, appeared in its crack form at a price as low as three dollars a dose, use among the poor exploded.

Libertarians suggest that individuals should be allowed to use any drug they wish because drug use is a victimless crime. Nonsense. Such suggestions, as well as those that legalization would reduce crime, are a mirage on the desolate streets of urban poverty. Shoot-outs among drug dealers might subside. But the shattering violence that accompanies alcohol and drug abuse would skyrocket. And when drugs become readily available, users are likely to do more drugs and less work, increasing their need to steal to finance their addiction, even though drugs cost less.

Proponents of legalization tend to focus on less addictive

(though still harmful) drugs such as marijuana, rather than highly addictive drugs such as cocaine, the bête noire of the legalization movement. Here the notion of "safe, casual" use is dangerously naïve. Casual users are notoriously poor judges of their chances of getting hooked. Dr. Kleber, who has treated thousands of addicts, has rarely met one who foresaw his or her slide into addiction. Unlike sedatives, which temporarily depress the desire for more drugs, cocaine use only stimulates more cocaine use. And marijuana is a big-time gateway drug: Teens who have smoked it are more likely to use another drug. Twelve- to seventeen-year-olds who smoke pot are six times more likely to use other illicit drugs and 85 times more likely to use cocaine than teens who do not smoke pot.

Clinicians who regularly see the ravages of addiction and families of the addicted are strenuous in opposing legalization. "The closer one comes on a regular basis to addiction, the less likely one would want to increase availability," says Dr. Kleber. "A crack addict, describing how he suffered chest pains suggesting a heart attack, and yet reached a few minutes later for more crack, has a chilling effect on arguments that more people should have access to this drug."

The flirtation with legalization is a cry of despair, born of frustration with the nation's lack of a comprehensive antidrug policy. We tolerate drug bazaars in southeast Washington, D.C., and Harlem that we swiftly stamp out if they appear in Georgetown or on the Upper East Side of Manhattan. We leave the war to be fought disproportionately by military and border personnel trying to interdict drugs and by police officers trying to contain mayhem in ghettos overrun with drugs and guns. We have yet to commit the resources to research, prevention, and treatment that this formidable foe requires.

Arguments for legalization are often based on distortions of the experiences of other nations or communities that have tried it. Switzerland opened its Needle Park in Zurich to drug users for a little over a year and promptly shut it when addicts destroyed the park, and crime and vandalism spread to neighboring streets and throughout the city. In late 1994, the Swiss were considering the use of troops to quell the violence of its open-air drug markets. When Italy decriminalized heroin possession and use, its emergency-room episodes and deaths from overdoses jumped to the highest level in Europe.

The Netherlands, which has long accommodated drug users and addicts, is building more treatment centers and jails so that it can force more addicts into treatment—or throw them in jail if they refuse. "People are absolutely fed up with all the troubles caused by drug addicts—car windows broken, noise, whole streets almost given up to the drug problem," explains Eberhard van der Laan, leader of the Social Democrats in the Amsterdam city council.

Reporting on the British experience and Liverpool, England, has been notoriously inaccurate. Contrary to popular American opinion, the British never pursued a policy of legalization. Though any physician could prescribe heroin, its purchase on the black market was illegal. Then in 1969, illegal heroin addiction and related crime came to England, as it had previously come to the United States, and several doctors misprescribed the drug. In 1971, the British made the prescription of heroin and cocaine illegal, except through a handful of specially licensed physicians. Though some one hundred are licensed, only seventeen doctors throughout the country prescribe any heroin and British public health officials estimate that doctors maintain no more than two hundred addicts on the drug, an apparent reaction to studies indicating that two-thirds of heroin-maintained addicts continued their criminal behavior.

One such doctor is John Marks, whose offices are in Widness and Warrington, outside Liverpool. News reports in the United States have depicted him as prescribing heroin for a large population of addicts in Liverpool and producing a dramatic reduction in the crime rate there.

In early 1994, Dr. Kleber and I visited Dr. Marks in his Warrington office, as well as national and local police and health officials in London and Liverpool. Dr. Marks said he had somewhere between two hundred and three hundred patients in his two programs, most of them on methadone, the rest receiving heroin. His statistics have not been independently reviewed, do not distinguish between methadone and heroin, and relate only to criminal convictions of his patients; the Liverpool police report no decline in the crime rate associated with his programs.

Arguments for legalization are notoriously short on details. Would we legalize all drugs or only some? Could they be marketed like alcohol and tobacco? How old would you have to be to get legal drugs? Old enough to drive a car? Would you have to prove you are already addicted? Could drugs be sold in pharmacies? In every neighborhood? If we legalize marijuana, would we legalize a potency of 1 percent, 10 percent, or highly potent hashish? If we legalize cocaine, would we allow the use of crack, a cocaine product? Would the Food and Drug Administration regulate quality and efficacy, as it does for other drugs?

Too many of us display a shoulder-shrugging sense that it is "they" who are afflicted, not "us," and that "we" can stop "them" from making "our" streets dangerous and clogging "our" courts by letting "them" stay high and happy. If drugs were legal, judges who came to the federal bench from corporate law practices and political fund-raising would have lots of time to try high-visibility commercial and white-collar-crime cases rather than deal with drug-related crimes involving the most vicious perpetrators and the most vulnerable victims. In short, life would be a lot easier for "us."

Legalization condemns drug addicts, and poor young African Americans and Latinos at highest risk of getting hooked, to a life of dependence and degradation. Congressman Charles Rangel, who opposes legalization, told me, "They're talking about my people. It's like saying, 'Let all those people who use heroin and cocaine—it's a limited problem and only affects the blacks, the minorities—let them have it. As long as they have it they won't be bothering me. They won't be robbing. They won't be committing crimes. So let's give it to them. Whether or not it destroys them, destroys their lives, that's not our problem.' "

At its best, America strives to give all of us the chance to develop our talents. Cornering millions of people into drug addiction insults this fundamental value and demeans the dignity to which everyone is entitled.

Our nation has yet to commit to substance abuse and addiction the financial resources and intellectual energy it has commandeered to fight other diseases, develop spectacular military technology, or master space. Until we do so, we should view attempts to legalize drugs as cop-outs that ignore the failures of such schemes in other countries and condemn poor Americans to a life incompatible with their inherent human dignity.

SELF-INFLICTED WOUNDS

In his epic, *A Study of History*, Arnold Toynbee concluded that great civilizations are destroyed by self-inflicted wounds—not by enemies from outside, but from within. The threat from substance abuse is not the only internal threat our nation faces, but it is certainly as pernicious and costly as any other. Nowhere is this more evident than in the hospitals, emergency rooms, and doctors' offices crowded with its victims and in the trail of shattered lives and families in every part of our nation.

By any measure—the cost to the health care system; the illness, injury, and agony visited on children, spouses, and parents; the impact on our schools; homelessness; reduced product quality and worker productivity; crime—the pandemic of substance abuse demands our attention. Individuals and institutions throughout society, in government, business, schools, media, sports, and entertainment, and in our homes, must take responsibility to confront this devastating scourge. If we face this threat honestly and forcefully, we can enter the twenty-first century with our heads held higher because we will have taken a giant step toward making the minds of our people clearer and their bodies stronger.

CHAPTER FIVE

TAKING THE PROFIT
OUT OF POOR HEALTH

Jesus said to them, "The healthy do not need a doctor; sick people do."

—*Luke 5:31*

Trying to contain health care costs and provide quality care to all without a thorough health promotion and disease prevention program is like trying to clean an oil spill from coastal waters without capping the ruptured well offshore. It can't be done. A generation of failed attempts has been trying to teach us this lesson, but like children who play with matches again after they have set the house on fire, we stubbornly refuse to learn from experience.

Despite federal, state, and corporate pressures to cut prices and the recent spread of managed care to increase efficiency, since 1970 health spending has climbed at more than double the pace of inflation—and twelve times the rate of population increase.

At the same time, without any such efforts, the cost of dental care has declined and our oral health has improved.

Why?

The reasons for the contrast between medical and dental care are many, but one rises in stark relief: the obsession of health care reformers with the delivery of medical care for the sick. This love affair has relegated the commonsense alternatives of disease prevention and health promotion to the role of dowdy wallflowers, while we shower financial attention on specialized medicine and research to invent new treatment technologies, creating a virtually limitless sea of ills and injuries that we can diagnose and treat.

The contrast with dentistry is stunning. Spending on dental care is rising at only about half the rate of increase in total health care spending. Individuals are going to the dentist less often for work on cavities. The nation needs fewer dentists, and those who pursue dentistry as a career are held to modest fees. Dental schools have closed and reduced the size of their classes.

This revolution has little to do with drilling, filling, and pulling sick teeth and treating infected gums, and much to do with prevention: fluoridation of the water supply, effective toothpastes that not only curb cavities but also stem tartar growth, habitual flossing and brushing after each meal, less sugar in our diets, and the decline in cigarette smoking. Children and adults who adopt the most modest preventive measures sharply cut their dental bills. During the 1980s, prevention saved nearly $100 billion in dental treatment. In 1994, half of all schoolchildren had no cavities, compared to 36.6 percent in 1980 and 28 percent in the early 1970s.

Society has made "dental hygiene" chic, and whiter, healthier teeth have become a prerequisite of beauty for women and handsomeness for men. We don't see it as health promotion and disease prevention, but that's exactly what it is—and it's working because cleaner, whiter teeth are an "in" part of our culture, not because government regulators or hard-nosed employers have imposed them on us.

Unfortunately, dental care is the exception to the rule of the American way of health.

About two-thirds of all premature deaths in the U.S. are preventable, as are most illnesses and injuries. Yet we devote little more than 3 percent of the funds we spend on health to such disease prevention and health promotion measures as prenatal care, vaccinations, smoking cessation, and persuasive education about the benefits of pursuing healthy life-styles.

Nowhere is the backbreaking load we place on treatment more striking than in hospital emergency rooms, where patient caseloads have risen to one hundred million a year. Dr. Melvin Konner captured this tilt in describing his visit to the Johns Hopkins Hospital emergency room:

> Almost before we get our bearings the bullet is gone from the young man's body, and wonderful fluids protect him from the ancient scourge of wound infection. Before we have time to become accustomed to her screams the woman laboring on the narrow, rickety stretcher has become the mother of a well-delivered baby. The questions of why the young man has been shot, and why the young woman gives birth so precipitately—an obstetrics term that evokes a vertiginous fall from a high place, a fall without any preparation—have a legitimate place in our discourse about health. But they have no place in the spare, utilitarian talk of the white-collared soldiers in the emergency room. They remove the bullet; they birth the baby.

As long as we neglect the root causes of problems such as violence and teen pregnancy, even the most ambitious reforms of financing and delivery will not cool the feverish spending on sick care. In America's after-the-fact system of care, there is always demand for more medical services and technology to treat ill health, to ease pain and suffering, and to push back the encroaching signs of death.

Health care American-style is a euphemism for sick care, which can be a spectacularly profitable enterprise for those who cure the ills, mend the injuries, and meet the demands of the sick. Pharmaceutical and medical-equipment companies, hospitals, managed-care networks, and doctors have their sights set on sick care for much the same reason Willie Sutton robbed banks: That's where the money is. Until we take the profit out of sick care, we will recite our prayers for affordable health care for all in vain.

THE POWER OF POSITIVE PREVENTION

The power of prevention shines through in the decline in deaths from heart disease. Most of the almost 50 percent drop in the death rate from heart disease since 1960 is due to changes in life-style, which can reverse even severe heart disease in as little as a year, not to pricey medical miracles such as transplants and coronary bypasses. Indeed, credit goes to simple changes that reduce the known risks of heart disease: quitting cigarette smoking, eating a low-fat diet, handling stress, and getting regular exercise. Alexander Leaf of Harvard Medical School, a preventive care expert, believes that as more Americans adopt such life-styles the number of heart attacks could drop another 60 to 80 percent.

Since 1960, the progress of high-tech medicine in treating heart disease has been wondrous, expensive, and palliative. However impressive their benefits, transplants, coronary angioplasty, bypass surgery, thrombolytic therapy, and antiarrhythmic drugs do nothing about the underlying disease that clogs the body's arteries. Each treatment temporarily eases the effects of the ailment. But without life-style changes, the deadly disease resumes its destructive march on the heart.

These alleviative measures come at high cost. The three hundred thousand coronary bypass surgeries performed each year cost more than $9 billion; the three hundred thousand angioplasties, $4.5 billion. Within a year, doctors need to repeat about 30 percent of angioplasties and about 10 percent of bypass surgeries, because the disease again blocks the blood vessel. Why? Largely because patients resume their old bad health habits.

Such advances in the treatment and management of heart disease have played a role in cutting the mortality rate from heart attacks. But by keeping people alive without curing the illness or changing their life-styles, they have also helped increase the prevalence of chronic heart disease, fill nursing homes, and hike hospital admission rates for congestive heart failure by 70 percent since 1973.

Of the six million Americans with coronary heart disease in 1994, roughly five hundred thousand died by year's end. Thousands more will develop the disease in 1995, filling hospital beds emptied by 1994's victims. And thousands more, who start smoking, become overweight, and don't exercise, guarantee that the lucrative demand for heart disease treatment will continue for decades to come. In America's system of sick care, meeting this demand—however costly—is where the money is for hospitals, cardiologists, and pharmaceutical and medical-equipment companies.

Cancer is similarly situated, with the big money focused on treatment. Yet if we put into action what we already know about this killer, such as the importance of not smoking, drinking moderately, and eating a high-fiber, low-fat diet, we could prevent more than half of all cancers.

In a system of health care rather than sick care, the measure of success would be the number of Americans who adopt healthy habits and enter the sick-care system less often or avoid it altogether. Those who promote and pursue such life-styles would be financially rewarded.

Americans don't like being preached to, but they can be persuaded. Changes in smoking habits are a telling example of how deeply embedded unhealthy behaviors can change, even in the face of billions of dollars of advertising from cigarette pushers. The common use of seat belts and child safety seats and the decline in drunk driving also illustrate how habitual behavior can shift.

Injuries of all kinds, which in 1994 will cost roughly $80 billion in medical spending, are ripe for this kind of attention and ingenuity. Among children, the leading causes of death are accidents such as car crashes, drownings, falls, and poisonings. "Injuries are an epidemic in this country and we can prevent them," says Mark Rosenberg, an injury prevention specialist at the U.S. Centers for Disease Control and Prevention. "If you had something that was 85 percent effective in preventing a disease, you would call it a vaccine. We have such measures for some injuries, but we have not been using them."

Injuries can be prevented by simple actions from keeping ice off the sidewalk and toys off the stairs, to creating an uncluttered, well-lit home for elders who are uneasy on their feet, installing smoke detectors, wearing a helmet while biking or roller-blading, using bases in softball games that give way when slid into, and keeping guns out of a child's reach, or, even better, out of the house entirely.

While the number of deaths in car accidents fell from 55,000 in 1968 to 43,500 in 1991, the number of deaths from guns rose from 24,000 to 38,000. At this pace, by 2003 guns will become the leading cause of injury-related death—a fate we could avoid if we apply the same imaginative energy and commitment to changing the gun culture that we have applied to changing the tobacco culture.

The limits of treatment and the potential of prevention have gathered respect lately because of the humbling AIDS epidemic, which, with death its certain outcome, has triggered treatment costs approaching $15 billion annually. The mysteries of AIDS have defied the best efforts of medical science to find a cure, but we know how to prevent its spread. Community-based education and the siege mentality that permeated the gay community are largely responsible for behavioral changes that slowed the transmission of HIV among gay men in major urban areas during the late 1980s.

Abetted by drug and alcohol abuse and unprotected sex, the AIDS virus still infects more than forty thousand people and kills about forty thousand individuals each year. By 1990, AIDS and related infections had become the leading killer of young men in sixty-four American cities—not only New York, San Francisco, and Los Angeles, but also Salt Lake City, Baton Rouge, and Kansas City.

Furthering this tragedy can be avoided by the use of condoms, the practice of abstinence, the exchange of used needles for clean ones, and the prevention and treatment of substance abuse. Don Des Jarlais of the National Commission on AIDS argues, "In a country with the resources of the U.S., we should be able to cut the rate of new HIV by three-fourths, maybe more." But the big profits and high profiles are in finding a cure for those infected, not in curbing the spread of the disease.

Another prime target for health promotion and disease prevention is the community of senior citizens and those about to enter their ranks. The prevalence of chronic disability among the elderly has dropped from 1982 to 1989; while the elderly population grew

15 percent, the number of chronically disabled elderly grew only 10 percent. We don't know the exact mix of prevention and treatment that caused this change. But much of the drop is due to rising living standards, exercise, healthier diets, and declines in smoking and heavy drinking. Even so, as Dr. Steven Schroeder, president of the Robert Wood Johnson Foundation, points out, one in seven Americans face major disability due to a chronic illness, and more than one-third of them do not seek routine or preventive care from their doctor.

Maintaining a good, calcium-rich diet can reduce the incidence of osteoporosis, which causes 1.5 million bone fractures a year (mostly among older women) at a cost of $10 billion. Avoiding hip fractures from osteoporosis would enable thousands of elderly women to live independently for many more years. Preserving mobility also helps curb depression among the elderly, who are likely to suffer this disorder.

With seventy-seven million baby boomers born between 1946 and 1964 getting older, the potential savings in reducing chronic medical problems among the over-sixty-five population are enormous. In 1993, the elderly, who represent 13 percent of the population, accounted for a third of the nation's health care spending. About 70 percent of Medicaid dollars go to the elderly for health and nursing-home care, and their doctor bills are climbing 35 percent faster than those of younger citizens. Average health care spending for a senior citizen is more than triple what it is for a young adult.

The goal of effective health promotion and disease prevention is not only to help people live longer, but, even more important, to shorten their period of dependence. Rebutting the argument that longer life necessarily increases health care costs, Dr. Alexander Leaf points out: "We are talking about keeping people as healthy as possible. True, we must all die, but the longer we can stay healthy within a fixed life span, the less morbidity we must suffer. And disease prevented is not necessarily disease postponed." Higher health care costs are not an inevitable consequence of living longer.

Many of the costs of prevention, from screening and diagnostic tests that detect and avoid more serious illness to public education campaigns to immunize every child and discourage teenagers from smoking cigarettes, will pay for themselves in the costs of sick care they avert. But even when they don't, they are worthwhile investments in individuals. As Princeton health economist Uwe Reinhardt points out, they will "produce a higher percentage of high-quality days in people's lives," even if they do not reduce "the claims of health care on the gross national product."

Promoting the health of the elderly can also contribute to maintaining a civil discourse between the generations, where tensions over the use of scarce resources are already simmering. The longer the elderly can take care of themselves, the less of an economic burden they place on the nation's resources. The less the burden, the less pressure from the younger generation for rationing care by bureaucratic fiat and experimenting with euthanasia. By taking better care of themselves, the elderly can help take the worst of the "me" out of the "Me Generation."

WHAT'S THE HITCH?

At a White House meeting, Bob Boorstin, a White House communications official, couldn't stand the mind-numbing abstractions of experts as they droned on for hours about the economics of including mental-health services in health care reform. He leaned across the table to-

ward Mr. Clinton, Mr. Gore, Mrs. Clinton, and Mrs. Gore, and reminded them of the psychotic manic episode that had landed Boorstin in the hospital for three weeks in 1988, producing a $14,000 bill. That, he said, is about the price of the preventive treatment he has received for three years to avoid another episode. Make the investment up front in preventive care, he implored, and you will avoid costly hospital bills.

　　　　　　　　　　　　　　—The Wall Street Journal, *October 27, 1993*

If large-scale efforts at prevention hold so much promise, why don't we put our resources where our rhetoric is?

OUR SENSE OF INVULNERABILITY

Since the early decades of the twentieth century, medical miracles and public health triumphs have given individuals a reason to believe that however they abuse their minds and bodies, science will find a way to repair them. Vaccines and pharmaceuticals can wrestle diphtheria, measles, scarlet fever, whooping cough, typhoid, meningitis, and polio to the mat. With modern medicine, hard drinkers, heavy eaters, and even couch potatoes who smoke can survive heart attacks and hypertension that would have killed them a few years ago.

Each day, television and newspapers report new discoveries and herald cures for all kinds of pain and heartache, from tension headaches, sagging eyelids, ulcers, chronic fatigue, and alcohol-induced depression to kidney failure, shattered knees, and hips crushed by overweight torsos. Each night, commercials promise quick relief from hangovers, heartburn, inability to sleep, blood-shot eyes, hemorrhoids, and backaches.

With this drumbeat of promises, it's not surprising that adult vigilance against health threats is on the decline. Although the portion of the population that smokes cigarettes fell from 40 percent in 1965 to 25.5 percent in 1990, the twenty-five years of steady decrease ended in 1991, when the smoking population ticked up to 25.7 percent. Since then male smoking levels have not declined and smoking among women and teens has increased. Health officials cite the lure of discount cigarettes (a third of all sales in 1993), $4 billion of tobacco ads crowded with glamorous young men and women who magically suffer no ill consequences from their habit, and the marketing of lozenges and nasal sprays to soothe the throat and clear the nostrils of the precancerous sting of cigarettes.

In 1992 more Americans were overweight, getting less exercise, eating less sensibly, feeling more stress, and sleeping less than they had in the 1980s. In March 1993, "bacon makers [were] in fat city," reported *The Wall Street Journal,* because demand for bacon, as well as for sausages and eggs, was making a comeback. Pollster Louis Harris warned that "the healthy life-style movement" could be "a passing fad like the Hula Hoop," as our self-delusion of invulnerability to other people's ailments reasserts its dominion in our human natures.

THE "SO WHAT?" SYNDROME, A.K.A.
"I'LL WORRY ABOUT THAT LATER" OR
"IT'S TOO LATE NOW"

A teenager's sense of immortality is understandable, but it can be lethal when mixed with the instability of adolescents and their temptation to strike every match. The most common health problems of teens stem from preventable causes: sedentary days with high-fat diets, substance abuse, risky sexual practices, and unsafe driving. Simply admonishing the three million teens who smoke that they are hiking their chance of premature death from heart disease, emphysema, and lung cancer sometimes seems like blowing in the wind. Concepts of death and disability are remote to them, the least of their worries.

Senior citizens rarely have similarly naïve notions of immortality, but they often believe it is too late to improve their health and fail to appreciate their capacity to defeat, or at least postpone, fragility and disability. Even past age sixty, quitting smoking produces health benefits. Regular, sensible exercise and even weight training can help prevent and delay dysfunctional consequences of aging. Inactivity in the hammock, the idealized picture of retirement, leads to muscle atrophy, lower aerobic capacity, bone loss, incontinence, and unnecessarily early dependence.

Older individuals, like youngsters, sometimes just make a decision to pursue immediate gratification despite the consequences. President Lyndon Johnson used to tell of an elderly gentleman who went to the doctor complaining that he was losing his hearing. The doctor examined him, found nothing wrong, and finally asked the patient how much he drank.

"A quart of bourbon and a bottle of good red wine each night," he responded.

"That's it," said the doctor confidently. "If you stop drinking, your hearing will get better."

Six months later, the elderly patient returned, this time complaining about further deterioration in his hearing.

"Have you quit drinking?" the doctor asked.

"No, Doc," the patient replied. "I still drink a bottle of bourbon and a bottle of red wine each night."

"You've got to quit, if you want to restore your hearing," the doctor admonished.

A year later the patient was just about deaf. When he returned to the doctor, he was asked again about his drinking.

"To be honest, Doc, I still drink a quart of bourbon and a bottle of red wine every night."

"God damn it," the exasperated doctor snapped. "What's wrong with you? Why don't you give up drinking?"

"To tell you the truth, Doc," the patient replied, "at my age, I like what I drink a lot better than what I hear."

The Petticoats of Privacy and Pluralism

Concerns about privacy can snuff out the best intentions to promote healthy behavioral change. Efforts to prevent disease and promote health require frank discussions that involve deeply personal matters related to alcohol and illicit drug use, mental illness, abusive relationships, violence, sexual practices, and religious values. Faced with such delicate personal terrain, doctors who don't want to lose patients and parents who can't believe their child could be smoking pot or sleeping around look the other way.

Family violence and the serious health problems it spawns often fester until they reach fever pitch because of misguided privacy concerns. Too many doctors fear to tread where Dr. David Baughan has the common sense—and guts—to go:

> In fifteen years of clinical and academic medicine, I have been frequently frustrated with the inadequacy of ethical discussions as they apply to privacy concepts and significant, expensive health problems, such as family violence and substance abuse, that I commonly detect in primary care. . . . I think the concept of beneficence should be elaborated to consider effectiveness. . . . Since patients come to me seeking treatment for the consequences of family violence . . . I am ethically obliged to offer treatment. The best treatment, the best hope

for restoration or achievement of health, requires that I address the "private" details of the family system. . . . While this must be done with respect for the sacred aspects of the family institution, not to enter the private world would result in token, ineffective beneficence.

Parental vision can be just as clouded by false notions of privacy, often complicated by denial. Many mothers and fathers tell me that they would never search their teenager's bedroom to look for drugs, alcohol, pornography, or condoms even if they suspected that their child was, say, drinking, smoking pot, or experimenting with promiscuous sex. Recoiling from "even the thought of such action," a mother claims to have "too much respect for my child's privacy" to do anything like that. This kind of misguided deference allows too many young Americans to persist in risky games with alcohol, drugs, and sex, and to pursue life-styles that can eventually get them into serious trouble, require costly care, and even destroy their lives. Parents should muster the courage to speak frankly to their children in the preteen and teen years about drugs, alcohol, and sex in order to prevent dangerous experimentation; but if they suspect drug use or unsafe sexual activity, they should not hesitate to act on their suspicions uninhibited by any false notions of teen privacy.

As the petticoat of privacy gives Americans a place to hide from aggressive health promotion and disease prevention efforts, the petticoat of anything-goes pluralism provides cover for our reluctance to talk about values. Due respect for America's cultural and religious diversity is one thing. Mealymouthed messages about behavior and conduct that bow to the notion that one belief is as good as another, that it's all relative, are quite another. With so many health issues (particularly in the arena of sexual conduct) engaging deeply held religious beliefs and cultural standards, doctors, nurses, teachers, and parents sigh with relief whenever they can hide under the skirt of pluralism.

Parents are often so confused about their own values that they refrain from "imposing them on their children," an attitude likely to gain momentum with the rise in religiously, socially, and culturally mixed marriages, where the least common denominator, rather than the highest standard, often sets the tone for parental compromise and guidance. The students of the sixties and seventies, most of whom experimented with drugs, have conflicts about their role as parents of the eighties and nineties, particularly in dealing with their own children's substance abuse.

Vituperative public debates over the content of sex education and its influence on teenage sexual activity have hobbled efforts to prevent teen pregnancy and the spread of AIDS, genital herpes, and syphilis, even though all of the above continue to rise among young people. In a sampling of primary care doctors who routinely asked their patients about smoking habits, only half asked about sexually transmitted diseases, a third about condom use, a fourth about sexual orientation, and a fifth about the number of a patient's sex partners.

Doctors who reluctantly engage patients in value-laden conversations look like high-wire enthusiasts compared to the gingerly caution with which politicians dip their toes into the water of health promotion when it involves sexual conduct. As the National Commission on AIDS notes, "Years of disagreement at the highest levels of the federal government over the proper message to give young people have helped to create a national atmosphere of confusion and controversy."

The tragedy is that candor does not require imposition of any single approach to the dangers of promiscuous sexual activity among teens. In a multicultural, multireligious society such as ours, there is no one proper message. Those who seek to impose their views on all—whether their priority is abstinence, monogamy, the promotion of condom use, or the characterization of homosexual sex as sinful and abnormal or its acceptance as moral—are as much culprits as those who scurry under the petticoats of privacy and pluralism to avoid dealing with the problem. These all-eggs-in-one-basket approaches usually end up offering nothing, allowing sexually transmitted diseases to prey upon those who are ill informed or morally adrift.

On such ethically charged health issues, our religiously and culturally diverse nation will never agree. But that does not require us to abandon sex education to the streets, steamy television soap operas, R-rated films, and raunchy pop lyrics. There is plenty of room for the Catholic bishops to insist that abstinence be the predominant way of life for teenagers, just as secular liberals with permissive attitudes about sexual intercourse among teens can encourage the use of condoms.

Health promotion begins at home, with parents who in the first instance must get their act together about their children. The church, school, and doctor can all help—indeed, sometimes they must substitute for parents—but the issues raised in areas of sexual activity and substance abuse are best handled in the family. Controversies that rend public schools, town councils, and even Congress often reflect the failure of parents and churches to fulfill their responsibilities.

When governments, public schools, and public health officials do get involved, they should discuss values. Sex education that ignores values is unlikely to stem the tide of teen pregnancy and spread of sexually transmitted diseases. It must incorporate a message of individual dignity and, to be most effective, the value of abstinence. California has discovered this among the 180,000 high-schoolers to whom it preaches abstinence. Maryland's program, which includes posters that say ABSTINENCE MAKES THE HEART GROW FONDER and VIRGIN: TEACH YOUR KIDS IT'S NOT A DIRTY WORD, is credited with prompting a 10 percent drop in teen pregnancy. Also effective are school-based health clinics, where nurses deal candidly and one on one with teens.

WHERE THE BUCKS ARE

Perhaps the biggest deterrent to health promotion and disease prevention efforts is the fact that the big bucks are in promoting unhealthy habits and treating poor health.

Doctors are not trained or paid to ask or counsel patients about disease prevention or health promotion. Only a quarter of accredited medical schools require a course in prevention, and among those that do, instruction comes to only a few hours. In an era when efficiency is everything, insurers are disinclined to reimburse physicians for spending another few minutes talking with patients, especially in an ambience of mistrust where they can't figure out how to police payments for such activity.

Private insurers argue that a beneficiary might use the coverage this year and then switch to another carrier, which would profit from the healthy results. Corporate managers remain unconvinced of the savings from companywide health promotion efforts, especially in a world of high personnel turnover. Today's employee may work tomorrow for someone else who will reap the benefits.

Government officials have their own set of short-term monetary concerns. Despite preachy rhetoric to the contrary, politicians resist allocating much money for health promotion. Prevention costs money now and saves money later, a serious handicap when, each year, Congress and state legislatures have to pass budgets with too few dollars to meet the immediate expectations of constituents, and when every two years most politicians must stand for reelection.

Finally, selling danger and poor health to American consumers is highly profitable. Tobacco heads the list of powerful, profit-driven interests. Despite overwhelming agreement that tobacco is the only legal product that maims and kills when used as intended, the cigarette and chewing-tobacco companies continue to push their wares on young Americans. Alcohol companies resist attempts to label their products and advertising with high-visibility warnings about the potential of beer and alcohol as drugs of entry for young Americans and their special danger to pregnant women. The gun lobby opposes restrictions on the sale of guns—even automatic weapons—and higher taxes on ammunition and gun dealers.

WHAT TO DO?

In 1979, in my last act as secretary of Health, Education, and Welfare, I published *Healthy People,* the first surgeon general's report devoted to health promotion and disease prevention, and the first to set goals for our people, such as reduction in infant mortality and improvements in teenage health. In 1990, the secretary of Health and Human Services, Louis Sullivan, issued *Healthy People 2000,* a second call to arms with updated goals. Both reports were cries in the wilderness of complacent self-indulgence, scarcely heard and largely ignored. But their pages demonstrate beyond a doubt that we know exactly what to do to create a healthy America:

Eat nutritious food, lots of fiber and little fat. Exercise. Don't smoke or use drugs. Avoid alcohol or use it only in moderation. Avoid the sun. Reduce stress. Learn the signs of mental illness. Learn how to spot skin cancers. Go to the doctor for periodic checkups and tests, such as Pap smears, mammograms, electrocardiograms, rectal exams. Get prenatal care. Get children immunized. Brush teeth after eating; get periodic dental checkups and fluoridation. Install smoke detectors. Wear seat belts. Don't drink and drive. For teens, practice premarital sexual abstinence or at least use a condom. Keep conflicts nonviolent. For older Americans, take calcium and other vitamin supplements. Shovel and salt sidewalks. Get the lead, radon, and asbestos out of houses and schools and the guns off the streets. And so on.

We are, after all is said and done, what we eat, drink, and breathe, and how we exercise and handle stress.

For America to move from sick care to health care, the trillion-dollar question is not what to do. It's why people and institutions don't do it. And one clear answer is that the profit is in poor health.

THE PROFIT IN SICK CARE

The financial incentives in America's system of care seem designed by a mad genius to encourage us to abuse our minds and bodies and discourage us from taking care of ourselves and our children.

Millions of Americans do not have health insurance, and among those who do, most policies create financial incentives to wait until sickness strikes before approaching a doctor or nurse. Uninsured Americans are less likely to be immunized, to receive early prenatal care, to have their blood pressure checked, and to seek medical care for serious symptoms. The uninsured have access to sick care in America—largely through hospital emergency rooms—but they do not have full access to health care.

The early-warning system of health care—Pap smears, immunizations, periodic physicals—is not a common experience of the uninsured; they see a doctor far less often than affluent Americans do. Most of the hundred million patients in emergency rooms during 1993 had nonurgent ailments that could have been treated in less-expensive settings or avoided altogether with routine preventive practices. The most common emergency-room diagnosis is ear infection.

On each visit emergency-room patients see a different doctor, who starts from scratch and repeats expensive tests. Just ask Armadella Kedrick, who took her daughter to the emergency room at New Orleans' Charity Hospital twenty times—and saw twenty different doctors. Her daughter suffered a mysterious recurring illness of fever and hysteria. When Kedrick finally ran into a doctor who remembered the patient, he told her to ignore the symptoms because her daughter was "playacting." Kedrick did so and the symptoms disappeared.

Even the insured often lack coverage for timely preventive care. In 1992, only half of the employees in fee-for-service plans had coverage for immunizations for children. At least a quarter of the four million two-year-olds in America have not been fully immunized. These failures are particularly dismaying given the demonstrated cost-effectiveness of immunizations. Measles-mumps-rubella vaccine returns fourteen dollars for each dollar spent; polio vaccine returns thirty.

Donald Henderson, former chair of the National Vaccine Advisory Committee, sees it as insane that insurers "will pay for treatments for acne or ingrown toenails, but they won't pay for immunizing children against measles and other life-threatening diseases." Because doctors are paid little to administer vaccines and pharmaceutical companies make little, if any, profit on sales, there is hardly any financial incentive for such providers to promote them.

Babies seem to be targets for denial of preventive care. For twenty years, Medicaid did not cover prenatal care for the first pregnancy of a teenager. Precious little is done to encourage poor mothers or pregnant women to seek preventive care even when they and their children are eligible for regular checkups and early treatment. In 1992, only 36 percent of eligible children participated in such federal programs. In Kentucky, Montana, Mississippi, and North Dakota the participation rate dipped below 15 percent.

In 1991, a million pregnant women received late prenatal care or none at all. In the same year, 290,000 low-birthweight babies were born, 53,000 of them weighing three pounds or less. As the National Commission to Prevent Infant Mortality notes, much as we might try, "No amount of high-tech medicine and machinery can replace a child's healthy development in the mother's womb." The commission might have added that there's no profit for medical equipment manufacturers or hospitals, and precious little for doctors, in a healthy baby.

Since 1985, the rate of low birthweight has been rising slightly while, surprisingly, the infant mortality rate has been falling. Why? Not so much because we are getting better at making sure babies are born healthy, but because medicine is getting better at keeping unhealthy babies alive at enormous cost—covered by insurers, of course. Most of the drop in infant mortality reflects advances in medical treatment and high technology rather than proper prenatal care and prevention.

Our emphasis on treatment comes at a high price. In 1992, the hospital-related costs of caring for low-weight newborns topped $4 billion. While low-weight infants represent 7 percent of births, their medical care accounts for almost 60 percent of health spending on newborns.

Few insurers cover periodic physical exams and fewer still underwrite all the appropriate tests given during such exams. Adults who seek to prevent heart disease can expect little encouragement from their insurers. Most carriers will pay $30,000 for a coronary bypass or $250,000 for a heart transplant, but not $2,000 for a cardiac rehab program that can curb and even reverse the disease by systematic exercise, controlling blood pressure, lowering cholesterol, and helping people quit smoking. Coverage of treatment for alcohol or drug abuse, or smoking cessation, is spotty at best. Medicare limits its coverage of preventive care to mammograms, Pap smears, and pneumonia, hepatitis B, and flu vaccines. Medicare and Medicaid rarely pay for periodic physical exams.

Plenty of public and private bucks are available to pay doctors to do something to us after we're sick, but only a few pennies (if that) are available to pay doctors to tell us how to stay healthy. As Dr. Seymour Post of Columbia's College of Physicians and Surgeons points out,

> Since medical insurance reimburses doctors far more for procedures than for spending time listening to and talking to patients about their illnesses, many doctors have, where possible, shifted to an increased use of procedures. Physicians prefer procedures, like passing tubes and high-tech computerized imaging, to spending the time discussing a patient's life-style or reactions to illness or even simply taking a proper medical history.

The lack of coverage for prevention and health promotion sends you and your doctor a perverse message: Even though you pay a fat premium each month, the costs of foresight and less expensive medical interventions will come out of your own pocket. But if you wait until the problem gets serious and costly, you will pay only a fraction of the bill. Indeed, the longer you wait and the more seriously ill you get, the tinier the fraction you pay and, in a fee-for-service system, the more money your doctor will make.

In theory, the financial structure of HMOs encourages their doctors to promote healthy life-styles to keep their costs as low as possible. HMOs receive fixed payments to cover the care of their patients; many put their doctors on salary. Prospective (versus retrospective fee-for-service) payment gives HMO doctors an incentive to keep patients healthy so that serious illnesses don't bust the annual budget.

In practice, some HMOs have done well at ensuring that their patients are fully immunized, get prenatal care, and have regular mammograms. But HMO physicians also report that pressure to see more patients more briefly is becoming paramount. The HMOs' drive to increase membership and profits presses them to be ever more efficient in the short run, even if it means shortchanging prevention and health promotion.

To transform America's medical system, we must take the profit out of sick care for both patient and doctor, and direct the money to the practice of health care. It should be financially attractive for patients to change their poor health habits and for doctors to offer more preventive services and counseling. Patients and doctors who default on these obligations should pay a price. "Individuals are moved by love and fear," President Lyndon Johnson used to tell me. "The trick to persuasion is to put together the right mix for each one."

To change course, we must:

Straighten the leaning tower of insurance for sick care. Health insurance is not property insurance, but the two share a common goal. With property insurance, the sole objective is to have the resources to pick up the pieces after loss or damage from a robbery or fire. Similarly, health insurance covers the costs of catastrophes such as cancer or heart attacks. Just as property insurers reward you for installing a burglar alarm, health insurance should encourage the insured to pursue healthy habits—and penalize them if they don't.

A homeowner's insurance policy will not pay to rebuild a house if the owner has deliberately set fire to it. But the health insurer pays the individual who sets himself on fire with self-inflicted diseases. Indeed, with most homeowners' insurance, the premiums go up if there is no water nearby to put out the fire and go down if smoke detectors, modern electrical wiring, and fire-resistant materials are used. Isn't it time for health insurers to reward healthy habits and penalize unhealthy behavior aggressively the way home insurers promote safe houses—and demote the owners of unsafe homes?

We must eliminate the precipitous tilt of health insurance toward sick care. Health insurance should pay for all preventive services, including compensating doctors to talk to patients. Patients who do not seek such services and physicians who do not provide them should be penalized. Failure to obtain periodic physical examinations and dental checkups (and timely fluoridation treatments during the high-cavity years) should be a cause for the patient to pay the insurer, as should the failure of parents to have their children get timely immunizations. Failure of high-risk individuals, like the elderly, to get flu shots in the winter should be a cause for them to pay higher premiums. Physicians who fail to offer preventive measures to patients should receive lower reimbursement for treating ailments that could have been avoided.

Even in a system of community rating, health insurers should reward good habits and penalize bad ones. Individuals with poor health habits—smoking, high-fat diets, not exercising, and not using smoke detectors or seat belts—have much higher health claims, $1,550 a year in one study, than people with better habits, $190 a year in the same sample. Life insurance companies commonly have higher premiums for smokers. Three life insurers owned by tobacco companies—CNA Life, Farmers Insurance Group, and Franklin Life Insurance Company—charge smokers nearly double the premium they set for nonsmokers because they know that smokers are about twice as likely as nonsmokers to die at any age. Making room for similar financial incentives in health insurance will help motivate individuals to take more responsibility for their health.

Increasingly employers and health insurers are offering carrots and sticks to promote healthy habits that reduce treatment costs. Mutual of Omaha covers the cost of a program that seeks to prevent and reverse heart disease with a low-fat vegetarian diet, exercise, stress management, and a support group. Some employers charge higher premiums to employees who smoke or who are overweight. Some will pay 80 percent of a nonsmoker's health care bills, but only 70 percent of a smoker's.

Others exclude coverage for certain conditions altogether, such as lung cancer related to smoking, or neonatal care related to prenatal alcohol or drug use. Camberley Hotel Company excludes coverage for injuries from bungee jumping, parachuting, skydiving, and scuba diving and sets a $5,000 limit on bills for injuries from drunk driving or illicit drug use.

Such sticks are valuable tools, but they must be used with decency and caution, and aimed at conduct that individuals can control or change. Companies see big savings if they can get at—or reduce—the 10 percent of the work force that snares 80 percent of health care claims. It is time to change the financial incentives that motivate the 10 percent, for the savings can be significant. But employers, as well as individual and public insurers, should temper their zeal by remembering that many, perhaps most, claims are beyond the control of the people who file them.

Require that individuals eligible for public programs take responsibility for their health. Those eligible for public programs should have their benefits conditioned on getting preventive care, an obligation that must be matched by an assurance of access to such care.

At least as important as trying to put welfare mothers to work is to get them to take advantage of prenatal care when they become pregnant, and to take care of themselves, the fetus they carry, and their children, if they are to remain eligible for cash payments. Maryland reduces welfare payments to parents who fail to get their children fully immunized; other states should tie payments to vaccination requirements as well.

Seniors on Medicare should be required to obtain periodic physical exams or face higher premiums. As Congress mandated in 1994, recipients of supplemental security income and Social Security disability payments who are drug and alcohol abusers should be required to get treatment as a condition of receiving benefits. Their taxpayer-funded payments should not be used, as U.S. Senator William Cohen and CBS's *60 Minutes* revealed was true in many cases, to support alcohol and drug habits where they refuse or neglect treatment.

Some suggest even firmer steps: Gregory Pence, a philosophy professor at the University of Alabama at Birmingham Medical School, urges public and private insurers to tell lifelong smokers, "Sorry, no lung transplants. You could have stopped smoking."

Use the malpractice system to encourage doctors and patients to practice prevention. The current professional responsibility and malpractice system encourages doctors to perform more tests and procedures rather than counsel patients. As a result, some twenty-five million unnecessary tests are performed in the United States each day, and all sorts of stomachs, chests, and women giving birth are cut open in order to avoid later litigation. Doctors who do not provide preventive services and counseling should be held accountable for malpractice when patients get preventable diseases.

Turning the potent incentives of the malpractice system and professional decertification toward providing preventive care can help change the doctor's mind-set from "When in doubt, unsheathe the knives and prescribe the pills" to "When in doubt, vaccinate, provide a full physical checkup, and spend a few more minutes talking about the patient's health habits."

The malpractice system can also be turned to encourage people to take better care of themselves. Individuals in auto accidents who were not wearing seat belts should be denied recovery for injuries and treatments that could have been avoided if they had buckled up. In 1994, Tennessee passed a law permitting defendants in auto accident cases to use failure to buckle up to mitigate damages. Virtually all other states prohibit the introduction of evidence of failure to use a seat belt to reduce damages; these laws should be changed.

Reward individuals who take responsibility for their health. Some large corporations that see the light of health promotion and its potential to brighten the bottom line have offered financial rewards to influence employee behavior.

In 1993, 15 percent of one thousand medium and large companies offered financial incentives for employee wellness, up from 12 percent only a year earlier. Honeywell pays its employees $200 to go through a "health promotion" program that includes medical tests and classes on prevention and early detection. Champion International credits $100 to employees who complete certain tests and preventive treatments. The company also educates employees to avoid unnecessary treatments and tests. "There are a lot of worried well," says Jeri Medea, Champion's director of health services. "They overuse the system."

In 1990, poor birth outcomes, such as low-birthweight babies, cost employers $5.6 billion. Rather than bankroll this expensive treatment, Levi Strauss & Company in San Francisco instituted a healthy birth program. The company paid pregnant employees $100 to sign up for prenatal care during their first trimester and stick with it for the nine months. In 1990, unhealthy births cost Levi Strauss $1.1 million; a year later, with its incentive for prenatal care, the bill was only $654,000.

As companies learn to boost their profits with such programs, they will get insurers to take the profit out of sick care for unhealthy babies. Prudential's Baltimore HMO pays its pregnant members ten dollars for each prenatal visit they make. These women receive customary checkups and screening, and nutrition and substance abuse counseling. Prudential's $80,000 investment in the plan's first two years has avoided spending $1 million on two dozen premature and low-weight births. This HMO treats a large Medicaid population and offers a lesson in how to use incentives, and not just penalties, to encourage recipients in public programs to take more responsibility for their own health.

To encourage workers to stay healthy, some employers pay them not to use their health insurance. When Forbes, Inc., paid its employees up to $1,000 a year if they filed minimal health claims, their cost of claims fell 30 percent. Dominion Resources paid seventy employees $800 each for not exceeding their deductibles in 1992.

Make good health accessible and fashionable. The first step is making preventive services easily accessible. The hard part is getting individuals to take advantage of them.

Public or private insurance coverage means little to a family in a rural area or urban ghetto with no primary care doctors or nurses available. Offering insurance for prenatal care does little good when the nearest primary care provider is a hundred miles away or waiting lists are weeks long.

In Chicago, a pregnant woman seeking care at a public clinic may have to wait 125 days to see a doctor. In New York, the Health and Hospitals Corporation, which runs eleven municipal hospitals, found that patients had to wait thirty-five days for a birth control consultation. When a Pap smear came up positive for cervical cancer, women stood in line for six weeks for follow-up tests. Long waits in the doctor's office are especially difficult for individuals who get paid only for hours worked.

Eliminating these barriers to care is important, but even if we expand the availability of primary care it is folly to rely on the *Field of Dreams* faith that "If we build them, they will come." Preventive services must be convenient and attractive, and it should be fashionable, not just sensible, to use them. The world marvels at America's genius at making lipstick and toothpaste fashionable and available in every neighborhood of the fifty states. We need to apply the same genius to health care.

People who work in school-based health clinics for teenagers know that if their offices are not clean, attractive, fun, and private, reluctant teens will never show. Embarrassment about pregnancy, immaturity, beliefs that prenatal care has little value, depression, inadequate transportation, couch potato habits, real or perceived time constraints—any number of reasons and excuses—keep women from seeking prenatal care.

Men and women alike often fail to make use of a range of available preventive services. For most of us, it's easy to conclude, "There just aren't enough hours in the day." The difficulty that the elderly experience getting up and out—and just plain laziness, ignorance, and failure to take a prescribed regimen of pills—contribute to the common failure to take advantage of available timely treatment.

To uproot this inertia, Florida Governor Lawton Chiles mounted a home-outreach program that cut the infant mortality rate for participating mothers. Volunteers and paid workers visited at-risk pregnant mothers and counseled them about how to have healthy babies. (Such visits are a common technique in Western European countries.) If "Avon calling" can sell cosmetics, why not use the same method to sell healthy baby care?

To reduce big-ticket heart procedures for its members, Health-Partners, a Minneapolis HMO, uses "naggers"—nurses who call and cajole members to take advantage of preventive services and make behavioral changes that will improve their health. United HealthCare Corporation, with twenty HMOs, launched a direct mail campaign to remind female enrollees over age fifty to get mammograms to screen for breast cancer. The result? Almost 60 percent got mammograms, twice the national average for HMOs and other managed-care programs.

The Health Care Financing Administration learned these lessons the hard way in January 1991, when it extended Medicare coverage for periodic mammography screening and urged doctors to install mammogram machines in their offices. Officials predicted that 4.9 million Medicare recipients would benefit. But in the first year, only 670,000 took advantage of the coverage. The failure to combine accessibility with persuasive advertising actually drove up the price of each screening as doctors tried to recover their overhead costs of the newly installed mammography machines from 14 percent of the patients they had anticipated.

A study of 1,500 employees at Johnson & Johnson, which covers the cost of immunizations, found that only 45.2 percent of the employees' children were fully immunized at age two. Many cited the difficulty of getting off work for a doctor's appointment and long waits at the doctor's office as deterrents.

The rate of polio vaccinations among one- to four-year-olds, which require three visits to a clinic or doctor, plummeted from 74 percent in 1965 to 44 percent in 1992. Dr. William Atkinson, a U.S. Public Health Service epidemiologist, noted that "Most [children] get one dose of oral polio vaccine and DPT [diphtheria, pertussis, and tetanus] vaccine, but fewer return for the second dose and fewer still for the third dose."

The successful development of a single-dose vaccine is long overdue, as are imaginative, savvy campaigns to get parents and their children fully immunized. Sister Sheila Lyne, the city health commissioner in Chicago, explained, "We don't want just the free vaccines. We need nurses and aides to get them out to the children who need them." And we need incentives to convince mothers to bring their children in.

Many adults need a dose of information and motivation about their own vulnerability to infectious disease. Some seventy thousand people die each year from pneumococcal infection, influenza, or hepatitis B, all of which can be prevented by vaccines. Lack of insurance coverage and primary care providers is only part of the problem. Better health education—and more attentive doctors and nurses—would help, as might increasing premiums for beneficiaries who fail to take basic preventive measures, and making it fashionable to get prenatal care and immunization for children and adults.

CULTURAL REVOLUTION: FROM SICK CARE TO HEALTH CARE

Joet Ranker, age 69. Condition: Congestive Heart Failure. Outcome: In 1989, Ranker was on the waiting list for a heart transplant because her heart was failing. Fifteen months later, after a strict regimen of diet, exercise, and drugs, she was off the list and on the golf course. Joet Ranker's cardiologist believes thirty percent of those on heart transplant lists can be treated this way.
—U.S. News & World Report, *November 22, 1993*

When it's hip to be healthy, we will have a healthy America. It must become cool to take care of ourselves, chic to exercise, fun to eat good foods. Teens should feel peer pressure *not* to smoke, *not* to take drugs, *not* to sleep around. Getting prenatal care, immunizations against childhood diseases, and periodic physicals has to be the thing to do. Knowing when to stop or cut back needs to replace the machismo of proving that we can handle high stress (popping a few pills on the side) or drink more beer or liquor than the next guy. Binge drinking in college should be as unwelcome as bad breath and body odor. Conceiving a baby during our teenage years must become decidedly uncool. The reckless abandon of unprotected sex must become a demonstration of stupidity, not sexual prowess.

The decision of television producers to show their characters using seat belts whenever they get into a car was far more potent in getting America to buckle up than all the laws passed in the fifty states. Mothers Against Drunk Driving, the popularity of beer-free high school proms (often prompted by the tragedies of death and permanent disability due to a teen's drunken drive), promotion of designated drivers in television sitcoms, tougher law enforcement against drunk driving, and the growing consensus that bartenders and bars should be held responsible for the damage caused by customers they serve to the point of intoxication—all this helped change the American attitude toward driving drunk, sharply reducing deaths and crippling accidents on the road even as the number of cars has increased. And all demonstrated how it is possible to change habits deeply entrenched in our culture.

The success of the antismoking campaign, which I started in the late 1970s, Surgeon General Koop revved up in the 1980s, and Surgeon General Elders kept going in the 1990s, derives less from our preaching than from the saturating coverage of television networks and radio stations. Because they could not accept advertising from cigarette companies, the electronic media gave the subject plenty of coverage and helped make smoking socially unacceptable for millions of Americans. That's why the beer industry fights so tenaciously against proposals to stop its TV advertising at events like baseball, football, and basketball games, which are watched by teenagers.

The enemies of a healthy America understand this. That's why the cigarette pushers fight so hard to keep glamorous human beings in their ads, pay film studios to have characters light up in movies and television shows, and oppose laws to guarantee smoke-free space. That's why every segment of society—public officials, employers, doctors, educators, priests, rabbis, parents, and individual citizens—must all unfurl the flag of cultural revolution. And that's why we have to find a way to talk about moral values in our communities and our country, respectful of diversity as well as mindful that clinical medical care, barren of values, is not suited to the problems that threaten the health of citizens today.

Skeptics know that the temptations of short-term gratification are a strong influence on human behavior, especially powerful for the young and the poor. Families in poverty live stressful, disorganized, where's-the-next-meal-coming-from lives, in which doctor appointments that require time off from work, special child care arrangements, or lengthy trips easily fall off the daily radar screen.

But even here, it takes only imagination—not Herculean powers—to enlist the poor in the cultural revolution. Marty Hiller, a Vietnam vet and psychologist, runs a free health clinic in Cleveland. He never fails to tell poor patients that they have the ability and responsibility to take care of their health. At the clinic, doctors, dentists, nurses, and therapists treat fifteen thousand patients a year. Whether they come to have a cavity filled, get a pregnancy test, or seek drug or AIDS counseling, Hiller serves them a dose of education on personal responsibility.

"Any national health care system will succeed only if the individual takes responsibility for his or her own health," said Hiller. "If we just assume there will be a system there to help me when I get sick or need help, it will reinforce the worst behaviors in the individual—and probably bankrupt society."

MANNING THE FRONT LINES OF REVOLUTION

Doctors, nurses, and other health care workers are pivotal in the creation of a culture of health care by providing information, advice, and counsel to patients and communities. A doctor who urges patients to stop smoking increases their chance of quitting. A physician's warning about the harmful effects of alcohol abuse ups the likelihood that the patients who enter employee assistance programs will stay sober. At Dartmouth, Dr. Koop is working to develop a "new kind of medical student," dedicated to health promotion and disease prevention and sensitive to the social and economic circumstances that influence a patient's health.

Too often, doctors miss opportunities, particularly with women. A 1993 poll found an alarming lack of basic preventive care among women. Though only 13 percent of the women lacked insurance, 35 percent had not had a timely Pap smear (including a quarter with incomes above $50,000); more than a third had not had a breast, pelvic, or physical exam; and 44 percent over age fifty had not had a mammogram. Although cost was a reason, Ellen Futter, chair of Commonwealth Fund's Commission on Women and Health, stressed "the lack of information and counseling from physicians. Too many women simply don't know what they should be doing to protect or better their own health."

Many women don't appreciate the risks of contracting sexually transmitted diseases, such as syphilis, gonorrhea, chlamydia, and herpes, which infect 13 million people a year, causing infertility, birth defects, blindness, and even death. In one poll, 72 percent of women under age twenty-five did not fear contracting such diseases. Doctors can help here by initiating discussions about sexual activity and its risks.

Teenagers also slip through the frazzled net of preventive health care because of physician neglect. Dr. William Jacott of the American Medical Association warns of the "tremendous gap in health care between the sixth grade and the pre-college or first employment exam. There's often no preventive care at all." Citing increases in drinking, smoking, and sexually transmitted diseases,

Dr. Arthur Elster, director of adolescent health for the AMA, added, "The health of many adolescents is going downhill" and "the biggest problems are behaviors that we can screen for and address." The price we pay for defaulting is high. Each year two and a half million teens contract a sexually transmitted disease. Each day three thousand children and teens start smoking—more than a million a year.

To be effective, doctors must tune into the particular circumstances of a patient's life. Older citizens may need reminders to take their medicine, help getting their prescriptions filled, and instructions on pill containers that pharmacists write in large, clear type. Some 60 percent of San Francisco's bus drivers who had been diagnosed with hypertension were going without treatment—despite full access to medical care. Why? Doctors had prescribed antihypertensive drugs that were diuretics. The drivers couldn't take them because bathrooms were inaccessible on their bus routes.

Whether the patient is young or old, working or unemployed, a lecture on the value of regular exercise and dietary fiber is of little use to someone living in a poor neighborhood where fresh fruits and vegetables are exorbitantly expensive, where jogging or walking on streets is dangerous, where drug dealers destroy playgrounds and public basketball courts, and where the purchase of a health club membership, treadmill, or stair climber is well beyond dreams or means.

Given the variety and complexity of persistent problems, doctors and their nurses need to learn the nonmedical systems that promote the health of families hobbled by unsafe housing, unemployment, illiteracy, poor nutrition, substance abuse, and other social and economic threats to health. At Johns Hopkins Hospital,

Carol Stansbury, a staff social worker, helps substance abusers, who repeatedly show up in the emergency room, get treatment, qualify for health coverage, and find shelter.

It also helps if doctors and nurses know, or can get help in, a language other than English. To reach people who don't speak English, a community health center in Oregon uses *promotores,* Spanish-speaking laypersons who roam the community to offer education and basic health services, screenings, and counseling.

CORPORATIONS AS CULTURAL REVOLUTIONARIES

Employers can plant seeds of cultural revolution. Johnson & Johnson launched its "Live for Life" program in 1979, to offer information and counseling on health, as well as programs for smoking cessation, weight control, stress management, nutrition education, fitness, and blood pressure modification, to twenty-eight thousand company employees. The program is free, including services such as fitness facilities. Over five years, annual hospital inpatient bills for each "Live for Life" participant went up 40 percent less than bills for nonparticipants. Baltimore Gas and Electric saves $15 million a year as a result of its wellness program.

In 1985, Steelcase, Incorporated, an office equipment manufacturer, ranked four thousand employees as high risk (high blood pressure and cholesterol, 20 percent or more overweight, high number of sick days, and use of regular medication) or low risk (lower levels on each indicator). The company offered employees smoking cessation, weight reduction, and stress management programs, and athletic club membership. From 1985 to 1990, many high-risk workers dropped into the low-risk category, and their medical claims came down with them—on average, from $1,155 to $537 annually.

Employers can also promote the health of their employees by establishing smoke-free workplaces (at the drug company Merck, the number of employees who smoked fell 25 percent during the first eighteen months of a workplace ban), insisting upon moderate (or no) drinking at office parties, and shifting the menu in the company cafeteria to healthy, low-fat foods.

Businesses can also be a catalyst outside the office walls, encouraging healthy, stable families that have sufficient time off from work to be together, helping to fund school-based health clinics and Head Start programs, and advocating health care priorities in the public sector. Finally, they can take a candid look at their own advertising to communicate their messages without glamorizing impulsive sex and violence.

The agreement by television networks to warn viewers about violent programs is, however limited, a form of prevention. The warning could help educate parents about the potential harm to their children and send a signal to all viewers that the use of violence, so common and evidently painless on television, should not be taken lightly. Video games should follow TV's lead.

GREENING THE GRASS ROOTS

Community leaders, teachers, health care workers, recreation organizers, social workers, clergy, and parents can learn to identify the health needs of their families and neighbors, and to nurture an environment in which individuals can actively protect their health. When Dr. David Satcher, director of the Centers for Disease Control and Prevention, visited a Nashville elementary school in 1993, he was appalled to find teachers smoking, exposing their students to secondhand smoke and providing unhealthy role models.

Smoking is far more prevalent among individuals with low incomes. More than one-third of individuals living below the poverty line smoke, compared to one-fourth of those with higher incomes. Liquor stores crowd the desolate landscape of urban ghettoes. Cigarette and alcohol companies plug their stuff as they paper billboards and sponsor social events in poor communities starved for recreation.

Jim Berry, a community leader in Washington, D.C., helped convince the district's lawmakers to impose a two-year ban on licensing new liquor stores in four of the city's wards. Berry counted more than a dozen stores that sell liquor, beer, and wine within a few blocks in his poor neighborhood. "We're absolutely surrounded," he said. "Everywhere you turn, it's booze, booze, booze."

Amid this battery of concerns, African-American politicians, hungry for campaign funds, can become enemies of their own people. In 1993, Illinois state legislators, with the support of African-American Democrats, opposed a fourteen-cents-a-pack cigarette tax increase. The Chicago *Sun-Times* reported, "Several of the black legislators articulated the view that smoking is a poor person's pleasure." Noting the campaign contributions that tobacco companies have made to black politicians, *New York Times* columnist Bob Herbert concluded, "The tobacco companies are buying the silence of the black leaders. And by accepting the money, and not speaking out against the awful dangers of smoking, those leaders are selling out their people. How many black bodies is a political contribution worth?"

GOVERNMENT: LEADER, REGULATOR, EDUCATOR, COACH, AND FUNDER

The words and actions of government officials play a fundamental role in establishing a culture of health care. Providing family planning and social services that help to prevent teen pregnancies, informing the public about the hazards of smoking, taxing cigarettes and alcohol, regulating environmental pollution, requiring that all workplaces be smoke-free, making lead paint illegal, and stripping public housing of this danger are only a few examples of what government can do, in addition to its more obvious role as financier and provider of medical services.

Too often the government defaults in its obligations. The Southern Regional Project on Infant Mortality found that in 1991, seventeen southern states spent over $5.7 billion to support families begun by adolescents, a 60 percent increase since 1987. The same states were spending only $110 million for primary prevention of adolescent pregnancy. "We are most definitely paying for the pound of cure," said Oklahoma Governor David Walters.

Although recalibrating such imbalances in funding is important, we must also acknowledge the limitations of what politicians and government regulators can do to prevent problems such as teenage pregnancy in the face of profound social forces. They can also do serious harm, as we learned when U.S. Surgeon General Elders publicly suggested a study on legalizing drugs, which implied that the hazards of drug use had been overblown.

The Centers for Disease Control and Prevention, armed with data that black Americans have a harder time quitting smoking than white Americans, has targeted an education campaign at black citizens. Praising the effort, Robert Butcher of the National Medical Association said, "It is hard to fight an industry that gives money and jobs to African-American people, but we must think about the cost to us in sickness and death." The tobacco industry, which has long targeted women and minorities, in a burst of cynical hypocrisy, called the campaign "paternalistic" because its focus on African Americans implied that "they need special health information."

What else can government—federal, state, and local—do to create a culture of health care?

• Provide reimbursement for a wide variety of health promotion and disease prevention services in federal and state health programs.

• Prohibit smoking in all public places and any place that receives federal funds, a move that the E.P.A. estimates would prompt one million smokers to quit, prevent up to 10,000 deaths from second-hand smoke a year, and deter 35,000 to 75,000 teenagers from ever lighting a cigarette.

• Place limits on TV advertisements of beer and wine.

• Prohibit cigarette advertising at sporting events.

• Eliminate the tax-deductibility of spending on advertising by cigarette companies.

• Prohibit sponsorship and advertising by alcohol and cigarette companies at inaugural festivities and other government events.

• Reduce the number of liquor licenses in poor neighborhoods.

• Enact higher taxes on guns and ammunition and tougher gun and ammunition control legislation.

• Promote healthy diets in the military, public schools, and social service programs.

• Create and protect safe places for children to play and exercise.

• Expand Head Start and other quality preschool programs that emphasize health promotion and disease prevention.

• Support home-visiting programs that encourage prevention and early detection of illness to enable the elderly and disabled to live independently.

• Fund the research necessary to learn what works in health promotion and disease prevention. Philip Lee, assistant secretary of health and head of the U.S. Pubic Health Service, has emphasized the "need for an initiative in prevention research" because "we know too little about what works."

YOU AND ME

The cultural revolution from sick care to health care begins with you and me—though most of us would prefer that it start with you, not me.

It's time for each of us to deploy the weapons of prevention and health promotion and adopt the life-styles that we know can make a difference.

CHAPTER SIX

A REALITY CHECK
FOR RESEARCH

In 1993, Fairfax Hospital of Falls Church, Virginia, asked a Federal District Court to clear the hospital of liability if it stopped treating a baby born in 1992 without a brain. The baby's condition, "anencephaly," is incurable and quickly fatal without medical treatment. The baby is permanently unconscious, without sensation or cognitive function, and has periodic respiratory crises that require treatment at Fairfax, where the intensive care unit costs $1,464 a day. The Court insisted that treatment continue, noting that the child's mother wants every possible scientific tool used to keep the baby alive.
    —The New York Times, *September 24, 1993*

Hazel Welch, age 92, managed to push her chronic leukemia into remission, but she could not walk unassisted and lived in a nursing home. When she collapsed from an ulcer, she asked her doctor, Sherwin Nuland, not to perform surgery. She said she had lived "quite long enough, young man," but he changed her mind. After the extensive operation, he sent her to the intensive care unit with a tube in her windpipe to help her breathe. In the days that followed, "she spent every minute of my twice-a-day visits staring reproachfully at me," said Dr. Nuland. Finally, when she could speak, "she lost no time in letting me know what a dirty trick I had pulled by not letting her die as she wished. I indulged her in this, certain that I had done the right thing, and with living evidence, I thought, to prove it. She had after all,

*survived." Two weeks after leaving the hospital, Hazel Welch suffered
a stroke and died.*
                              —*Sherwin Nuland,* How We Die, *1994*

The roots of modern medical practice lie deep in the nation's research community, which is busy exploring the mysteries of body and mind, inventing machines, concocting potions and pills, and devising surgical procedures to stretch the envelope of human life. Those who decide where to invest research dollars can determine where doctors will direct—and patients will demand—that health care dollars be spent.

The great American research volcano has been phenomenally successful at spewing forth treatments to fend off death with long-shot surgical, chemical, and mechanical therapies. Once new ideas erupt, however, it seems impossible to contain their use and misuse if they respond to a bedrock tenet of our health system: Keep people breathing, whatever the cost or quality of their existence.

It is in our American nature to democratize everything from education and medical care to VCRs and automobiles. We pride ourselves on the speed with which every advance becomes widely available. Nowhere are the incentives and pressures greater to hit the accelerator of democratization than when medical discovery offers hope of a longer life—whatever the odds.

Innovations that offer even marginal benefits in the quest to prolong life swiftly become required routine in hospitals, outpatient centers, and doctors' offices under the legal, financial, and ethical dictates that shape the practice of medical care. Terminally ill cancer patients are commonly admitted to hospital intensive care units and tied to ventilators—at a cost of tens of thousands of dollars per patient, though fewer than one in four survive more than three months at home.

This blind pursuit of even the most tattered shreds of life—as experienced in the case of the Falls Church baby, or the critically sick ninety-two-year-old knotted in tubes in an intensive care unit—can drive despairing men and women to plead for death in order to escape a medical establishment that insists on keeping them alive, however artificially or painfully. And it can be prohibitively expensive. Harvard economist Joseph Newhouse believes that new technologies account for as much as half of the growth in U.S. health care spending since 1940.

Such innovation, of course, pays homage to the most basic of all human instincts, the desire to stay alive. But is the American research community—the National Institutes of Health, great medical research and teaching centers, pharmaceutical giants, and biotechnology venture capitalists—so enamored with the exotica of cutting-edge science and the chance of hitting a billion-dollar jackpot that it is failing to serve the needs of our society? Are our research centers becoming laboratories for an elite corps of Dr. Frankensteins who revel in playing God with an abandon that threatens the dignity of the very lives they are trying to save, extend, and even create?

Much radiation and chemotherapy have sent otherwise deadly cancers into remission. But some chemotherapy so tortures terminally ill cancer victims that it seems designed more to satisfy the curiosity of mad scientists than to cure patients. The search for knowledge is essential to improving the human condition; most problems arise in the application. As we subject patients to such treatment and devise artificial hearts and all manner of organ transplants and, on another frontier, as we probe the mysteries of genes to define and deliver perfect babies, it is time to ask whether medical research has lost touch with the reality of the problems that individuals in our society face.

The need for a reality check for America's medical research

community stems from its neglect of questions whose answers could reduce the increasing years of dependence among the elderly. Researchers have failed to address adequately the pandemic of substance abuse and addiction, the urgent need for persuasive preventive and health promotion measures for all ages, old and young, and the special needs of adolescents who are distinctly vulnerable to the lure of addictive substances and reckless sex.

WHERE IT ALL BEGINS: THE RESEARCH BUDGET

The 55-year-old woman died of natural causes, but had suffered from arthritis, osteoporosis, and malnutrition; her teeth were rotten and an improperly set broken leg had led to a bone abscess. The infant, probably a girl, was malnourished too. Her last weeks had been marked by spinal meningitis. The man had been sedentary and overweight; his death at 50 was sudden, perhaps from a heart attack. The Calvert family lived in a different era: colonial America. Their remains were found in 1992 in unmarked graves in a Maryland cornfield, a discovery which provided grim evidence of the harshness of 17th century life.

—Time, *April 18, 1994*

The saga of American medical research is a glorious one, and we must now bring our research resources and genius more into line with the needs of this age and our civilization.

No doubt, if the Calverts were alive today, modern medicine could add another twenty years to Mrs. Calvert's life before a death from "natural causes." It could rescue the child from her meningitis, and Mr. Calvert would probably undergo a cardiac bypass or angioplasty to lengthen his life by a decade. But most of what ailed the Calverts in the "harsh" seventeenth century—the arthritis, the osteoporosis, the child's malnutrition, the heart dis-

ease caused by excess weight and a sedentary life—would probably still afflict them today, for America's researchers have made far
less progress in keeping people healthy and out of the sick-care
system than in providing exotic treatments to lengthen their life.

When how we spend our research dollars has such direct impact
on how we spend our health care dollars, and when most of the
money invested in basic research and almost half of what we pay
for health care comes from the common treasury—us taxpayers—
then publicly funded research should focus on preventing, curing,
and alleviating ailments that will provide the greatest good to our
society and the largest number of its people.

The nation spent some $30 billion on research related to health
care in 1994. The federal treasury directly bankrolls almost half.
The balance comes from commercial and nonprofit institutions,
such as drug companies and foundations, which enjoy substantial
tax breaks.

The National Institutes of Health lead the health research effort
with an $11 billion annual budget. The 320-acre NIH campus in
Bethesda, Maryland, is home to hundreds of laboratories, a 540-
bed hospital, and 17,000 employees, up from 140 at its birth in
1930. How NIH spends its money depends not only on the judgment of experts who choose the most promising lines of research,
but also on the wishes of the White House and the Congress,
which listen to advocates for particular concerns such as AIDS and
cancer.

In 1994, the NIH devoted $6 billion—more than half of its
budget—to basic research, which represented roughly 90 percent
of the nation's investment in this area. Basic research has no
immediately apparent profitable application; scientists try to solve
fundamental mysteries in the hope that the knowledge they un-
cover may somehow prove useful. Their work has delivered star-

tling breakthroughs: the discovery of the structure of DNA (deoxyribonucleic acid) and RNA (ribonucleic acid), oncogenes that trigger cancerous cell growth, brain transmitters that have become targets for the treatment of psychotic illness, and the AIDS virus.

It is the applied-research arm of the NIH, pharmaceutical companies, and medical-device enterprises that have lost touch with many of America's fundamental needs. Applied research takes the discoveries from basic research and tries to use them to treat particular illnesses. Political forces that make certain diseases fashionable drive the direction of this research, as do the legal requirement that publicly owned corporations maximize profits and the abiding obsession of our people with postponing death.

Any number of dramatic incidents can make a disease fashionable. Watching cancer eat away at an ebullient political leader like Hubert Humphrey, seeing John F. Kennedy's sister Rosemary suffer from mental health problems, being awed by the courage of First Lady Betty Ford after a mastectomy for breast cancer—these human experiences draw millions of dollars into research efforts to prevent future tragedies. That is the way of the world and always will be.

But more systematic, organized ways to make diseases fashionable, however well intentioned, may not serve the national interest. I remember the great philanthropist Mary Lasker and her friend Florence Mahoney listening to Lyndon Johnson complain about delays in getting Congress to pass his legislation to create centers for research on heart disease, cancer, and stroke throughout the nation and to approve the sharp increases he had recommended in funds for cancer and cardiovascular research. "Oh, Mr. President," they chorused one afternoon in the Oval Office, "we wish we could do more to help."

"You sure can," LBJ snapped back. "You have what those senators and congressmen need," he said.

The two fashionable ladies looked puzzled.

"Money," he said after a dramatic pause. "Lots of money. Use more of it to help those in Congress who support my health programs."

The ladies did. And they had quite an impact as more than two dozen Great Society health bills made their way through the Congress into the law of the land.

The legalization of political action committees has influenced the nation's research agenda. Wealthy trustees of medical centers make contributions to encourage members of Congress who support the research agendas of their institutions. Pharmaceutical companies seek to tilt NIH dollars into areas they see as most likely to produce profits. Tobacco interests have no problem with research into lung cancer and heart disease caused by the use of their product, but they don't like to see federal funds spent on addiction research (which might help individuals shake the nicotine habit) or on finding ways to persuade young Americans not to smoke.

Effective advocates can be key to focusing attention on neglected areas. Congress earmarked $263 million for NIH research on breast cancer in 1994 (compared to $90 million for lung cancer, $71 million for colorectal cancer, and $50 million for prostate cancer), a 34 percent jump in one year. (And this doesn't count the $210 million that Congress earmarked for breast cancer research in the Department of Defense.) Reflecting the growing clout of women in the House of Representatives, the NIH has mounted a long-overdue $625 million, fourteen-year research project on osteoporosis, heart disease, and breast and colorectal cancer in women.

Too often, however, politically fashionable diseases and the pervasive desire to postpone death fill America's research dance card, while disabling ailments that afflict millions of our people do not get the attention they deserve. This contrast between the ample funding that marks research into trendy ailments and the paltry resources devoted to unfashionable debilitating diseases is cruelest with respect to the nation's failure to commit adequate resources to research into the causes of and cures for substance abuse.

The oldest and youngest are especially shortchanged by our research investments. In 1994, NIH spent only $420 million on research related to aging, even though the over-sixty-five population (which accounts for a third of all hospitalizations) will double to 65 million people in a generation, and the eighty-five-and-over population will almost triple by 2030. This amount includes almost everything NIH spends on Alzheimer's disease and osteoporosis.

In 1994, NIH spent only $555 million on child health care, even though children are the most innocent and, in the long run, the most expensive victims of substance abuse, addiction, and lingering physical and mental disabilities. Curbing ailments in infants and children offers one of the most cost-effective health care investments.

CROSSING THE BOUNDARY BETWEEN LIFE AND DEATH

Attending the birth and nurturing the growth of high-tech innovations in American health care are the doctors and nurses in the nation's prestigious teaching hospitals. Funded by public tax dollars, private donations, or capital from companies hoping to profit from miracle pills and procedures, these medicine men and women test and try the exotica of American medicine to find the Lazarus in every intensive care patient.

Of the nation's hospitals, 408 are affiliated with 125 medical schools. These teaching hospitals perform cutting-edge research, while providing clinical experience for troops of medical school graduates. Magnets for the best specialists and subspecialists in the country, they audition the latest instruments, machines, drugs, and procedures on seriously ill patients and grease the passage from experimental treatment to routine medical practice.

The best and brightest who work these corridors are eager to satisfy the demands of patients who expect up-to-the-minute marvels. In 1983, doctors performed coronary angioplasties, threading a balloon-tipped catheter through the arteries, on only thirty thousand patients; by 1990, the number of angioplasties had jumped to three hundred thousand. Before 1987, doctors did not do a single cholecystectomy (gallbladder removal) with laparoscopic instruments and tiny incisions; within five years, 80 percent of all gallbladder removals were done this way and the total number of operations had soared as laparoscopic gallbladder surgery became as routine as pulling a tooth.

Such technological progress rarely means lower costs. In the Alice-in-Wonderland world of America's health care system, when costs go down, costs go up. Laparoscopic surgery is less expensive than traditional gallbladder removals, but doctors perform the new method on so many more patients that the total bill for gallbladder surgery has risen.

The most expensive technologies quickly become de rigueur at community hospitals. Once a hospital has a new machine, its next-door neighbor buys a duplicate to compete for patients and doctors. The latest in high technology is the "Gamma Knife," a $3 million machine that radiates brain tumors. Although its clinical value is unproven, hospitals are scrambling to buy it. "People want bragging rights," explains Larry Atkins, president of American Health Services Corporation, which owns a subsidiary that installs Gamma Knives. "They want the chance to say: 'We have it and you don't.' "

The crown jewel of many hospitals is their intensive care unit, where doctors deploy the latest highest-tech treatments to fend off impending death. America's hospitals have ninety-seven thousand intensive care beds, devoting about fourteen thousand of them to neonatal care, three thousand to pediatric care, twelve thousand to cardiac care, and the remainder to general medical and surgical care, many for patients with terminal cancer.

Patients who teeter on the edge of death in intensive care beds seek a thread of hope among the beeping machines, monitors, artificial ventilators, blood pumps, glaring spotlights, and harried nurses and doctors who labor to defy the odds and sustain life. For this reason, many revere the wizardry of hospital intensive care as the American medical system at its best.

Dr. Steven Schroeder compared four major teaching hospitals in Western Europe to the University of California hospital in San Francisco, a typical American teaching hospital. The American hospital had more intensive care beds, placed "much greater emphasis on research," and was "more aggressive" in providing intensive treatment to very sick and dying patients.

In contrast, the European teaching hospitals were "less expensive, less technology intensive, staffed by fewer employees and physicians," and "occupied by less severely ill patients." European physicians, Dr. Schroeder concluded, are more inclined to help people with terminal ailments die comfortably in their homes. They emphasize "quality of life" more than their American peers, and they say to our physicians, "You guys don't know when to stop."

When Dr. Sherwin Nuland reflected on the case of ninety-two-year-old Hazel Welch, he concluded that, by operating on her, he had won out over the "riddle" of human illness, but he had "lost the greater battle of humane patient care." In retrospect, he "would not have been so quick to recommend an operation. . . . The effort was not justified, no matter what success might have resulted, and I was not wise enough to recognize it." Yet in his next breath, Dr. Nuland admitted that it was "a lie" to imply that he would have acted differently. "I know I would probably have done exactly the same thing again, or risk the scorn of my peers," he confessed.

Even when American patients plead to forgo extraordinary measures and simply ask for pain relief, it's not easy to change the norms of medical practice. Believing that not using all available treatments might be professionally unethical and even illegal, doctors often act contrary to their own humane and moral instincts.

A survey of fourteen hundred doctors and nurses found that half admitted to acting against their conscience and overtreating terminally ill patients, especially in using ventilators, cardiopulmonary resuscitation, and artificial nutrition and hydration. Strangely, this commitment to prolonging life does not necessarily extend to easing the passage to death. Concerned about side effects or addiction to painkillers, doctors and nurses acknowledge undertreating for pain, often ignoring patients' requests for relief.

Extraordinary efforts to prolong life are not reserved for the elderly. The nation's best medical minds and machines are also turned on to keeping premature, low-weight babies alive, whatever the expense and permanent scars. Doctors can now keep alive an infant born after only twenty-three weeks in the womb, although the baby will likely suffer brain damage and other severe disabilities such as blindness. More and more infants born with severe congenital defects, such as spina bifida or malformed hearts, survive each year, another tribute to costly, high-tech neo-natal intensive care units.

Advances such as these are largely responsible for doubling, since 1960, the proportion of children who are chronically dis-abled to 7.4 percent of all boys and 5.4 percent of all girls in 1992.

"Specialized medicine," much of it neonatal care, "is the Pied Piper" at Jackson Memorial Hospital, concedes Bernard Fogel, dean of the University of Miami School of Medicine, which is affiliated with Jackson. On a typical day in 1993, Jackson's neona-tal unit housed three babies, side by side in incubators. At birth, each weighed little more than a pound. The care for each infant cost $2,500 a day, a total of $400,000 per baby after the 160 days of hospitalization that each required.

What about their futures? "Two of the three babies were badly brain-damaged," Dr. Fogel said. "All three had problems relating to their mothers' substance abuse. One had been exposed to the AIDS virus in the womb. One will clearly need to be institutional-ized. Their care will cost tens of millions of dollars if they live to be forty or fifty years old." Most of these costs could have been avoided with prenatal care and health promotion to wean the mothers off cigarettes, alcohol, and drugs.

Joseph Amato, a specialist in pediatric cardiothoracic surgery, sees the other side of the coin. In 1992, Catherine Grotto was born with a severe congenital heart defect that robbed her blood of oxygen. When the obstetrician cut the umbilical cord, she turned blue. If she had been born only a decade earlier, she would have died. But in 1992, Dr. Amato could offer hope.

"The father came to me, devastated," says Amato. "He said, 'This is my baby. You have to save her.' " The chances of saving her were only one in five, but Amato offered to try. He immedi-ately performed one of three surgeries necessary for her to live. She survived. Amato performed the second surgery in 1994, and he is confident that Catherine will be able to live a normal life—if she makes it through the third operation.

Meanwhile, after a five-month stay in the intensive care unit, Catherine's medical bills hit $500,000, breaking the limit of Grotto's insurance policy. But, Amato says, "We always find some grant, some state assistance. We would never refuse a child." He acknowledges that "twenty percent or twenty-five percent is not a good success rate." But, he points out, no one—not the doctor and certainly not some government or insurance company bureaucrat—knows in advance whose child will survive to enjoy a normal life, whose will be seriously disabled, and whose will die.

The desire for the perfect baby—for flawless reproduction, uninhibited by natural limitations such as parental age, premature birth, or congenital defects—has prompted major investments in neonatal research, experiments with new methods of prenatal diagnosis, and development of ways to tinker with fertility and the fetus. Once a disappointment that inspired adoption, infertility is now the launching pad for a battery of exotic tests and procedures. The results have led to unthinkable new powers—such as cloning human beings and freezing embryos for some future use—and jarring headlines, such as one in *The Washington Post* on January 11, 1994, that asked, SHOULD EGGS FROM FETUSES OR CADAVERS BE USED TO HELP WOMEN BECOME PREGNANT? and another in *The New York Times* on June 5, 1994, that announced, NEWLYWED HOPES TO USE SPERM OF DEAD SPOUSE TO START A FAMILY.

Gloria D'Arrigo knows all too well the medical industry that our research investment in fertility has spawned. In 1982, her pregnancy ended in a miscarriage. Since then, she has had two laparoscopies, four hysterosalpingograms, twenty-two postcoital tests, more than a year of intrauterine insemination, one in vitro fertilization, and two gamete intrafallopian transfers. She has spent $25,000 from her own pocket; her insurer has put up another $30,000. But in 1993 Gloria D'Arrigo was still not pregnant. "Eleven years ago, the doctor led me to believe I'd become pregnant," she said then. "And he tells me that to this day."

Many hospitals have begun to advertise their lucrative specialty services. Facing stiff competition in the metropolitan area, Mount Sinai hospital boasted to potential customers reading *New York* magazine:

> For thousands of couples grappling with the pain of infertility, nature frequently needs a little help. And that's what we provide. . . . We offer a wide range of highly sophisticated infertility services from IVF [in vitro fertilization] to GIFT [gamete intra-fallopian transfer]. Including micromanipulation techniques and advances such as Circumferential Zona Thinning. We're even one of the first hospitals in the New York area to have a fully-licensed ovum donation program.

Amid the emphasis on developing new techniques for infertility treatment, prenatal diagnosis, and neonatal care, which have brought such joy to many parents, researchers accord remarkably little attention to developing effective primary care and preventive interventions for the health problems and disabilities that threaten and afflict millions of children and teenagers, or to finding ways to persuade teenagers not to become pregnant, and if they do, to persuade them to obtain high-quality prenatal care.

THE DOUBLE EDGES OF THE RESEARCH SWORD

The publicity machine of medical miracles keeps us transfixed, gazing in awe at the razor-sharp edge of health care research, which creates and prolongs life that just a few years ago would have been lost. But there is also a jagged edge to this sword.

Our scientific genius has given the world surgical anesthesia, microsurgery, pacemakers, computer-driven artificial limbs that mimic the real thing, antibiotics, and diagnostic imaging tools that produce living-color pictures of our internal organs. If that genius has also given us addictive drugs to abuse, chemical and radiation treatments so savage they can dehumanize, and faulty mechanical heart valves, no matter. Medical technology promises that human life, which for so many centuries had been "nasty, brutish, and short," can now be comfortable and long.

Biomedical and pharmaceutical research has produced a host of psychoactive drugs, tranquilizers, and antidepressants. When first discovered, there was little debate about their possible effects. Those who thought about the matter at all assumed that a new day was at hand, when thousands of mental patients, who had been sentenced to lives in institutions, could begin to live in the free air of their homes and communities.

These drugs have made a significant contribution to treating mental illness. But a tragedy of our day is the dumping of mental patients, many of them without homes or families, out of hospitals and into communities and prisons ill equipped to care for them. Could we, by asking the right questions in the past, have foreseen and prevented such tragedies?

We have chosen—without thinking and without asking the

right questions—to use tranquilizers, antidepressants, and sedatives freely to ease the stress our society imposes on the human spirit. Each day more than a million Americans take Prozac. Why? "This seems to be the perfect postindustrial service-society drug," said Dr. David Rothman of Columbia University. "You simply say to yourself—day in, day out—this is going to be a tough one. Bring me my Prozac."

Each night millions of Americans cannot sleep without a sleeping pill. Each year Americans consume billions of tranquilizers and sedatives. Is this promiscuous use of pharmaceuticals the best way to deal with stress? Should we not ask whether more fundamental changes are needed in life-style and work-style, and in the way we nourish our bodies and souls?

Pharmaceutical fixes may make life more comfortable, but by concentrating so much of our dollars and brains on extending the life of the near dead, we have produced a population that, on the whole, is sicker. Willard Gaylin, professor of psychiatry at Columbia University, puts it this way: "Good medicine does not reduce the percentage of people with illnesses in our population; it *increases* that percentage. There are proportionally more people in the U.S. with arteriosclerotic heart disease, diabetes, hypertension, and other expensive chronic diseases than there are in Iraq, Nigeria, or Colombia." In the United States, people with these ailments survive; in other countries, they die. Indeed, if "good medicine" in the United States keeps sick people alive, the best medicine keeps the sickest people alive.

No one would reverse the tide of the sparkling miracles of American research, which have brought profound joy to many. But the success of our researchers in keeping sick people alive should make us wonder what we could achieve if we devoted the same kind of resources, energy, and imagination to the challenge of keeping people healthy in the first place. In the absence of such a commitment, the scope and cost of innovative sick care will expand infinitely.

THE LIMITS OF REGULATION

Each medical drug or device must receive the imprimatur of the Food and Drug Administration before doctors can use it. But the FDA does not control *how* doctors decide to use it. The FDA approves products, not procedures; once it releases a new drug or device onto the market, the medicine men and women determine when to let us have it and for what ailments. FDA approval is the starting gate for promoters and patients to pressure physicians.

In 1993, Genentech, a biotechnology company, jubilantly trumpeted a study showing that the company's drug tissue plasminogen activator (TPA), which breaks up clots that clog arteries, was more effective than a rival drug, streptokinase. But TPA had two drawbacks: it helped only one out of one hundred patients who did not benefit from streptokinase, and it cost $2,200 a dose, ten times more than streptokinase. Is it worth it?

"It used to be that doctors had to find a reason to use TPA. Now they're going to have to find a reason not to use TPA," exulted G. Kirk Raab, Genentech's president. Indeed, by early 1994, sales of TAP had risen 43 percent, as physicians prescribed the drug, in part fearing malpractice charges if they missed that one-in-a-hundred patient.

In 1990, the FDA approved a device to monitor pregnant women in their homes for signs of premature delivery. Whether this device prevents premature births is unclear, but its sales promptly soared above $200 million a year. "The worst thing is that these devices have been put into widespread practice before they were studied, driven by an entrepreneurial spirit," complained Dr. Fredric Frigoletto, chief of obstetrics at Massachusetts General Hospital.

In 1989, after the death of comedian Gilda Radner from ovarian cancer, thousands of women demanded a test to screen for the disease from their doctors, who often complied even though the test's reliability was in doubt. The procedure has since proven to produce a high rate of false positives, prompting the National Institutes of Health to conclude in 1994 that indiscriminate use of the test produced a rash of unnecessary surgeries on healthy women. "In many cases," said NIH spokesman Bill Hall, "surgeons are opening up women who have no ovarian cancer."

LIMITING PHYSICIAN DISCRETION

Where the FDA lacks the power to tread, insurers and managed-care organizations are jumping in with both feet to curb the abandon with which doctors dispense new products and procedures. Under pressure from cost-conscious corporate employers and deficit-plagued governments, they are withholding reimbursement for long-shot therapies, experimental drugs, and, in the bottom-line world of managed care, even FDA-approved use of drugs for what they consider marginal purposes.

In 1993 the FDA approved the drug tacrine because it can stall for six months the progression of Alzheimer's disease, which robs its victims of their personalities, independence, and ultimately their lives. But only 40 percent of Alzheimer's patients respond to tacrine, and then only at high doses that frequently cause liver damage. Kaiser Permanente's HMO in northern California has discouraged its doctors from prescribing the drug, and other HMOs have followed suit.

The most severe tension between physician and payer arises in the area of medical procedures, like surgery. Here no FDA approval is required as a precursor to the use of new techniques. The medicine men and women are on their own.

Most insurers refuse to pay for "experimental" treatments, although the line between "experimental" and "proven effective" can be murky in the American health care labyrinth where what's "experimental" today can be "proven effective" tomorrow in saving someone's life. Doctors charge that this tightfisted attitude will squelch innovative uses that could save lives and provide new knowledge. At the same time, the need to temper physician zest for supporting, conducting, and applying new procedures has become a topic of concern within the medical community. Dr. David Grimes admonished in *The Journal of the American Medical Association:*

> Physicians must demand the same high standards of science for new operations as we do for new medicines. The alternative is uncontrolled human experimentation. . . . "Doing everything for everyone" is neither tenable nor desirable. What *is* done should be inspired by compassion and guided by science—and not merely reflect what the market will bear. As physicians, we are ethically bound to be sure that the tests, procedures, and treatments we provide are worth the money, pain, and inconvenience that they cost.

If doctors are ethically bound to be sure that "tests, procedures, and treatments . . . are worth the money, pain, and inconvenience that they cost," then we must ask whether the researchers who provide the building blocks for these innovations should not also accept some ethical constraints on where they put their energies and resources.

WHERE SHOULD THE MONEY GO?

How we invest research dollars sculpts the shape and cost of health care in America. It affects not only who lives, but how we live. If our research is to serve the goal of sustaining a decent life, we need to reallocate the nation's health research budget. We must:

Give as much attention to the leading causes of disability for the elderly as we give to the leading causes of death. Research should seek to prevent and treat not only what causes people to die, but what threatens their ability to live with dignity and independence and savages the quality of later life.

At 4 percent of the NIH budget, aging research is small potatoes for one of the three major causes of disease and dependence (genetics and the environment are the other two). In the mid-1990s, we do not even know precisely the answer to the question, What should older people eat? The recommended daily allowances for elderly diets are extrapolated from those determined for younger people, without adjusting for biological changes of aging.

The National Academy of Sciences Institute of Medicine report *Extending Life, Enhancing Life: A National Research Agenda on Aging* points out that better understanding of aging "will lead to interventions that may delay or even reverse disability." It urges research to answer questions like these: Why do individuals differ so in aging changes of bone, brain, and heart? What preconditions for aging may be set early in life, perhaps even in utero? What's the role of genetic and environmental interactions in individual aging patterns?

A catalogue of disabilities serves to restrict the independence of the elderly. Some two million seniors are severely demented. Millions suffer incontinence; sixteen million are handicapped by arthritis. Deafness hinders ten million; blindness and other visual problems, more than nine million. Three million have diabetes. Osteoporosis afflicts nine out of ten women over age seventy-five, threatening them with permanent dependence should they slip or fall. Some three hundred thousand people, most of them women sixty-five or older, suffer hip fractures each year.

Although these conditions rob the elderly of their independence, they will not be found among the leading causes of death. Yet such problems often lead to a nursing home. On any given day, a total of 1.5 million people, 75 percent of them women, live in nursing homes, twice the 800,000 in a hospital each day. In 1994, roughly seven million seniors needed long-term care. The number will rise to fourteen million in the next generation.

Dementia tops the list of causes of institutionalization. As many as half the individuals in nursing homes are heavily sedated by antipsychotic drugs, a common treatment for behavioral problems (aggression, verbal abusiveness, restlessness, agitation, wandering) symptomatic of dementia. On any day, 25 percent of nursing-home residents are bound by such restraints as lap belts, wrist or leg tethers, or vests that tie them to a chair or bed.

Better understanding of the debilitating problems that trigger dependence could avoid this tragic finale for hundreds of thousands of senior citizens and lead to more humane treatment and even independent living. It could also reduce health care costs. Treating and caring for the four million Americans who suffer from Alzheimer's costs about $100 billion a year. Long-term care in a nursing home is so expensive that even the original, generous Clinton administration proposal for universal coverage did not cover it. Each month the onset of disabilities that create the need for nursing-home care is postponed can cut $5 billion a year from the nation's nursing-home bill.

Although, on average, people born today can expect to live to age seventy-five, most experience a healthy life span, free of disabilities, disease, and impairment, to only sixty-four years. We must focus more research on the next eleven years, when aging, accidents, and illness impair mobility and brain function, reducing individuals to degrading states of disability, dependence, and despair. Unless we do, our current priorities will give us a brave new world with millions of people—as Dr. Robert Butler, Chairman of the Department of Geriatrics and Adult Development at New York's Mount Sinai School of Medicine, puts it—stuck with "quantity of life without quality of life." And they will give us a world of escalating social and economic pressures to kill off the old or to medicate and warehouse them out of sight. That's why Dr. Butler wants the budget of the National Institute on Aging increased to $1 billion.

Focus research on interventions to prevent and treat conditions that sap the health of children and teenagers. The threats to the health of children and teens are very different from those early in the twentieth century. Then, the most serious health problems for children were pathogens rampant in the air, water, or sewage system, causing dysentery and infectious diseases such as influenza, measles, and tuberculosis. Public health measures, sanitary engineering, vaccines, and child labor laws have all but eliminated these threats for most children.

Other concerns have replaced them. Since the mid-1970s, children have suffered the highest poverty rate of any age group in America. In 1994, fifteen million children—including almost one of every two African-American children—lived below the poverty line. Many poor children grow up soaked in unhealthy conditions: distracted, depressed, single parents, or no parents; transient communities; poor nutrition; violent crime; unsafe housing; widespread substance abuse and addiction. They are more likely to get sick, and when they do, they get sicker longer and are more likely to die than are the children of affluent parents.

Twelve million children do not get basic preventive care, such as periodic physical exams or immunizations. Instead, kids get asthma, measles, and whooping cough and suffer the consequences of malnutrition. They get chronic ear infections that hold them back in school. They don't get eye exams and glasses that would help them read or see the classroom blackboard. They suffer from lead poisoning that goes undetected until its damage is done. They struggle with mental health disorders that hobble their development into productive, nonviolent human beings.

These and other health problems that most afflict children and teenagers will not be solved by universal health insurance. Many of the twelve million children who have not gotten basic health care have been covered by Medicaid or other insurance. Even filling gaps in the infrastructure by building more health clinics and providing easily accessible primary care, though important, will not do the job.

For many problems we know what to do. What we don't know is how to get poor young parents, their children, and teenagers to do it. We have a remarkable capacity in this nation to get individuals to buy Sony Walkmans, all kinds of cars, stereos, refrigerators, and T-shirts. Our pharmaceutical companies are clever at devising easy-to-swallow pills and delayed-action capsules that make it unnecessary to remember to take medication every four hours. But we have put little research effort into learning how to get individuals who feel alienated from established social and health institutions, and those who suffer from depression or other chronic mental illness, to take advantage of readily available help and health care resources.

High-risk behaviors, such as fast driving and experimenting with drugs and alcohol, are commonplace among teenagers. Sexual activity and the presence of its sinister sidekicks, AIDS and other sexually transmitted diseases, have increased since the 1970s. Most high-schoolers have sexual intercourse; one in five has already slept with four or more partners. Many were high on beer or pot and had not used a condom during their latest intercourse. One in four sexually active teens will get a disease such as gonorrhea or chlamydia. Although the number of teens infected with AIDS (555 reported cases in 1993) is still relatively small, the number more than tripled from 1992 to 1993.

Our brightest minds should focus on two particularly vulnerable periods of development: early childhood and early adolescence. As Dr. David Hamburg explains in his powerful book, *Today's Children,* early childhood is "characterized by rapid growth, specific environmental needs, maximal dependence on caretakers, great vulnerability and long-term consequences of failures in development." In early adolescence (ages ten through fifteen), puberty strikes, the junior high school years begin, and temptation rises to adopt high-risk behaviors, such as cigarette smoking, alcohol and drug abuse, truancy, careless driving, poor nutrition, and sexual experimentation.

Research should focus on these fragile periods of transition for children and on what it takes to motivate parents, children, and teens to pursue healthy life-styles and take advantage of available medical care. The importance of motivating teenagers to pursue healthy life-styles cannot be overstated—nor can our failure to devote adequate research funds in this area, for it is in the limbo of life between childhood and adulthood that we adopt habits that set the tone—and too often seed the illnesses—for the rest of our lives.

Protect the basic research budget from being blown in the fashionable political winds. The will of the people should influence public spending on research. But micromanagement of the NIH budget by a Congress afflicted with a disease-of-the-month mentality is a threat to America's preeminence in biomedical research.

Until advocates organized, Congress turned a deaf ear to the murderous spread of AIDS during the early 1980s and allocated little for research on the mysterious disease because it was seen as an affliction of homosexuals and drug addicts. Pushed by angry advocates and entertainers who raise big political bucks, and shocked by public reaction to the deaths of movie star Rock Hudson and the child Ryan White, Congress flooded AIDS researchers with $1.3 billion by 1994, up from $64 million in 1985.

Lyndon Johnson invented this strategy in the 1960s, and the success of AIDS research advocates has served as an up-to-date model for others in the 1990s. The trouble arises when advocacy pushes Congress to override thoughtful experts who evaluate research proposals. Alluding to the peril of politically driven research, the Institute of Medicine report *Extending Life, Enhancing Life* concludes that because "many major advances in science have been unanticipated . . . it is essential to maintain the traditional primacy of investigator-initiated studies, the source of many research breakthroughs."

A congressional floor debate, driven by PAC money and freighted with emotional appeals, is sometimes the worst forum to decide where to place precious research dollars. In 1992, Congress decided to fund a $20 million trial of a potential AIDS vaccine and directed the Army to conduct the tests. Federal health officials had said the trial was ill conceived, but Congress wasn't listening. Why not? The vaccine's manufacturer had hired Russell Long, former chair of the Senate Finance Committee, to lobby for the experiment, and he got the directive written into law in an extraordinary appearance on the Senate floor. The Pentagon stopped the trial in 1994.

In a world where every dollar going to Peter must be taken from Paul, when Congress earmarks funds for specific projects, it is telling NIH officials to make room by killing less politically attractive research.

The easiest bystander to mug on the NIH campus is basic research, which rarely enjoys the protection of special interests. Yet by addressing fundamental questions, such as the mysteries of abnormal cell growth and the immune system and the secrets of the brain, basic research can produce breakthroughs that lead to preventive measures and cures for all sorts of destructive ailments. The applied-research community, including the profitable pharmaceutical industry, depends heavily on these discoveries.

AIDS researchers, for example, have been hobbled by our poor understanding of how the immune system works. Dr. Anthony Fauci, director of the National Institute of Allergy and Infectious Diseases, has noted, "Early on in the epidemic, there was a rush to get as many drugs as possible into clinical trials, and we were judged not necessarily on the quality of the science, but on how many patients were in these different clinical trials." Now, amid widespread pessimism about prospects for a vaccine or cure anytime soon, he senses a "reappreciation of the importance of answering many of the basic questions in pathogenesis, and using that as a basis of designing treatment strategies."

Congress should resist disease-of-the-month allurements, commit itself to the importance of basic research, and acknowledge that the nation's health research effort is underfunded. America spends only three cents of every health care dollar on research. Between 1980 and 1993, funding for health research rose 11 percent a year on average, but much of the increase occurred in private industry, which boosted spending at a 15.3 percent rate. Meanwhile, the federal government increased its budget only 7.4 percent annually. In 1993, commercial enterprises, which rarely fund basic research, accounted for 51 percent of the nation's health research budget, up from 31 percent in 1980. The federal government, which finances virtually all the nation's basic research, accounted for only 39 percent of the total research budget, down from 59 percent in 1980.

At a time when complex challenges such as AIDS, substance abuse, and the recondite influence on health of genetics, aging, and the environment demand the government's attention, federal funding has fallen far behind the capacity of our scientific genius. In 1987, 35 percent of research applications to the NIH received awards. By 1994, the award rate had plummeted to 20 percent.

The scarcity of public money for worthy projects has pushed many researchers into the arms of profit-minded funders. Noting this migration of money and talent, Arthur Caplan of the University of Pennsylvania's Center on Bioethics, asks, "Are we going to continue to bring the bottom-line mentality into the laboratory? Are we going to raise a generation of scientists whose first impulse is to patent, or to keep a trade-secret rather than share news with their colleagues? This is tearing at the very moral fiber of academic research." Indeed, the pots of gold at the end of the research rainbow have tempted more than one academic scientist to play fast and loose with the facts.

Senators Tom Harkin, the Iowa Democrat, and Mark Hatfield,

the Oregon Republican, have proposed legislation to place 1 percent of all health insurance premiums in a medical research trust fund, which would be allocated to the NIH. "Until we make this investment," Harkin noted, "the debate will largely be about paying bills, not preventing them, and long-term improvements in quality and cost reduction will be sacrificed to short-term fixes." Such a fund could provide the NIH with resources to attract an ample number of talented young scientists who are key to keeping America at the center of biomedical research. As pressures to cut treatment costs squeeze teaching hospitals, it's especially timely to fund more research through the front door.

Attend to the moral implications of our scientific genius. The contest to remain civilized has for centuries been the struggle of moral sensibilities to keep pace with the development and application of knowledge. In pluralistic America, which has provided such fertile soil for inventive genius, it has been especially vexing to maintain a moral and ethical balance as one scientific and technological discovery piles onto another.

We see this lack of balance on our urban streets where our cleverness in devising addictive drugs and rapid-fire weapons has left in the dust of despair our ability to harness the reckless energy of youth and eliminate persistent poverty amidst plenty. We see it internationally where our skill in creating devices of destruction has overtaken our capacity to prevent war and terrorism. We see it in our entertainment, where our creativity in producing dramatic motion pictures and television programs has normalized porn over performance, violence over virtue, shock over sensitivity.

Nowhere does our inventiveness pose a greater challenge than in the arena of biomedical research. As our scientists blur the lines between life and death, suicide and murder, male and female, treatment and torture, genetic accident and genetic engineering, animal, artificial, and human body parts—as they stir life in glass bowls and suspend it for decades with their cryogenic wizardry— we must invest the time, energy, and resources needed to think through the ethical, human, and moral implications of their incredible discoveries. We must infuse science with morality as well as genius, nourish discovery with a reverence for ethics as well as excellence, and complement our intellectual sextants with a moral compass.

Though I hope it happens more often, only once in my private law practice can I remember a pharmaceutical company executive raising the ethical and moral implications of a discovery. James Burke, the chairman of Johnson & Johnson who steered the company through its Tylenol poisoning crisis in the early 1980s, called to ask me who I considered to be the best medical ethicist in the nation. My answer was immediate: Richard McCormick, the Jesuit priest who had served on the first U.S. Department of Health, Education, and Welfare Ethics Advisory Board, which I had established to advise me as secretary, and the author of numerous books and articles on the subject.

I asked Jim Burke why he wanted to know. "We are looking at a pill that will abort a fetus after intercourse, possibly even weeks after conception," he said. "We need to think through the ethical and moral implications of developing and marketing this thing. I want to consult the best minds in the country about it." We need more researchers with such ethical and moral antennae.

Take the human genome research project. No single health research undertaking has prompted such high hopes and deep fears. With a 1994 budget of $127 million, the National Center for Human Genome Research is working to map the location of some one hundred thousand genes that occupy the twenty-three pairs of chromosomes in each human cell. To date, scientists have located more than three thousand genes. They've found a glaucoma gene on chromosome no. 1; a gene defect related to colon cancer on chromosome no. 2; and the gene that causes Huntington's disease on chromosome no. 4. They've even learned that a genetic defect on the X chromosome may predispose men to aggressive behavior, and they're closing in on the genetic link to manic depression.

Unfortunately, locating the gene doesn't guarantee the existence of effective treatments; developing genetic therapies and cures that work could take anywhere from a year to a century. In the short run, however, genetic screening can help detect a disease, such as kidney cancer, in its earliest stages, when treatment is more likely to be successful. Surgeons at Washington University in St. Louis removed the thyroid glands of fourteen youngsters when genetic tests had revealed a mutation known to lead to a potentially fatal carcinoma.

In the long run, genetic research opens up spectacular potential to understand how to preserve health and counter disease before it starts. It also harbors the seeds of holocaust and the potential for frightening political manipulation, privacy invasions, and discrimination on a scale previously reserved for racial, religious, and ethnic hatreds.

Employers could use genetic information to deny jobs to people with predispositions to costly diseases, disabilities, or disruptive personalities. Concerned about such possibilities, a National Academy of Sciences panel called in November 1993 for legislation to deny genetic information to employers or health insurers without the individual's consent. The panel cited the "debacle of the 1970s with respect to sickle-cell screening," when carriers of the sickle-cell gene, most of them African Americans, lost jobs and paid more for health insurance, even though there was little or no evidence of higher risk of illness.

In the absence of therapeutic options, the most common use of genetic knowledge is to counsel couples about their risk of passing a genetic flaw to their offspring. Armed with information about their genetic makeup, couples may decide either to adopt or to conceive a child. They can then use prenatal diagnosis technologies to evaluate the genetic makeup of the fetus. The availability of abortion lets parents decide whether they like the genetic constitution of the forthcoming child or want to dispose of the fetus— for any number of reasons, from Down syndrome or Tay-Sachs disease to the child's gender or skin color. Preimplantation technologies allow parents to choose among embryo collections, discarding those not selected.

This potent mix of technology and knowledge dumps impossible choices in the laps of parents. Current legal mandates and ethical guidelines encourage doctors to inform their patients fully and then leave the decisions to them. In 1993, when scientists discovered the mutation on the gene that causes hemophilia, *The New York Times* reported the news: "Now that [the mutation] has been identified, it will make genetic counseling and prenatal diagnosis possible." For what? Until researchers devise effective fetal treatments or genetic therapies, which are not expected before the year 2000, parents have little choice but to abort the pregnancy or prepare for the child.

Not all genetic information is as clear as the link to hemophilia or gender. More often genes conspire with environmental and behavioral factors to produce unpredictable impacts on health and personality. Rather than offering a new pantheon of "preexisting certainties" for individuals to face and insurers to scrutinize, most genetic factors create a set of "preexisting propensities" freighted with lots of surprises.

Bonnie G. (who would not allow the release of her last name) and her husband learned in midpregnancy that their fetus had suffered severe kidney damage. The child might be born normal, need dialysis or an organ transplant, or die shortly after birth. Bonnie and her husband "went home that Friday night numb and stayed at home all weekend, trying to understand, trying to figure out what to do." With only three weeks to go before an abortion would be illegal, the couple frantically sought advice from relatives. After more tests offered encouraging—but indefinite—information, the couple decided to continue the pregnancy and hope for the best.

In another time, one might ask whether the use of such technology is worth the agony. But the existence of these medical powers in the American way of health makes the question irrelevant; they are available, so they will be used.

The researchers who created these powers and most of the doctors who make them accessible to parents will be long gone when the parents must attend to the emotional and moral ramifications of their wrenching decisions. But the promotion of prenatal technologies, which can discern increasingly subtle nuances in the fetus, tells parents that assessing their future child's qualities is possible. Once you have the information, what are you supposed to do with it? Go home and decorate the baby's room? Have an abortion? Get a divorce and find a spouse with more desirable genes? Until researchers develop treatments and measures beyond abortion, we are stuck with knowing our genetic flaws (and those of our children), but not being able to do much about them.

For example, as more parents use prenatal diagnosis to learn a child's gender, sex selection of a child becomes tempting. To avoid the emotionally vexing (and for millions, morally unacceptable) procedure of abortion, researchers are devising sperm-sorting techniques to identify semen samples that are rich in X (female) and Y (male) chromosomes. With early success rates as high as 80 percent, samples can then be artificially inseminated into the woman depending on whether she wants a boy or girl.

If this makes you squeamish, just wait. As genetic tests become available for everything from mental disorders and creative talent to sexual proclivity, obesity, height, and hair and eye color, the natural limits of this pursuit are hard to fathom. Given that it is already possible to rent a womb, genetic information could spawn a profitable market for sperm and eggs with "desirable" genetic qualities and "attractive" physical attributes.

As we continue to satisfy our natural hunger for discovery, we must keep in mind that our nation has another striking genius—the ability to turn the quest for perfection into for-profit ventures, such as those pandering to people more concerned about being cosmetically perfect than about the risks and costs of surgery and hospitalization. For a price, medical innovations already serve those who want larger breasts or the perfect nose, thighs, hips, eyelids, and chins. For a price, they can also serve people who want the perfect baby. The biotech business, nascent in the early 1980s, blossomed into a $50 billion industry of two thousand companies in 1994, nourished by academic researchers licensing their patents for hefty royalties.

The attitudes and mores that drive biomedical research and the use of its inventions are not developed in a cloister. They reflect the moral standards and serve the ambitions of the society in which they are shaped.

Scientists must accept responsibility for the dangers as well as the benefits of their discoveries. Those who seek to discover new worlds are obliged to do their part to make them brave and not brutish. Every researcher, and we taxpayers who pay the bills, should subject research with the power and potential of the genome project to rigorous moral scrutiny and as much foresight as we can muster. To this end, Congress has mandated that the National Center for Human Genome Research devote 5 percent of its budget to the study of ethical issues embedded in this profound endeavor. Some such allocation might be appropriate for the entire NIH budget, and private industry should consider a set-aside.

The legal system, short of breath and ideas as it seeks to catch up with our scientific genius, ties the hands of the growing number of doctors who would like to respond to their patients' pleas for a merciful transition from life to death. Political leaders who funnel resources to projects devoted to extending life rather than eliminating disability and dependency, or who focus resources on the last years and months of life rather than the earliest years, are making value judgments that define the nation's biomedical research agenda.

Religious leaders who neglect the education of their congregation on the spiritual value of not prolonging life with every (or any) available extraordinary means must bear responsibility for the misguided Christians and Jews who believe they have an obligation to keep their parents, their spouses, or themselves alive with every machine and medicine that science has to offer.

Are the fruits of American biomedical research nourishing our civilization and enriching our lives, or are some to be as destructive to human dignity as the bite of the apple that blew away the Garden of Eden and left Adam and Eve ashamed of their natural, naked human beauty? That is the question. To ask the question is not to oppose progress; it is to demand that progress serve a decent human end. The answer rests with our nation's priests and rabbis, lawyers and judges, politicians and philosophers—and with you and me—as much as it does with our scientific geniuses and superspecialists.

There is no higher calling for our intelligence and energy than the pursuit of knowledge, and investments in basic and applied biomedical research hold extraordinary promise to improve the quality of life for each of us. But we will fulfill that promise only if we look hard at the priorities to which we direct such research— and even harder at the way we use its fruits.

CHAPTER SEVEN

BUSTING THE
MEDICAL MONOPOLIES

The medical monopolies are busting up all over.

The trumpets of technology and economics are blowing down the walls that have protected doctors, dentists, and hospitals and separated health insurers, hospitals, pharmaceutical companies, and physicians—often at the expense of patient care and efficiency.

The most prominent, powerful, and well-protected monopoly in American medicine is that of physicians, established early in the twentieth century. As the century ends, it's time to ask whether perpetuating this and other health care monopolies—for pharmacists, dentists, drug companies that hold lucrative patents, plaintiffs' lawyers who control malpractice litigation, doctors and hospitals who have the power to set and self-police their own standards of professionalism—serves the patient's need for excellent, affordable, and compassionate care, or whether it simply protects the interests of the monopolists.

Whether the medical monopolies have been good or bad—or a mixed bag—for American patients and health care, the forces intent on their collapse are gaining such momentum in the final years of the 1990s that the survival of those monopolies in the next century seems unlikely. The health care implications for Americans may be as profound as the political implications of the transfer of authority over the city of Jericho for Israelis and Palestinians.

THE DOCTORS' MONOPOLY

Nursing is not the same as doctoring. As nurses who've become physicians have pointed out: Nurses do not know what they do not know.
—Daniel Johnson, Jr., M.D., Speaker, American Medical
Association House of Delegates

In the game of medical monopoly, doctors want to manage all the hotels and real estate and keep nurses in supporting roles, fluffing the pillows, emptying the bedpans, and keeping the guests clean, fed, and happy. But with the stakes so high in prestige, professional satisfaction, and financial rewards, it's not surprising that the nurses believe they are ready for a bigger part.

The tension between physicians and nurses has grown as the financial stakes have risen and as technology has empowered paramedicals to perform many diagnoses and treatments once reserved for doctors. The fact that the nation's corps of nurses is overwhelmingly female at a time when women are pressing for higher status, more opportunity, and more money adds to the pressure for change.

The elaborate system of licensing doctors and prohibiting all others from practicing medicine was created in the early years of the twentieth century in response to a report in 1910 by Abraham Flexner, a young layman educator from the Carnegie Foundation for the Advancement of Teaching. The report exposed the racket medicine had then become—riddled with lousy schools, inept faculties, and quack doctors. The most a professor of a Philadelphia medical school could claim for its students was "that nobody who is absolutely worthless gets in." Following Flexner's report, almost half the medical schools in the United States closed their doors as states stampeded to establish licensing boards. Well-trained doctors were given a stranglehold on the practice of medicine, an understandable response to Flexner's shocking revelations. Since then, state medical boards, controlled by doctors, have drawn the professional boundaries for nurses and doctors.

Prior to the 1930s, when doctors started to tighten their control over who could provide what medical care, nurses often worked independently, made drug therapy recommendations, and attended to the prevention and treatment of common ills and injuries. After muckraking journalists, progressive reformers, and doctors crusaded for regulation of pharmaceuticals to discourage deceptive advertising of quack remedies, state governments designated physicians as the only providers who could select a patient's medication.

Doctors thus became the powerful gatekeepers between drug manufacturers and patients, and this monopoly to prescribe drugs has served them well. It has cemented them at the top of the medical tower and enhanced their social and economic standing. Drug companies needed doctors to prescribe their products, and patients needed doctors to give them access to the miracle medicines discovered during World War II and the second half of the twentieth century.

Nurses also enhanced the hegemony of doctors by placing limits on themselves. In 1955, the American Nurses Association declared that nursing should not include "acts of diagnosis or prescription of therapeutic or corrective measures." In their effort to professionalize the boundaries of nursing, the nurses fenced themselves in.

In the early 1960s, nurses began to demand a greater role in health care, as more sought postgraduate degrees, raising expectations for what they could contribute as full-time professionals. At the same time, health policy experts began to worry about a shortage of doctors and nurses to meet the nation's burgeoning health care needs.

The enactment of Medicare and Medicaid in 1965 greatly increased the demand for health care providers. Almost overnight, more than twenty-eight million elderly and poor Americans were brought into the health care system. In response, Duke University and the University of Colorado founded the nation's first education and training for physician assistants and nurse practitioners, beyond the two to four years of schooling for registered nurses.

In the mid-1960s, Congress passed legislation launching a decade of federal programs that supported nurse practitioner training and employment. In 1980, encouraged by such public initiatives, the American Nurses Association scrapped its restrictions on the profession of nursing, and in an extensive Social Policy Statement adopted this open-ended definition: "Nursing is the diagnosis and treatment of human responses to actual or potential health problems."

The fence came down, the stature of nurses rose, and thousands entered the profession. In addition, there were twenty-seven thousand physician assistants with degrees from one of fifty-eight accredited training programs in medical schools, teaching hospitals, and the armed forces. Under physician supervision, they provided a broad range of medical services to diagnose and treat many common ailments. By 1994, there were more than one hundred thousand advanced-practice nurses who increasingly have postgraduate degrees: nurse practitioners, certified nurse midwives, clinical nurse specialists (*e.g.,* in cardiac or cancer care) and nurse anesthetists.

Together, these professionals can deliver up to 80 percent of the primary care that family physicians normally provide. In many states, these nurses have the power to prescribe drugs. Yet government and private insurers balk at paying directly for most of their services, preferring to reimburse the doctors, hospitals, clinics, and nursing homes that employ them. Insurers believe this protects them from paying for needless or duplicate care; doctors like the greater control it gives them.

Despite such lingering restrictions, nurses have helped fill holes in the porous infrastructure of American health care. In rural and inner-city communities, nurse practitioners are often the only source of medical care. As family doctors retire from rural practices, these communities increasingly turn to nurse practitioners as replacements.

When Claude Hardwood retired in 1990 after practicing as a family doctor for 34 years, the citizens of Glasco, Kansas, population six hundred, lost their only doctor. Instead of attempting to lure another physician to the rural community, Hardwood turned his practice over to Debra Folkerts, a certified family nurse practitioner. Some disgruntled patients left to go to a physician-run practice, but new patients were attracted to the nurse practitioner because of her reputation for personalized care. She, and the nurse practitioners who succeeded her, handle 75 percent of their cases without conferring with a consulting physician, who visits her clinic only one afternoon a week.

In the expansive 135,000-square-mile region of West Texas, Sister Nancy Hansen, a pediatric nurse practitioner, and Sister Carol Boschert, a certified physician assistant, are the only medical providers in Presidio, a hundred miles from the nearest doctor at a hospital in Alpine. Using interactive video, when necessary they consult with physicians, and their discussion is preserved on video-tape.

Rural populations are not the only underserved Americans affected by the shortage of primary care providers. Many urban residents and senior citizens across the country require more intensive, ongoing medical care than overworked primary care physicians can supply.

In Tucson, Arizona, nurses run the seventeen-community health centers of Carondelet Health Care Corporation in mobile home parks, churches, and senior centers. These nurses provide six thousand individuals with comprehensive physical exams; monitor their blood pressure, cholesterol, and blood sugar levels; and diagnose and treat routine ailments like urinary tract infections. Working in easily accessible locations, the nurses see their patients regularly and can detect even the slightest change in a senior's health. This continuous care promotes geriatric health and cuts costs by allowing seniors to live independently in their homes and reducing or eliminating lengthy hospital stays.

Certified nurse midwives are a source of care in areas without an obstetrician or where obstetricians no longer deliver babies because of exorbitant malpractice insurance premiums. In Cooperstown, New York, the obstetrical department of Bassett Hospital employs nine nurse midwives and four obstetrician-gynecologists. The nurse midwives manage all prenatal care and deliveries, with physicians on call to intervene only if problems arise. The department's cesarean rate is 10 percent—well below the national average of 24 percent—with no increase in infant mortality even though these nurse midwives serve an indigent population often plagued by substance abuse and teen pregnancy.

On the whole, nurse midwives can provide prenatal care and

handle normal births with the same quality of care as can obstetricians—at far less cost. Midwives use less anesthesia and perform less fetal monitoring, delivery-related surgical incisions, forceps deliveries, and artificially induced labor. While their C-section rates are lower than those of obstetricians, their average rates of prematurity are only 4.5 percent, compared to 10 percent among doctors. The average hospital stay for their patients is two days, compared with almost three days for doctors' patients. Much of their success stems from their more attentive prenatal care and reluctance to resort to high-tech interventions unless clearly necessary.

Under pressure to check medical costs, federal and state governments are encouraging greater use of nurse practitioners. Medicare has begun to reimburse nurse practitioners directly and state Medicaid programs are employing them to help stem rising costs. The $115,000 average income for primary care doctors is more than twice the average earnings of nurse practitioners.

In Coatesville, Pennsylvania, Joanne Moser and another nurse practitioner staff a medical office three days a week, with a physician on hand the other two days to treat the sickest patients. Serving the area's predominantly poor population, these nurses together receive the equivalent of one doctor's salary and they see more patients. Pennsylvania's Medicaid program reimburses the practice whether the patient sees a doctor or a nurse practitioner. "This is the way that primary health is headed, like it or not," says their consulting physician, David Cooper.

In 1993, the U.S. Public Health Service awarded the University of Maryland's nursing school $655,000 to operate Open Gates, a primary care clinic in inner-city Baltimore. Run by nurse practitioners, the clinic delivers primary care in adult medicine, geriatrics, gynecology, and pediatrics to six hundred clients. "When people can't afford care, they delay until they get very sick and end up at the emergency room—or they may go there because they don't know where to go and they're not that sick," said Dr. Mildred Kreider, who supervises the clinic. "We're trying to save the system some money."

Patients, who normally don't care about saving the system a cent when it comes to their own care, laud nurses for the caring and attentive nature of their treatment. William Pottenger of Tempe, Arizona, described why he prefers Margaret Manchester, a nurse practitioner, over a traditional family physician: "Nurse practitioners listen to you as an individual. Doctors study so hard they get set theories in the mind. They don't always listen, and they're very limited as far as their personal involvement."

Some twenty-two million Americans live in urban and rural areas with shortages of primary care physicians. Passing a law giving them the right to care is no assurance they will get it. As Dr. Steven Schroeder points out, "If we got there tomorrow with a health reform plan, we wouldn't have the physician work force to make it work."

Expecting the nation's medical schools to produce the thousands of family doctors needed to provide primary care is like waiting for Godot. We'll be cooling our heels a long time for someone who may never arrive. Of America's six hundred thousand physicians, almost four hundred thousand are specialists and more than two hundred thousand are primary care providers. With retirements and only fifteen thousand physicians graduating from medical school each year, even those most determined to increase the ranks of primary care doctors do not expect their number to grow more than two thousand to three thousand per year. Mary Mundinger, dean of Columbia University's School of Nursing, warns that it could "take a hundred years" to get the number of primary care physicians we need to provide care to all Americans at affordable cost.

The medical stars are in place for a major expansion of the roles and number of physician assistants and nurse practitioners, and an end to the medical monopoly of doctors. But the change will not come easily.

WHOSE FINGER WILL CONTROL THE HEALTH CARE BUTTON?

Throughout the 1990s and perhaps into the twenty-first century, the turf wars between doctors and nurses over who can do what to patients will be waged in the trenches of federal, state, and local legislatures, hospital boardrooms, rural clinics, HMOs, and insurance companies across the nation. The skirmishes center on whether nurses should be given keys to the medical kingdom—the unfettered power to diagnose ailments, treat patients, write prescriptions for drugs, and admit and release patients to and from hospitals. But appropriate roles for nurses and the future of the physician monopoly are far too important to be resolved solely by the interested parties.

Firing an early shot, the Clinton administration included in its health care reform proposal a provision to preempt state laws limiting the freedom of nurses to practice medicine. Doctors, led by the American Medical Association, have attacked this provision—and any others—which would require them to share with nurse practitioners and other non-physician providers their authority to give patients entree to the world of medical miracles. Dr. M. Roy Schwarz, a top AMA executive, put it this way: "Some [nurse practitioners] are asking for independent practice privileges, and some of us are rather alarmed. When the concept evolved, it was never envisioned they would play doctor."

Doctors invariably begin by launching a weapon that targets the first and foremost worry of every American patient: quality of care. Doctors point to nurses' lack of training to diagnose rare, often deadly diseases, and to handle the complex array and interaction of pharmaceuticals available for prescription. After eight years of education in college and medical school, doctors spend at least another four years—many another seven to ten years—in training. Beyond nursing schools of two to four years after high school, nurse practitioners rarely train for more than one or two years.

Doctors charge that savings from greater use of nurse practitioners are exaggerated, because they refer so many cases to physicians who have to repeat the examination to get the right diagnosis. And doctors note that plaintiffs' lawyers will still want to stick their hands in the physicians' deep pockets. If we are going to be held liable for the actions of these nurses, doctors argue, then we should have tight control over them.

Nurse practitioners counter that, in the realm of primary care, they can "play doctor" as well as or better than many M.D.'s. They cite recent studies showing that, within their scope of practice, nurse practitioners provide care of equal quality to doctors— and are even better at controlling blood pressure in patients with hypertension, reducing the weight of obese patients, easing pain or discomfort in adults, and reducing anxiety and limitations on activity that afflict patients with chronic medical problems such as arthritis. Candice Owley, chairwoman of the Federation of Nurses and Health Professionals, makes the point this way:

Advance practice nurses wouldn't be performing heart surgery or cesareans. Instead they'd be providing the kind of basic health care Americans need most. You could call on them when you had a sore throat, or your child's asthma acted up, or you needed advice on how to cut fat from your diet. Do people really need a physician with 11 to 13 years of expensive education and a corresponding six-figure income for such services?

With respect to their knowledge of pharmaceuticals, nurse practitioners note that doctors change only one-tenth of one percent of the prescriptions they write. To the charge that their referrals to specialized doctors will result in duplicate exams and costs, nurse practitioners ask, "Don't family doctors today already make such referrals, a practice that suits specialists just fine?"

The struggle to redraw the turf of American medical practice should be resolved quickly, for its economic and gender components hold the potential to make it acrimonious. Whatever the rhetoric about professional responsibilities and quality care, there is a rough financial underbelly to recasting the roles of doctors and nurses—who gets paid, how much, for what.

The doctors want to protect their turf, status, and income, while the nurses feel unappreciated, underpaid, and suppressed. Even the most enlightened young doctors—saddled with $100,000 in debt (sometimes twice that amount) and weary of accusations that they make too much money—fear the increased use of alternative providers. But nursing professionals, buoyed by their sisters in other fields such as politics and law, are fed up with what they see as condescending economic and sex discrimination.

The battle lines have formed. The American Medical Association has for decades been one of the most effective and well-financed lobbies on Capitol Hill. In this arena, the nurses are playing catch-up from far behind, but they're learning. In 1992, the American Nurses Association and other nursing organizations gave $330,000 to 254 congressional candidates; by mid-1994, they had anted another half million dollars. In 1993, nurses gobbled up twelve of the forty-seven slots in the professional advisory group for First Lady Hillary Rodham Clinton's Task Force on Health Care Reform.

Both sides insist they want a fair fight, but the last blow America's health care system needs is a bare-knuckled, shoving-and-kicking brawl of the professions—and the sexes—who deliver health care to our people. The way to avoid that is to act quickly and fairly, as both professions are sworn to do, in the patients' interest. That interest requires opening major elements of the practice of medicine to the nursing profession.

STRIKING THE BALANCE: THREE TIERS OF MEDICAL PRACTICE

For the nation, the issue is: What will it take to get high-quality, affordable health care to all Americans? Two essential ingredients are the best-trained specialists in the world and an ample supply of medical professionals who can efficiently provide quality primary care.

To ensure this mix of reliable quality and maximum access, we need to stop fighting the last war, scrap the conventional wisdom that we have too many specialists, and take advantage of the increased capability that modern diagnostic and treatment technology has given non-physician providers. It's time for a top-to-bottom reorganization of the way we deliver medical services. We should develop a three-tiered medical system: non-physician practitioners, primary care physicians, and physician specialists.

The first tier—the front line of delivery—should be the non-physician practitioners: physician assistants, nurse practitioners, and certified nurse midwives. These professionals are capable, reliable, and cost-efficient. The revolution in medical diagnosis and treatment techniques gives them the ability to fill many primary care needs. They can be trained, and should be licensed, to diagnose ailments, treat common diseases, prescribe drugs, admit patients to hospitals, and release them. The federal government should finance their training in properly accredited schools as it has done for doctors.

The second tier should be composed of primary care physicians: the family doctors, pediatricians, and general internists, including geriatric practitioners. These physicians should handle the more complex cases that do not require specialist care and be available to consult, guide, and, where appropriate, supervise the non-physician practitioners. We should increase the number of primary care doctors; they remain central to the delivery and coordination of compassionate, effective, and efficient care by both nurses and specialists. But we should recognize the corps of trained non-physician practitioners as the major and timely new source of primary and preventive care.

The third tier should be specialists, ready to provide the best and most sophisticated medical care. The conventional wisdom that we urgently need to slash the number of specialized physicians is an idea whose time has passed.

We need a strong, extensive, and affordable army of specialists who are well prepared to distribute efficiently the goods of complicated medical discoveries to our people. With the inventory of medical knowledge and the complexities of medical care increasing every day, doctors spend substantial portions of their time reading and consulting simply to stay abreast of the latest research. Experts attribute much of the disturbingly wide variation in medical practice to doctors' inability to keep up with advances in their own fields.

Primary care doctors have no hope of keeping up with the

dizzying pace of change in the many fields of health care. It is as important for primary care providers—nurses or doctors—to have specialists available in person, on interactive video, or by helicopter as it is for nurses to have family doctors to consult.

In some urban centers such as Boston, major teaching hospitals and medical schools churn out enough specialists to glut the marketplace. But inhabitants of other regions throughout the nation, and selected populations such as the poor and elderly, often lack timely access to specialized care. At least 40 percent of the American people live in areas where the population is not concentrated enough to support high-tech hospitals or HMOs that provide most specialty services. Reducing the number of specialists could further jeopardize the quality of care for these individuals.

The problem is not that we have too many specialists, but rather that specialist care is too costly and not accessible to large numbers of Americans. Specialists should develop standards of care to use expensive diagnostic and treatment procedures only when necessary. Incentives—from how specialists are paid to medical malpractice reform—should be shaped to encourage efficiency, not knee-jerk resort to high-cost technology. The physician payment system should continue its movement toward closing the gap in pay between specialist and primary care doctors. Professional organizations, such as the American Medical Association, should adopt and enforce ethical norms that require specialists to seek ways to serve all areas of the nation and all segments of the population at affordable prices.

The medical profession—and the corporations and insurers who reimburse physicians—must also guard against the needless costs of overspecialization and educate their patients to do so as well. In ancient Egypt, as Ira Rutkow's book *Surgery* records, "specialization was carried to absurd lengths. For instance, around certain pharaohs and their courts virtually every organ or sickness acquired its own specialist. One royal personage had one physician for his right eye and another for his left eye. In the Old Kingdom there was Iry, who was 'keeper of the king's rectum.' " In 1994, American medicine shows symptoms of similar hyperspecialization, which contributes lots to the wealth of the hyperspecialist and little to the health of the patient.

Specialists can support efforts like that of the Rural Cancer Outreach Program at the Commonwealth University Medical College of Virginia in Richmond to serve small hospitals in the state. Oncologists from the college travel to three rural hospitals every two weeks to treat patients and train doctors and nurses to perform chemotherapy.

Spending on specialists can be contained. In the specialty of cardiac care, which accounted for $80 billion in treatment during 1994, physicians in forty cities have formed a network to provide heart surgery, angioplasty, and other cardiac services at reduced fees for large corporations, managed-care plans, and government programs such as Medicare. Participating doctors expect to pare the cost of a heart bypass operation by as much as 50 percent.

"If we can standardize care, then we can really tackle the issue of costs by figuring out where the fat is in the system and getting it out," says William Knopf, a heart specialist in the Atlanta Cardiology Group. Network members are developing preventive services to link up with frontline primary care doctors and physician assistants. If networks such as this one streamline procedures, reduce hospital stays, and eliminate unneeded tests, we can increase the access to the finest specialist care—but only if highly trained medical specialists are available.

What makes American medicine the world's envy is our enormous research capacity and our preeminence in solving complex medical mysteries and calling the most difficult diagnoses. That's why individuals come from every nation to seek diagnosis and treatment here. With new discoveries, knowledge, tests, complex procedures, and miracle drugs unfolding daily, the best hope for rapid dissemination and democratization of the greatness of American medicine rests in those who have the specialized training to absorb and distribute the latest and best to their patients.

LEVERAGING THE DOCTORS' MONOPOLY

Physician control over the practice of medicine has given many doctors the ability to leverage their economic power through the technique of self-referral: a doctor sends patients to laboratories, radiology centers, or other health care outlets in which he has an interest, and he gains financially from the tests or treatments provided.

Self-referral has repeatedly been shown to produce more tests and treatments for patients and higher charges for them. Medicare patients whose doctors own laboratories are subjected to 45 percent more lab tests than other Medicare patients. Thirty-eight percent of MRI scans requested by self-referring physicians have been found medically inappropriate, as compared with 28 percent of those requested by doctors who sent patients to an independent MRI center. The use of MRI scans is 54 percent greater among doctors who own MRI centers than among those who do not.

After years of criticism and fractious internal debate, the American Medical Association condemned this conflict-infested practice in 1991. But their sluggish and weak response did not help doctors trying to make the case that they deserve more autonomy and to continue self-regulation. In 1993, Congress passed a law (effective in 1995) prohibiting doctors from sending their Medicaid and Medicare patients to their own laboratories, imaging and rehabilitation centers, and other health-related businesses. Since then, congressional and state reformers have pressed to extend such restrictions to all referrals by physicians.

Doctors have leveraged their economic power in the most surprising ways. In 1993, the Clinton administration suggested shifting liability for malpractice from the doctor to the health care delivery organization (the hospital or HMO). Both doctors and trial lawyers quickly knocked this idea of "enterprise liability" off the table, and the political contributions they made to members of Congress and the Clinton presidential campaign ensured it would not get up from the floor.

The opposition from trial lawyers was expected, but the physicians' resistance was startling because they had so long clamored for malpractice reform. However, it was then discovered that doctors and state medical societies own 40 percent of medical malpractice insurers, whose business—and profits—could have been gutted by the enterprise liability concept.

THE DENTISTS' MONOPOLY

We specialize in treating cowards. We use nitrous oxide when necessary. Expect to leave our office SMILING!
—An advertisement for Samuel Rudick, a New York City dentist, promising to treat "tooth decay . . . a gentler way—no drill, no injection, no pain, 10 sec. per tooth"

The dental profession's monopoly is under siege from the revolutionary advances in preventive oral health and the rise of the dental hygienist profession. Preventive care for oral health, including fluoridation and tartar-reducing toothpastes, have sparked fierce competition and aggressive advertising, saved Americans nearly $100 billion in dental bills during the 1980s—and emptied many dentists' waiting rooms.

The number of dental school graduates has steadily declined since 1980. In 1991, for the first time, dental hygienist graduates outnumbered their dental school counterparts. The average annual growth in total real dental expenditures was only one percent between 1980 and 1993, compared to 6 percent for total health care spending. The increase in income for dentists over that period barely kept in step with inflation.

Registered dental hygienists, who graduate from some two hundred nationally accredited dental hygiene educational programs, are nipping at the dentists' heels, as they perform clinical, educational, and preventive services, ranging from cleaning teeth to, in some states, filling them. Although good dental hygiene has reduced costs over the last decade, giving dental hygienists greater access to patients and direct compensation could drive costs down by millions more.

An experimental project in California found that independent dental hygiene practices offer safe, quality care, cut costs, and increase access to oral health care for underserved segments of the population, including poor and disabled residents of rural areas. Almost 90 percent of dental hygiene practices in California accept new Medicaid patients, compared to only 16 percent of the state's dentists. Participating hygienists refer patients who require more sophisticated care to dentists.

"Dental hygienists are preventative professionals. Our focus is prevention," says Toby Segal, a dental hygienist taking part in California's pilot project. "We concentrate on providing solutions for oral health care problems before they become costly and time-consuming."

By providing high-quality care and linking their future to primary and preventive care, dental hygienists have earned the right to greater professional autonomy. But, with slim economic pickings, it's not surprising that dentists advocate laws to require that any patient who wishes to be treated by a dental hygienist must first see a dentist. In 1994, only four states, Colorado, Wisconsin, Michigan, and Washington, allowed dental hygienists to practice independently. The success of the California experiment, and pressures to cut costs and provide dental care to all, should lead other states to permit hygienists to set up their own practices outside the dentist's office, freestanding or in hospitals, nursing homes, or other centers for health services.

There is one matter on which dentists and dental hygienists shout hearty agreement: universal coverage of dental services for the 150 million Americans who lack dental insurance. That would not only improve oral health; it would give them a much bigger pie to fight over.

THE PHARMACISTS' MONOPOLY

The local pharmacists' monopoly over filling prescriptions is being shattered not by changes in the law, but by changes in the marketplace. There was a time when skilled local pharmacists were uniquely privy to the mysteries of stirring potions and mixing powders, and providing them to patients dependent on their expertise and counseling. Today, with modern pharmaceuticals, patient-friendly packaging, color-coded pills, and informative inserts approved by the Food and Drug Administration, many pharmacy tasks can be performed by anyone who can read labels, count pills, and isn't color-blind.

To the local pharmacist, it must seem that the entire health care system is lined up to attack. Large corporations have trimmed the pharmacist's role and revenues by pressuring employees to use generic drugs, limiting reimbursement to the price of such drugs, and cutting deals with retail drug chains to reduce fees for filling prescriptions. Many employers are sidestepping the local pharmacist altogether, turning instead to mail-order companies to dispense pharmaceuticals, particularly for individuals with chronic diseases that require long-term medication such as hypertension pills and insulin. Managed-care organizations—HMOs, PPOs, and networks of hospitals, clinics, and nursing homes—now dispense their own pharmaceuticals and keep the prescription fees, if any, for themselves.

The saga of Martin Wygod and Medco Containment Services, Inc., which he founded, tells the tale. In 1984, Wygod asked me to join the nascent company's board of directors. He was setting up large mail-order drug-dispensing operations in states that gave pharmacists wide discretion to substitute generic drugs for brand-name prescriptions. He would then approach large corporate employers and offer to manage their employees' prescription drug benefits at far less cost than the companies were then paying for brand-name drugs. With enough customers, Wygod could leverage his buying power to extract deep discounts from pharmaceutical companies.

It was win-win for the employers and patients, both of whom would pay less. (I thought it was a fabulous idea, but I declined to be on his board because I was writing about the subject and wanted to be free of any possible conflicts of interest.)

That was 1984, when Wygod had about a hundred employees

and counted his customers by the thousands. By 1993, Medco was a mail-order giant with six thousand employees, thirty million customers (most dependent on long-term prescriptions), and $1.8 billion in revenues, up 35 percent over the prior year. Among Medco's blue-chip clients were General Motors, General Electric, Unocal, Siemens, and Capital Cities/ABC. According to Medco, in 1993 the average annual prescription cost to a beneficiary in its plan was $166.78 compared with $266.30 for an unmanaged major medical plan. Medco officials claim to undercut average retail pharmacy prices by at least 25 percent.

In 1993, Merck & Company, the world's largest pharmaceutical manufacturer, acquired Medco for $6 billion in cash and stock as drug companies and others moved to acquire their own mail-order dispensing arms. SmithKline Beecham bought Diversified Pharmaceutical Services and Eli Lilly & Company purchased PCS Health Systems, the country's largest manager of drug benefit programs. Sears, Roebuck inserted a drug mail-order form in its catalogues. Caremark International, a nursing-home and hospital chain, combined mail-order pharmacies with retail networks, in which pharmacists dispense drugs by mail, provide counseling by phone for outpatients, analyze prescriptions, and suggest discount substitutes for managed-care groups.

The low-cost dispensing system of mail-order houses is based on economies of scale, negotiating volume discounts with drug manufacturers, computer automation, pharmacist consultation by phone, and campaigns to persuade doctors to change brand-name prescriptions to generics available at lower prices. These aggressive sales tactics have become a point of contention with local drugstore pharmacists.

Most provocative is Medco's move beyond the world of negotiating discounts for large-volume purchases and making generic substitutions, now practices widely accepted in the medical field. Under its Prescriber's Choice program, Medco's pharmacists, who speak with doctors and patients by phone, lobby physicians to change prescriptions to drugs that are chemically different, albeit therapeutically similar, and, of course, less costly.

Wygod argues that companies such as Medco have constructively "turned from a passive dispenser of drugs to a proactive deliverer of managed care and cost containment." He insists that the ability of local pharmacists to meet with patients is outdated and costly. "Face-to-face counseling is window dressing," says Del Konnor, executive vice president of American Managed Care Pharmacy Association. "We're in the forefront of patient information, and we offer telephone consultation in the privacy of the patient's home before, during, and after the prescription is dispensed."

The pressures from mail-order drug dispensers, HMOs, networks of hospitals, and other providers, and the ongoing competition from chain pharmacies, have trimmed the profits of individual pharmacists. Although the overwhelming proportion of prescriptions is still filled by independent local pharmacists and chain drugstores, profits for storefront pharmacists fell 50 percent from 1970 to 1994.

The shifting fault lines in the prescription drug market have also shaken up drug manufacturers, which enjoy their own monopoly in the form of a seventeen-year patent on their pharmaceutical inventions. Increased competition among pharmacy rivals as well as changes in federal law and the pharmaceutical industry's desire to fend off further government regulation has led drug companies to cut prices and profit margins. The U.S. Department of Labor reports that prescription drug prices rose an annual average of 3 percent in the first nine months of 1994, compared with 8 to 12 percent annually during the prior decade; earnings for drug companies in the first nine months of 1994 were among the lowest in ten years.

Moreover, the drive by mail-order houses and HMOs to encourage patients to use generic drugs whenever possible has been so successful that drug companies have adopted an "If-you-can't-beat-'em,-join-'em" strategy of selling generics in addition to their traditional stock of brand-name drugs. Some companies now sell brand-name drugs and identical generic rivals at the same time.

Trying to maneuver around cost-conscious managed-care physicians, drug companies, which normally advertise to doctors and pharmacists, have begun drumming up demand for their products by marketing directly to patients. Most visible are television ads for Nicoret gum or nicotine patches for those who want to quit smoking. But more ads in newspapers, general-circulation magazines, and on television push prescription drugs for everything from high cholesterol and depression to baldness—always reminding the patient to consult a doctor (whose signature the patient must have in order to get the medicine).

To circumvent FDA restrictions on direct marketing of drugs to consumers, many companies seek to increase awareness about a disease with the hope that patients will ask their doctor for the right pill. Pfizer ran ads in *The New Yorker* warning its readers about the signs of depression. "A message in the interest of better health," said the ad; it did not mention that Pfizer manufactures Zoloft, a drug for depression similar to Prozac. Abbott Laboratories, which makes a pharmaceutical for enlarged prostates, offered readers of *The New York Times* a "test" that asks questions like "Do you urinate often, especially during the night?" and advises, "If you answered yes to any question, you should see your doctor."

Unsatisfied with the boundaries of ordinary print advertising,

Upjohn offers 800-numbers for curious consumers and orchestrates talk-show appearances to publicize obsessive-compulsive disorder, a disease that afflicts some four million Americans. Upjohn's role in the promotions is rarely mentioned prominently, but the company hopes to create demand for its drug Luvox, a treatment for the disease. "Obviously it's not all altruistic," admits Upjohn's public relations director, Philip Sheldon. "We want to be part of the treatment."

The competition among pharmacists, drug companies, and mail-order houses is so fierce that the only monopoly likely to survive (as it should) in this corner of the health care industry is the patent that pharmaceutical companies enjoy as a reward for their long-shot research efforts.

But even the patent monopoly will be of less value as large corporations, managed-care plans, hospital networks, and insurers develop formularies—lists of drugs from which doctors must select if the patient is to be reimbursed. In order to get on the formulary list, pharmaceutical companies have to offer steep discounts even for their patented drugs.

There is a real threat here to the resources pharmaceutical companies will be able to commit to future endeavors. Patents are the honey that keeps billions of investment dollars buzzing to drug companies for innovation and discovery. Public policymakers and politicians must walk the line between holding down prices of newly patented drugs and maintaining financial rewards sufficient to encourage big investments in high-risk research. Turning this trick requires fancier footwork than the big-foot stomping that drug companies invited with their pricing practices from 1983 to 1993.

THE DOCTORS' AND LAWYERS' MONOPOLY

When John Rounsaville Jr., a 44-year-old father of three, checked into a hospital for routine back surgery, he expected to be released in a day or so. Six months later, when he left, he was strapped to a wheelchair, having suffered catastrophic damage to his brain and nervous system. Five years later, a jury found that "an incompetent anesthesiologist" had injected Rounsaville with ten to twenty times the recommended dose of a sedative. After hearing evidence that several of the doctor's colleagues had let him continue to practice—even though they knew he had physical disabilities related to a stroke and admitted drinking a pint of vodka a day—the jury awarded Rounsaville and his family $13.6 million.

—The New York Times, *April 9, 1994*

A doctor who was arrested and charged yesterday with fondling a patient in a medical office was permitted to practice medicine in New York even though state regulators knew he had been convicted of sexually assaulting a patient in New Jersey four months earlier. The doctor pleaded not guilty to the charges yesterday. If he can post bail, state health officials said, he will remain free to practice medicine.

—The New York Times, *May 6, 1993*

In 1992, my daughter was seriously injured in a car accident, and we are now close to settling the claim with the insurance company. She will need several more specialized surgeries, and will probably be left with residual problems. . . . We are expecting a significant settlement. However, the amazing thing about our case is that the legal fee (a 25 percent contingency fee) to settle the insurance will far surpass the total medical costs to date.

—*Letter to the Editor*, Los Angeles Times, *January 9, 1994*

The bout between trial lawyers and doctors over medical malpractice places the two professions in opposite corners of the ring, but both enjoy a pair of privileges shared by few other professionals: monopoly over their services and self-regulation.

The physician monopoly over how and when doctors are disciplined helps shield the medical profession from airing, before patients and public, questions of competence and willful neglect. The monopoly of plaintiffs' attorneys, covered by their own blanket of self-regulation, protects lawyers who promote litigation that drives up malpractice premiums and the nation's bill for defensive medicine, terrorizes doctors, and often exploits patients.

Medical malpractice insurance premiums come to some $10 billion a year. The bill for defensive medicine—the tests and procedures doctors use to protect against lawsuits or, in court, to defend against allegations of malpractice—may well exceed $25 billion. Steep as they are, these costs have not led hospitals and doctors to drive bad apples from the medical barrel and have not fairly compensated victims of negligence.

Most victims of medical negligence never file claims. Of those who do, only a small percentage produce convincing evidence of negligent injury or willful misconduct. Dr. Troyen Brennan, a professor at the Harvard School of Public Health and an expert in medical malpractice, likens the situation to "a traffic cop giving tickets to large numbers of motorists who are not speeding, but failing to give tickets to many speeding motorists."

Most of the money spent on malpractice litigation goes to lawyers, insurance companies, and courts, not to injured patients. Typically, plaintiffs' attorneys skim 25 to 33 percent off the top of any damage award. These attorneys normally take expenses on top of their fees.

A decade-long Harvard University study of New York State hospitals disclosed that, on average, seriously injured patients who litigated received compensation below their financial losses, while those with minor injuries often recovered amounts far in excess of their losses. In New York hospitals, researchers identified twenty-seven thousand patients as victims of medical negligence in one year, with more than a quarter of them seriously injured or killed. Projecting the findings nationwide suggests that, as a result of medical delinquency just in hospitals, some eighty thousand people die each year and almost four times that number are injured. Yet, in a year, only twenty-five thousand plaintiffs receive damages in suits charging injury or death related to malpractice.

The most disturbing aspect of the present malpractice system is the damage it does to the quality of care. In many parts of the country, professions such as obstetrics, gynecology, and neurosurgery have been crippled by the sheer cost of malpractice insurance. In New York, one out of six obstetricians has stopped delivering babies, up from one out of ten in 1990, and most obstetrics residents who train in New York leave to practice in another state. This exodus is not surprising when medical malpractice insurance for a New York obstetrician can cost more than $100,000 a year.

Obstetrics is a high-risk medical profession because parents who feel their baby's health problems could have been prevented are quick to sue a doctor who may be culpable. Juries moved by the sight of a suffering child and distraught mother are quick to grant multimillion-dollar judgments. Because defects traced to birth may not show up for years, obstetricians who see each pregnancy as a potential time bomb are likely to engage in defensive procedures that may create their own risks for mother or child.

A 1993 analysis of more than sixty thousand births reveals the link between malpractice premiums and high rates of cesarean births. Patients whose doctors and hospitals pay high premiums for malpractice insurance are three times more likely than patients in areas with low premiums to have a cesarean, a surgical procedure that lengthens a mother's recovery time in the hospital by three days and can increase the risk to mother and child. Most doctors admit doing more for patients than is clinically appropriate because of the threat of being sued.

Lawyers, who control when and how a member of their profession will be disciplined, have manipulated the malpractice system to their own financial benefit, often with little concern for their clients' interests. To protect their monopoly over malpractice disputes, trial lawyers oppose efforts to encourage arbitration rather than legal action controlled by lawyers. One study by economists at the State University of New York in Buffalo found lawyers motivated more by money than by the merits of each case. The worse business gets, the more likely malpractice lawyers are to take on weak or frivolous cases. "As you get more lawyers relative to the business available, previously unattractive cases become more attractive," explains Lawrence Southwick, an author of the study.

Trial lawyers are intent on increasing their business. As the balloon of medical concerns has expanded to include everything from receding hairlines to small breasts, lawyers have pressed to lower the threshold of litigable claims. In a wave of "cancerphobia suits," they charged employers with exposing employees to cancer-causing substances and sought compensation for their employees' fear that someday they might contract cancer as a result. After a string of victories for fearful plaintiffs in California, the state's supreme court moved to make such cases more difficult to win, noting that because exposure to carcinogens is so common, "all of us are potential fear-of-cancer plaintiffs," a fact that presents a nirvana of litigation to unscrupulous plaintiffs' lawyers.

Doctors, quick to finger lawyers as greedy ambulance chasers, have done plenty to fire the hot coals on which they practice medicine. By failing to police themselves through medical associations charged with enforcing professional standards, doctors have helped spark the distrust that makes injured patients easy pickings for the plaintiffs' bar.

With meager resources and staffs handpicked by doctors, state medical boards rarely discipline physicians for malpractice. Although an estimated three hundred thousand Americans are injured or killed each year because of medical negligence in hospitals, state medical boards took less than 3,100 disciplinary actions against doctors in 1991. Some states take an average of two years or more to investigate complaints of incompetence or misconduct.

A troubling symptom of how poorly doctors regulate themselves is the wide variation in the number of disciplinary actions taken by different state medical boards. The state medical board in Alaska takes almost twenty-two actions for every thousand physicians; the Massachusetts board takes only 1.5. Such discrepancies cannot be pinned solely on differences in physician competency. Variations arise from the resources and effectiveness of each board and the tendency of hospitals and physicians guilty of negligence to settle with patients—and to make part of the deal the patient's agreement to keep mum.

Perhaps the central flaw in physician self-regulation is the fact that doctors are loath to report colleagues they deem incompetent. It is more in the interest of clinics and hospitals to ease offending physicians out of their institutions quietly than to go public with charges of incompetence that could expose them to court proceedings and loss of patients. This suits many state medical boards just fine because they suffer from a chronic lack of adequate resources to investigate charges and take disciplinary action.

Even where physicians are found guilty of improper and unethical conduct with respect to their patients, state medical authorities often fail to pull their licenses to practice. In New York, Robert Willis, the psychiatrist treating Joan Weill, wife of The Travelers Inc. chairman Sanford Weill, invested in the stock market using confidential information she had revealed during their sessions of psychoanalysis. Dr. Willis was caught red-handed, cashing in on stock deals he made with what he had learned from his patient. He pled guilty to two counts of securities fraud and was sentenced to five years probation. In 1992 the state medical board found him guilty of improper and unethical conduct, but did not revoke his license.

Contrast the action the Securities and Exchange Commission took against Martin Sloate, the broker to whom Dr. Willis passed the inside information about American Express, Shearson, and BankAmerica that he had gained during his psychoanalytic sessions with Mrs. Weill. The SEC filed charges against Sloate; the federal district court in Manhattan found that he had knowingly violated the securities laws and he surrendered $161,000 in illegal profits and penalties. In 1994, an administrative law judge barred Sloate from the brokerage industry. If Mr. Sloate needs a psychiatrist to help him through his difficulties, he can consult Dr. Willis, who is still registered to practice as this book goes to press.

Even if the frazzled safety net of physician-controlled state medical boards snags a doctor, there is little to stop him or her from treating patients in another state. In 1986, Congress established the National Practitioner Data Bank to collect and store information, reported by hospitals and insurers, on adverse actions against physicians that involve licensing, hospital privileges, malpractice claims, and settlements. But the data bank, which has information on more than sixty thousand doctors and other health professionals and must provide this information to hospitals that request it, has been hobbled by bureaucratic delays and lack of funds.

Incredibly, patients have no legal right to the information, and physician organizations resist any efforts to give it to them. "The public has more information on the performance of a breakfast cereal than on the performance of a heart surgeon," complains Oregon congressman Ron Wyden.

Equally surprising, state medical boards are not required by law to check with the National Practitioner Data Bank about the disciplinary history of a doctor arriving from another state. Hospitals are required to check with the data bank when hiring or reappointing doctors, but medical clinics or group practices are not. Thus has the "gypsy doctor" been born—the physician who flees one state, which has investigated or disciplined him or revoked his license, to seek haven in another state, which may well neglect to check on his past professional conduct.

The rise of the gypsy doctor has produced tragic results. Mary Miller, a police clerk in Putnam, Connecticut, had been trying to conceive a baby for six years. Beginning in December 1991, she visited a new gynecologist, Steven Weber, with a complaint he treated as a cervical polyp. During Ms. Miller's second visit, Dr. Weber failed to realize that she was pregnant and damaged or killed the embryo during a cervical exam. He called Ms. Miller back for a third visit and performed an abortion without her knowledge or consent. The following day, bleeding profusely, Ms. Miller was rushed to the hospital.

Dr. Weber had previously lost his license to practice in New York after a series of negligent acts led to the death of two infants during childbirth, one woman losing her uterus and another almost bleeding to death. The New York State medical board reported the license revocation to the data bank, which led Florida to reject an application from Dr. Weber to practice there. But Dr. Weber simply moved to Connecticut, where he also had a license to practice. Ultimately an unrelated investigation conducted by Connecticut Blue Cross/Blue Shield alerted state officials to New York's disciplinary action against Dr. Weber. He finally lost his Connecticut license. (Fortunately, Ms. Miller became pregnant again.)

With a record demonstrating that physicians and lawyers have little interest in healing themselves, the self-regulation monopolies these professions enjoy should be busted.

First, state disciplinary boards should be composed of a majority of nonphysician members. States should give these boards the resources to fulfill their obligations to investigate patient complaints of malpractice.

Second, doctors themselves, and the hospitals, managed-care plans, and clinics where they practice, should be held responsible when they fail to report physicians who are incompetent, provide substandard care, or are guilty of negligence. These physicians and institutions should be held liable for some of the damage by doctors who commit malpractice after they are permitted to leave stealthily. After all, these doctors are free to harm another patient because the physicians and institutions failing to report them were protecting their own financial interests.

Third, malpractice actions to recover damages should no longer be the monopoly of plaintiffs' lawyers. Health insurance contracts and agreements with managed-care providers should routinely provide that patients, doctors, hospitals, and HMOs receiving payments must arbitrate most claims of malpractice, with limits on recovery for pain and suffering and legal fees. The arbitration should be binding in the absence of willful misconduct.

Fourth, where malpractice claims are filed, systems similar to that of California should be adopted by all states. In the absence of willful malfeasance, California limits recovery for pain and suffering to $250,000, and reduces the proportion that lawyers get paid as the amount of the award arises. Beyond $250,000, recovery should be limited to amounts needed to pay medical bills, replace lost income, and accommodate the costs of any lingering disability.

Fifth, physicians should develop standards of care to guide them in ordering up diagnostic tests and treatments. Doctors who comply with those standards should not be held liable for negligence. (Maine is experimenting with this remedy.) Doctors should be held responsible for incompetence and negligence, and for failure to follow adopted standards, but not for acts and events that only God can control.

THE HOSPITAL MONOPOLY

Another self-serving bastion of monopolistic control can be found in the temples of medicine, where the homogeneous grays, greens, and beiges of hospital halls, gowns, and masks cover vivid variations in quality.

The leading organization for evaluating the quality of the nation's 6,500 hospitals and accrediting those that meet minimum standards is the Joint Commission on Accreditation of Healthcare Organizations. In 1994, the JCAHO accredited five thousand community hospitals and more than three thousand other health care organizations that offered mental health, ambulatory, home, and long-term nursing care.

Founded in 1951, the JCAHO is a nonprofit organization whose history dates back to the early years of the twentieth century. In 1912, a group of physicians founded the American College of Surgeons, which committed itself to setting standards for hospital quality, in order to recognize institutions that met the highest ideals and "stimulate" those that did not "to raise the quality of their work." The task proved more formidable than the dedicated doctors anticipated because many hospitals were little more than boardinghouses for the poor and the sick, and medical records were skimpy or nonexistent.

In 1917, the College of Surgeons established its first criteria and began a field survey, expecting to approve at least a thousand hospitals. But at a conference in New York City on October 24, 1919, the college announced that after surveying 692 hospitals, including some of the nation's most prestigious, only eighty-nine met the standards. Though the college made the numbers public, in order to keep from the press the list that identified the hospitals, college members burned it that night in the furnace of the Waldorf-Astoria Hotel.

For the next four decades, the college pursued its mission. By 1950, the number of accredited hospitals grew to 3,290, more than half of those in the country. In 1951, overwhelmed by the growing complexity of assessing the quality of care, the college turned over its work to the newly formed Joint Commission on Accreditation of Hospitals (later renamed the Joint Commission on Accreditation of Healthcare Organizations), composed of representatives from the American College of Surgeons, the American College of Physicians, the American Hospital Association, the American Medical Association, and the Canadian Medical Association (which later withdrew to develop its own accreditation system).

The JCAHO is directed by a twenty-eight-member board (seven appointed by the AHA, seven by the AMA, three by the College of Physicians, three by the College of Surgeons, one by the American Dental Association, one representative of nursing, and six private citizens, handpicked by other board members). It designs standards for hospitals upon which Medicare and state licensing agencies rely when conducting their own reviews.

Most of the JCAHO's work has been hidden from the public eye, and the organization, which in 1993 collected $84 million from its clients, permits hospitals of dubious quality to retain accreditation. Sidney Wolfe, director of the Public Citizen Health Research Group, charges that because of the JCAHO's reluctance to rescind accreditation and its refusal to open its records for public viewing, "choosing a hospital remains a crap shoot for most Americans." Almost one-third, or about 1,700 of the 5,208 hospitals surveyed by the JCAHO between 1986 and 1988, failed to meet one or more of its standards, he says. Yet their doors remain open and their accreditation stands.

In 1993, the JCAHO vowed to develop specific performance measures and to release more information to the public. Despite resistance from hospitals that claim performance standards are flawed and want to maintain secrecy, Dr. Dennis O'Leary, the JCAHO president, promised an era of public accountability: "Our database should serve as a national information resource that will permit accurate comparisons of quality across most of the nation's hospitals."

But by whom? Will the JCAHO give patients the information they need to compare one hospital to another? The general public? So far, the JCAHO has made only limited public disclosure. Without full public disclosure, low-quality hospitals that endanger patients will keep their doors open with the JCAHO imprimatur—a frightening situation no one seems to deny. When Bruce Vladeck became administrator of the Health Care Financing Administration in 1993, he bluntly attacked low-occupancy, low-quality hospitals: "If you have a hospital doing under two hundred heart [operations] a year, you're killing people and costing more," he told reporters.

Closing a hospital is as hard as shutting down a post office or military base. New York's governor Mario Cuomo met fierce resistance to shutting a state mental hospital that spent $3.3 million a year to care for fourteen patients—$236,000 each. (When he finally managed to shut it down in 1994, it was converted to a 750-bed prison to accommodate the state's growing number of drug offenders.)

Although 509 community hospitals closed between 1982 and 1992, lots more should have. In 1994, the nation had a quarter of a million excess hospital beds at a cost of some $10 billion a year. Many rural communities would better invest their money in a paramedic team and a helicopter rather than in maintaining empty hospitals where doctors and nurses don't perform procedures often enough to maintain minimum levels of proficiency. The JCAHO has been of little or no help here.

What is needed is a federal nonpartisan, independent commission, similar to the one that has assumed the politically perilous task of recommending military base closings, to identify low-volume hospitals, from which all federal support, including Medicare and Medicaid reimbursement, should be withdrawn.

Accreditation of hospitals is too important to be left solely to hospital administrators, physicians, and other health professionals. If the JCAHO is to set standards for safe and quality hospital care, then its board should have a majority of members from outside the profession, and each team it dispatches for periodic review of individual hospitals should have at least a 25 percent public membership. When the JCAHO so reconstitutes—and when it stops keeping secret the deficiencies of hundreds of American hospitals—then its promise to make itself and the hospitals it protects publicly accountable can be taken seriously.

SO WHAT?

The consequences may be unpredictable, but the trends are clear: During the late 1990s and into the next century, the medical monopolies that have been so set in America's health care firmament will be breaking up. Market forces; public and private demands to contain costs; economic interests of employers, doctors, nurses, hospitals, lawyers, pharmacists, and pharmaceutical companies; political ambitions of governors and congressmen—all these and lots more are reshaping the way medical care is being delivered in our nation.

Is busting the medical monopolies good or bad for American health care?

To the extent it increases our attention to health promotion and disease prevention and encourages providers to talk to patients, it is certainly good. An increased role for nurses holds the promise of such patient care—both by the action of the nurses themselves and by the competitive pressure they will put on doctors to take similar steps.

To the extent it opens up the medical profession and the plaintiffs' bar to more public scrutiny, busting the self-regulation monopoly is a move in the right direction, as would be a complete overhaul of the hospital accreditation monopoly.

The pressure on pharmaceutical companies for lower prices also goes in the right direction, but it carries potential dangers of trimming the profits that provide the resources such companies are willing to invest in innovative pharmaceutical research.

On the whole, breaking the strangleholds of doctors, dentists, hospitals, lawyers, pharmaceutical companies, and pharmacists, opening their work to public scrutiny, and increasing competition should help get patients more attentive care at more affordable prices, and it should enhance the excellence of American medicine.

But the history of America's changing health care system makes it prudent for us to be prepared for plenty of surprises along the way. In the race to efficiency, merger mania among providers is fundamentally recasting the shape of American health care. As today's medical monopolies break up, a new group of conglomerates is assembling the pieces. These combinations can wring out a system drenched with waste. But conglomerate medicine can also produce bottom-line behemoths who submerge the human needs of their patients. Competition among all sorts of providers—various managed care organizations, fee-for-service doctors, networks of hospitals, nursing homes, physician practices, outpatient centers and clinics, insurers, for-profits and nonprofits—is important. But competition should not be permitted to crush caring.

CHAPTER EIGHT

FREE THE CONGRESSIONAL 535

*President Clinton probably didn't have lawyers, lobbyists, and public
relations types in mind when he said his health care proposal would
be a "net job gainer." But for Washington's permanent class of influ-
ence-peddlers and image-shapers—those who profit whenever the policy pot is stirred—the debate over health care is the biggest windfall
of the '90s. Steve Rabin, Washington-based executive vice president of
the public relations firm Porter Novelli, which made more than $1.5
million from new health care business in 1993, expects that total
spending on the effort to influence the outcome of reform will quickly
top $100 million. "I've never seen so much activity around a single
piece of legislation in my 15 years in Washington," says Rabin.*
                        —Baltimore Sun, *September 27, 1993*

*Money inside the beltway alters all the decisions that are made. It's
like the Little Shop of Horrors. You can't feed this plant enough.*
                        —*Representative George Miller (D-CA)*

The threshold move in any effort to shift Washington's focus
from sick care to health care and enact and maintain sensible
reforms that promote healthy behavior is not partisan politics or
gridlock, but campaign finance reform to free the Congressional
535 from the leash of political action committees and other

special-interest groups, whose twenty-five thousand lobbyists and thirty thousand special-interest associations have surrounded Capitol Hill.

With the business of health care constituting America's biggest industry and one of its most prolific job generators, partisanship and ideology take a backseat to the struggle over money, as those who pay the trillion dollars in health care bills fight to pay less and those who receive the trillion dollars scramble to get more—or at least hang on to what they've got.

The human stakes don't come any higher: No diagnostic test, surgical procedure, or medicine is too expensive or unnecessary when my spouse, my father, my mother, my child, or I am in severe pain or the victim of a life-threatening disease. During my years as secretary of Health, Education, and Welfare and since, I have been called on on more than a hundred occasions to recommend a doctor. Not once was I asked how much the doctor cost.

Those who pay the bills and those who get paid often lose sight of the ailing spouses, parents, and children because they're so bedazzled by the glitter of gold in treating them. The human situation can be wrenching, but it's the economic stakes that make the continuing contest to change America's health care system the political gang war of the century. And as long as the big bucks are in treatment and the profits are in sick care, that's where members of Congress and influential lobbyists will center their efforts; there are precious few political contributions to be found in health promotion and disease prevention.

WEALTH CARE REFORM

Not since Franklin Roosevelt's New Deal in the 1930s and Lyndon Johnson's Great Society in the 1960s had Washington seen such an attempt to redistribute wealth in America as President Clinton put into play in 1993 and 1994 when he proposed to overhaul health care delivery and financing.

Roosevelt and Johnson aimed to redistribute wealth from rich to poor. What makes the 1990s battles over health system reform so unprecedented—and a financial bonanza for members of Congress—is that they involve redistribution of wealth among the most powerful, moneyed interests in the nation. These interests are armed to protect their own financial jugulars—and to go for the other guy's. To understand health care reform, you must think wealth care reform.

Nearly every president since Harry Truman has tried to push major health care reform through Congress, but only Lyndon Johnson succeeded. The failure of so many attempts to enact reform cannot be chalked up to partisan bickering in the trenches. Nor can it be charged to a divided government which, for most of the years since 1969, has ruled the nation with a Republican White House and a Democratic Congress. The impasse on health reform and the enduring protections for special interests are tribute to the flood of private money and political action committee (PAC) contributors who have acquired veto power in key congressional committees over any proposal that seriously threatens their narrow interests.

Congress is the main field of battle, with plenty of nasty skirmishes at the other end of Pennsylvania Avenue and lots of brush wars in state legislatures and city councils. By their own design, the 100 senators and 435 representatives, who pick the winners and losers and decide how big the prizes will be, are locked in a system of legalized bribery. Each health care interest petitioning the Congress or a key committee can legally line the legislator's pockets with money to buy a little more time to plead its case, kill a bill, or tilt the fine print its way. What in other branches of government would lead to impeachment, imprisonment, or both, in the U.S. Congress leads to reelection.

The lessons of Lyndon Johnson's legislative street fight should not be lost. Though Johnson dealt from Herculean political strength, he still had to pay the private-interest pipers to enact his program. After assuming the presidency in November 1963, Johnson cited Medicare as a top priority in his first message to Congress. "We are going to fight for medical care for the aged as long as we have breath in our bodies!" he shouted—and he meant it. Yet even he, the shrewdest legislator to occupy the Oval Office, could not get either the Senate Finance Committee or the House Ways and Means Committee to report out his bill.

In late 1964, Johnson mustered the votes on the Senate floor to attach Medicare to a Social Security benefits increase that had passed the House. In the House-Senate conference, Johnson could not get the House to accept the Senate bill. As a result, shortly before the 1964 congressional and presidential elections, he killed the Social Security increase, no mean feat in a time when the lack of automatic cost-of-living increases (which were not established until 1972) left it to Congress to hike benefits on the eve of every election. But without pent-up pressure from the elderly for the increase in the 1965 Congress, LBJ feared that he would not be able to pass Medicare.

A few weeks later, Johnson won the presidency by the greatest landslide in American history—61 to 39 percent. He carried into office with him not only a two-to-one Democratic House, but a liberal majority in both House and Senate. Even with an unprecedented electoral victory and the phenomenal public support he enjoyed in the early years after Kennedy's assassination, Johnson could not cobble together a majority for Medicare and Medicaid in the House Ways and Means Committee.

To do so, he had to abandon the authority his proposed bill gave the government to set reimbursement rates and accept the methods hospitals and doctors preferred. Johnson realized what would happen. He almost immediately started to press Congress for cost containment. Unless Congress acted, Johnson predicted in March 1968, health care costs would hit $100 billion by 1975 and the cost of medical care for an American family would double in seven years. Pressured by lobbyists for physicians, hospitals, and insurers, Congress failed to act. By 1975, America's health care bill hit $133 billion; each family's bill doubled in less than six years.

After several unsuccessful attempts to work with Congress on cost containment, in 1971 a frustrated Richard Nixon slapped wage and price controls on health care for almost three years. As soon as he lifted them, the pace of increase in health care costs jumped into the double digits. Nixon's proposal to mandate that employers cover employees was stillborn as it emerged from the Oval Office, and his move to expand vastly the number of HMOs was strangled in bureaucratic red tape spun by the American Medical Association's drive to preserve the fee-for-service payment system.

President Jimmy Carter tried again to stanch the flood of spending with a bill to hold the rise in hospital charges to one and a half times the rate of increase in the overall cost of living. (At the time, those charges were running at two and a half times the Consumer Price Index.) Two years later, the bill was defeated on the House floor, largely due to opposition from well-organized for-profit hospitals and the AMA.

President Bill Clinton proposed to reshape the health care system with a 1,342-page bill designed to ensure universal coverage, create a system of state-controlled purchasing alliances, and establish a mandate that all employers provide health care benefits to their employees. Clinton put his stack of chips on health reform as no president had since Johnson, but he lacked Johnson's hand of political cards.

Clinton had won election by a mere 43 percent of the vote—less than the 46 percent Democrat Michael Dukakis accumulated in losing to Republican George Bush in 1988. Clinton faced more sophisticated lobbyists with deeper pockets. He had to deal with a health care industry of insurers, doctors, hospitals, pharmaceutical companies, medical-equipment manufacturers, unions, managed-care companies, HMOs, and nursing homes, each seeking to protect its take of a business rollicking along at a trillion-dollar-a-year clip. And he faced a more complex health care system, an aging population, and a technology revolution that required intricate legislative fixes.

Moreover, Clinton's ability to ram legislation through Congress was only an echo of the deafening power enjoyed by Johnson, who presided over a far mightier executive branch with lots more patronage, and had an uncanny shrewdness and zest for using it in legislative battle. By the time the Clinton safari settled in the White House, Congress had become King Cong of the Washington jungle.

Congress had given itself the power to raise its own campaign funds by legalizing PACs and by creating enough committees and subcommittees (more than 100 in the Senate; almost 150 in the House) so that virtually every senator and most representatives could have a senior position. Incumbency had become a priceless asset in raising funds; during the 1992 cycle, the American Medical Association gave $2 million to incumbents in Congress—both Democrats and Republicans—but less than a quarter that amount to challengers. Members had also learned the power of a prolific legislative pen to give out patronage directly rather than leaving the goodies for the president to dispense.

So President Clinton was left to speak in broad principles and assume the role of cheerleader for the nation. In the same address in which he sent Congress his health care reform bill, he stressed his willingness to compromise on just about everything in it. He knew that if Congress acted, it would draft the reforms its way and in detail unthinkable in the 1960s. Congress knew that Clinton would have to sign anything it chose to send him and declare victory.

Unless we change the way political campaigns are bankrolled, health care reform in the late 1990s will become like tax reform in the sixties, seventies, and eighties—stretching years into the twenty-first century as members of Congress leverage health care reform proposals in order to raise money to scare off political opponents, buy television time, and win the next election.

Without public financing of congressional campaigns and air-tight limits on private contributions, special interests will continue, as *Time* magazine describes it, "the blatant, shameless greasing of congressional palms" to twist health care legislation to their advantage, and the worthy goal of quality care for all at reasonable cost will be trampled in the melee over money.

THE ROUTE TO HEALTH CARE RICHES:
FIRST STOP, YOUR MAN OR WOMAN IN CONGRESS

For every Texan on the House Energy and Commerce Committee, there is a doctor back home—a specialist who can call in teams of campaign workers and prescribe balms of campaign cash during the periodic bouts of heartburn known as elections. For Rep. Craig Washington, a Democrat from Houston, the "key contact" is internist Regina Kyles. She helped organize medical students to canvass part of Washington's district in his tough reelection primary fight and initiated a fund-raising letter on his behalf last month. "They'll have my ear and the opportunity to present their case at any time," Washington said. "It's human nature that you should be grateful to people who help you in your time of need."
                                        —The Washington Post, *March 8, 1994*

By putting forth a health care proposal, Jim Cooper, the mild-mannered House Democrat from the most rural district in Tennessee, has become the toast of health care providers and insurance companies, which have channeled tens of thousands of dollars to his campaign for the Senate. At one breakfast hosted by Washington lobbying firm Cassidy and Associates, Mr. Cooper collected more than $14,000 from about two dozen drug company executives.
                                        —The New York Times, *April 19, 1994*

The representatives and senators in the 103rd Congress of 1993–94 constituted the first national government that PACs and other private contributors paid more than a billion dollars to put in place. Without public financing for future campaigns, these elected officials and their successors-in-interest were not about to slap the wrists of the hands that delivered the billion bucks, much less get into a bare-knuckled fight with their PACs. For members of Congress who aspire to reelection, appeasement is the favored approach because their time of need is now and forever.

Private contributions for House elections soared to a record $407 million in 1992. PAC and other contributions to elect the three classes that constituted the 1993–94 Senate totaled $653 million. These sums do not even include the millions in "soft money" slipped to party committees as under-the-table support for congressional candidates. Altogether, private money—almost a third of it from PACs—paid handsomely for lots of access to the best government it could buy.*

So long as private money clogs the corridors of power in the nation's capital, presidents can be expected to tailor health reform proposals to take into account the concern of big-bucks contributors and to trim recommendations so that a beholden Congress will find them politically acceptable.

Of all the moneyed cats prowling the halls of Congress, the players in the health care industry are among the fattest. From 1980 through 1994, health industry PACs and individual donors acknowledged some $200 million in contributions to Congress and candidates. Congress bagged nearly half the total, close to $100 million, in only two election cycles, 1992 and 1994, as it became clear that health care would be on its agenda throughout the 1990s and into the twenty-first century, and that government was getting deeper into the industry's pants each year. Typical of many donors, Integrated Health Services, Inc., a chain of nursing homes, hedged its bets, in 1993 passing $115,000 in soft money to the Democratic National Committee and $100,000 to the Republican National Committee.

These big bucks create a high-stakes pot for individual members

---

*The 1992 presidential candidates also depended heavily on the largess of private donors. In addition to $175 million in public funds, the candidates spent about $100 million in private contributions, not including their slice of the "soft-money" pie or the $60 million that H. Ross Perot took from his own pocket.

of Congress. That's why committees in the House and Senate wrestle for jurisdiction. In the House, three committees vie for big pieces of health care bills: Ways and Means, which oversees Medicare and taxes; Energy and Commerce, which watches over Medicaid and other health matters; and Education and Labor, which presides over employer-employee relations. In the Senate, the battle for jurisdiction is between the Finance and the Labor and Human Resources committees.

Whoever sits on the committees that get jurisdiction has the deep-pocket interests paying for access not only now but forever. That's like giving each committee member a book of blank checks to have signed by health care industry groups for as long as he or she wants to stay in Congress. Jurisdiction over the health care industry is as close to a money tree as you can grow in the shaded marble corridors of Capitol Hill.

According to Common Cause, from 1983 through 1993, health care industry PACs gave $6 million to members of the House Ways and Means Committee and $5.5 million to members of the House Energy and Commerce Committee. The PACs also gave about $5.5 million to Senate Finance Committee members and $3 million to Senate Labor and Human Resources Committee members. Richard Wade, vice president of the American Hospital Association, which puts plenty into the pockets of House Ways and Means Committee members, pulls no punches: "That's our gatekeeper committee in terms of health stuff."

Direct political contributions are not the only way to sway Congress. Lobbyists also give money to legal defense funds, established by members of Congress such as Senator Bob Packwood and Representative Dan Rostenkowski to defend themselves in ethics investigations and criminal cases (and to the fund established by President Clinton to pay lawyers defending him in the

Whitewater inquiry and sexual harassment suit). Industry reps donate to "leadership PACs," set up by congressional leaders such as senators Bob Dole and Ted Kennedy, who then divvy the goodies as they see fit.

The Texas Medical Association, which deployed Regina Kyles and other doctors to influence legislation in Washington, is one of many well-heeled players in the business of health care that have harvested the legislative rewards seeded by political donations. In the late 1980s, when the federal government moved to recover $13.5 million in Medicare payments that it said had been mistakenly sent to Texas doctors and patients, the Texas Medical Association sprang into action. TMA lobbyists wrote legislation to thwart the government's effort and got Texas representatives Ralph Hall and John Bryant to sponsor it. The measure eventually passed as an amendment to the budget reconciliation bill. In 1992, when Medicare stopped reimbursing doctors for interpreting electrocardiograms, a TMA doctor again visited Bryant, who then cosponsored legislation to reverse the Medicare change.

"It's a clever system," said Bryant. "They're active in their district, they volunteer for your campaign, and when there's something important going on, their professionals call you. There's only so many hours in a day, and when you're trying to figure out who to fit into your day, you obviously pay attention to the people who help put you there." Put another way, a constituent's crisis is a member's opportunity to collect a political contribution.

To understand the thrusts and parries in health care debates and to separate partisan rhetoric from political reality, think of health care reform as throwing a trillion-dollar pot of gold up for grabs. At bottom, legislative scrambles over health care reform are not political contests between Republicans and Democrats or ideological battles between liberals and conservatives. They're bare-fisted brawls over who gives and who gets from the rich business of providing care to the sick.

THOSE WHO ANTE THE TRILLION DOLLARS

On the night that President Clinton relaunched health care reform in his State of the Union Address, the lobbying arm of American small business was already at work to kill it. The strategists were up late compiling intelligence on lawmakers and organizing grass-roots support for an early congressional contest they felt reasonably confident of winning. John Motley, chief lobbyist for the National Federation of Independent Business, was preparing for trench warfare in the House Energy and Commerce Committee. "You pick the battleground that you have the best chances of success in," said Motley. "You want to fight them to a standstill . . . prove to them they can't possibly bring this [bill] to the floor" and win.
—The Washington Post, *February 15, 1994*

For those who pay the bills—presidents, Congress, governors, state legislators, corporate CEOs, small businesses, and patients—reform is a game of hot-potato economics, played out in frenetic attempts to toss the blistering bills of sick care to someone else.

The feds try to pass the hot potato of rising costs to the states by mandating broader Medicaid coverage while cutting their share of Medicaid payments, and to the private sector by mandating employer coverage of workers, holding down Medicare payments to doctors and hospitals, requiring individuals to pay higher Medicare premiums, and delaying the age of eligibility for coverage. States seek to toss the hot potato back to the feds by manipulating the Medicaid system, and to the private sector by cutting back on coverage for the indigent, which leads health care providers to charge the privately insured more to cover their losses.

Employers, who provide insurance for some 148 million workers and dependents, are eager to get rid of their own health care
costs. Large corporations balk at paying for care for employees of
small businesses that don't offer workers health insurance and for
government programs like Medicaid that don't pay enough to
cover the cost of care.

Many public corporations rushed to hand off the hot potato of
health care costs when they were required to bring such obligations out of the closet and account for them on their books, cutting
profits and holding down stock value. They foisted the hot potato
into the hands of individual employees by increasing their share of
premiums, deductibles, and copayments, and penalizing those
who didn't use HMOs and preferred providers. They hired more
part-time employees (to avoid paying health care benefits associated with full-time workers), encouraged more overtime (to
avoid new hiring), and trimmed retiree benefits.

THE HOT-POTATO POLITICS OF THE EMPLOYER MANDATE

Virtually all nations that have adopted universal coverage have
built on their existing systems. The British system did not stem
from an English infatuation with socialist principles in 1946. Almost every doctor and nurse in England was in the military at the
end of World War II and the government had taken over the
nation's hospitals, which had been overwhelmed by war casual-
ties. After the war, the British national health plan simply legislated the status quo. Similarly, Germany's universal coverage plan
built upon the worker guilds and sickness funds that performed a
health insurance function similar to the role employers and insurers play in the United States.

The American link between health care benefits and employment dates back half a century to World War II. So it is no wonder that three presidents—Richard Nixon, Jimmy Carter, and Bill Clinton—proposed to build on the existing system, where most Americans have received their health care coverage through the employment relationship, by requiring employers to provide a basic package of benefits for their employees.

The beauty that three presidents have seen in the employer mandate is that it takes so much of the cost of universal coverage off the federal budget and lays it onto private, state, and municipal employers. President Clinton was especially attracted to this beauty when he thought he could dress the biggest payroll tax rise in American history in the drag of premiums for health insurance. The beast that scares state and corporate employers is a package of benefits mandated by a Congress that has no responsibility to fund them. What is disturbing about most proposed mandates is that they are limited to sick care, and do not require employers to offer health promotion benefits, such as smoking cessation, periodic physical examinations, opportunities to exercise, timely employee assistance for substance abuse, and stress reduction programs, as well.

Small businesses, many represented by the National Federation of Independent Business, cry the loudest about being burned by any requirement that they cover their workers—and they should. Three-fourths of the uninsured work (or are dependents of workers), and most work for small enterprises. As a result of cost shifting in 1993, businesses that employed more than one hundred workers paid $20 billion in health care costs for employees at companies with fewer than twenty-five workers (who usually have no insurance).

The National Association of Manufacturers, which represents

businesses producing most of the nation's manufacturing output, estimates that its members fork over some $12 billion a year, almost 30 percent of the health care bill they pay, for treatment of individuals who are not on their payrolls. Seven billion dollars of that picks up the tab for workers in other sectors of the economy, notably service and retail industries, including hotel, retail, and fast-food chains. The rest supports public programs such as Medicaid and Medicare, which don't pay most hospitals and doctors enough to cover the cost of care.

Retailers and hotels, which traditionally have not covered many of their employees, balk at any mandate to provide health care benefits because they fear it would shred their paper-thin profit margins and threaten their survival. These and other service industries shift billions in health care costs not only to other businesses, but to federal and state governments.

Faced with competition from foreign companies whose governments pay workers' health care bills, global American corporations in the 1990s support national health plans that they condemned in the 1970s as galloping socialism. General Motors, Ford, and Chrysler were quick to jump into bed with the Clintons because the administration's plan would have been worth about $3 billion a year in savings that they could have used to lower prices, reinvest, or distribute in dividends to shareholders and wages to workers. The cost of health care benefits for each car produced in the United States is $1,200, twice the cost for each car made in Japan and shipped here. Clinton's plan would have cut that spread.

State governors have grown increasingly wary as they delve into the devilish details of national reform plans because they expect the feds to foist on them two big burdens: higher bills and more political responsibility if reform fails to deliver. The Reagan revolution taught most every member of Congress that it is politically better for the feds to mandate benefits and let states and cities raise the necessary taxes to finance those benefits, than for the feds to tax and tax and let the states and cities spend and spend.

The states are also turning to the courts to get rid of the hot potato of costs. California and Florida have sued the federal government to recoup state funds spent to provide medical care to illegal immigrants that the federal government failed to intercept at the border. In 1994, Mississippi, Minnesota, West Virginia, and Florida filed suits against cigarette companies to recover Medicaid and other taxpayer costs related to the treatment of diseases and disabilities caused by tobacco.

Individuals—you and I—are in harm's way of being hit by these costs as governments and corporations frantically toss them back and forth. Senior citizens have the American Association of Retired Persons and some workers have powerful unions to protect them. But the rest of us stand alone against the danger of being dropped from a retiree plan, losing a job and health coverage with it, becoming ineligible for a narrowly focused government health program, suffering from a disease that doesn't fit the insurer's jigsaw puzzle, and paying a bigger share of premiums and bills.

For us, cost shifting is a cruel mirage; it does nothing to make the system more efficient. As long as that's where the action is, the game of hot-potato economics will become more frenetic and, whether as higher taxes, premiums, out-of-pocket costs, foregone wages, or higher prices, the hot potato of costs will land in our laps.

THOSE WITH THEIR HANDS IN THE POT

Although most people have never heard of him, Michael Bromberg may be the man to watch as Congress wrestles with the issue that will affect every American. Chief lobbyist for the Federation of American Health Systems, representing for-profit hospitals, his influence is a product of an encyclopedic knowledge of politics and policy, a shrewd sense of timing, access to key members of Congress, and money; every two years, the Federation's PAC gives $250,000 to House and Senate candidates. By the time President Clinton gave his big speech on health care, Bromberg had already managed to kill both a tax and short-term price controls on hospitals.
                                        —The Washington Post, *February 6, 1994*

For those who get paid—insurers, doctors, nonprofit and for-profit hospitals, unions, pharmaceutical companies, medical-equipment manufacturers, HMOs, nurses, mental health providers, podiatrists, chiropractors, pharmacists, radiologists, other suppliers of services, and their satellites and parasites—reform is a fight to protect their share of the trillion-dollar health care pot—and maybe even take a bigger portion.

Humorist Art Buchwald captured the rush to get a scoop into the pot during an evening talk to the 1993 Renaissance Weekend audience in Hilton Head, South Carolina, which included President and Mrs. Clinton. After mentioning Norman Cousins's belief that humor was increasingly helpful in curing people, Buchwald looked right at the president and first lady and said, "Mrs. Clinton, we humorists want a piece of the action you are handing out in your health care reform package."

The roughest arm-twisting is likely to come from those who have the highest stakes in providing and financing sick care: hospitals, doctors, nursing homes and home health care, pharmaceutical companies and over-the-counter-product manufacturers, insurers, and others such as dentists, podiatrists, optometrists, psychologists, physical therapists, public health workers, researchers, and construction workers. They, and others who get the sick-care bucks—medical-equipment manufacturers, lawyers, and investment bankers—can be expected to scrap among themselves with a brass-knuckled brutality rarely seen in Washington.

In 1965, when we in the Johnson administration were pushing to pass Medicare and Medicaid, a handshake with the head of the American Medical, Pharmaceutical, or Hospital association was sufficient to commit the entire membership. We needed to negotiate with only one insurance industry representative. In the 1990s and into the next century, any restructuring of health care amid evolving economic interests in a market undergoing tumultuous revolution will pit individuals and institutions within the same profession against one another. The most blood is likely to be spilled *within* each group.

Doctors in one specialty are pitched against doctors in another. For-profit hospitals stand to gain from competition on the basis of price and restrictions on the ability of patients to seek care outside their home areas. Teaching hospitals will lose patients and doctors if such competition and geographic restraints prevail, and if government limits the numbers of specialists they can have as residents each year.

Pharmaceutical companies that get their biggest profits from generic drugs take to the legislative streets against those who make big bucks from patented drugs. Medco and the American Association of Retired Persons, which make millions filling mail-order prescriptions, tend to favor plans that set up large purchasing combines. Local pharmacists favor broad coverage for pharmaceuticals, but fear further erosion of their incomes under any plans that emphasize managed care.

THE MEDICINE MEN AND WOMEN

Family practitioners and pediatricians reach for higher reimbursement rates and a broader role as "gatekeepers" for patients who seek health care services. Surgeons and neurologists resist any reduction in their take and try to thwart the momentum of managed-care programs that reduce their autonomy in providing high-tech, high-priced treatments. Doctors in HMOs line up for reforms that push patients their way, as fee-for-service colleagues resist changes that will dilute their income stream and warn that cost controls will jeopardize quality care for their patients.

Once a virtual monolith, the American Medical Association in 1994 claimed only 290,000 members—less than half of the practicing physicians in the United States. Numerous medical specialty groups, from neurologists to oncologists, march to their own economic drummers. Although AMA officials sing the refrain of support for universal coverage, Dr. James Todd, the association's executive vice president, acknowledges the discordant notes in the verses of specialties and subspecialties as "disagreement about the best way to reach this shared vision."

In 1992, the nation's second largest doctors' group, representing eighty thousand internists, the American College of Physicians, supported a global budget cap for private and public health care spending, an idea that the AMA "unequivocally opposes" for fear it would lead to rationing both care for its patients and fees for its physicians. The AMA initially supported employer mandates. Then, torn between its interest in eliminating nonpaying patients and its concern for members who as small businesses would be required to provide health care benefits to employees, the AMA reversed itself and opposed any employer mandate, only to switch again to tepid sympathy for the idea a few months later. In the

1960s or even the 1980s, that would have been the last word. In the 1990s, the Clinton administration had no trouble assembling a coalition of ten physician groups, claiming to represent about three hundred thousand doctors, to support such a mandate.

During the Johnson administration, if the president had proposed that the national government take over paying for the health care system, the chorus of denunciation attacking socialized medicine would have been sung by all doctors. In 1994, this proposal was called the single-payer plan, and officers of the American College of Surgeons, with fifty-two thousand members, testified strongly in its favor because they saw it as less intrusive to their practice and more accommodating to their high-income status than the alternatives. Then a flood of phone calls from irate surgeons quickly prompted the ACS leadership to reverse its position.

Representative Fortney "Pete" Stark, the California Democrat who now chairs the health subcommittee of the House Ways and Means Committee, ridicules this cacophonous drumbeat of doctors as economic self-interest. "Organized medicine makes a lot of noise on Capitol Hill," Stark concedes. But, he adds, "Unfortunately, greed is a far stronger instinct than the Hippocratic oath."

More important than the volume of their noise is the depth of their pockets, and the doctors put the jingle of their coins behind their voices. The AMA is the premier PAC donor to Congress. From 1991 to 1994, the AMA and related PACs shoveled $8 million into the pockets of senators and representatives. And that does not include the millions that individual doctors have sent to Congress. That is why, as health economist Uwe Reinhardt says, "what the head of the AMA thinks in the shower in the morning is much more important than the aspirations of ten million Americans."

THE TEMPLES OF MEDICINE MEN AND WOMEN

America's great teaching centers, rural community hospitals, urban public hospitals, and for-profit institutions are like pit bulls tearing at the same slab of financial meat.

The teaching hospitals scratch to hang on to billions in state, federal, and private subsidies in order to conduct research, train the next generation of specialists, and sharpen the cutting edge of American medical practice that attracts patients from all over the world. They oppose any limits on the number of specialists they train, noting that the best and brightest medical residents are one of the few bargains in the health care system. "The residents represent cheap labor, and if we have to replace them with clinician-nurses, you're talking about doubling the cost of each position," says Dr. Paul Marks, president of Memorial Sloan-Kettering Cancer Center. When teaching hospitals are located in urban areas, as many are, these residents also provide high-quality care to large numbers of impoverished individuals.

Also in large cities are nonteaching hospitals, which can be public or private. Many of them serve a high percentage of Medicaid and uninsured patients, financed in part by an added subsidy from the federal government. Most proposals for universal coverage would end this special allocation, called a "disproportionate share" payment, which has led governors such as liberal Mario Cuomo of New York and conservative Pete Wilson of California to fight the same battle in Washington.

For-profit hospitals demand a level playing field for all hospitals in any system of universal coverage. To them, that means turning off the spigot of federal subsidies (unless they get some) and tax exemptions, which nonprofit hospitals currently enjoy.

Whatever their angle, the temples of the medicine men and women back their prayers for relief with big contributions when the basket is passed. During the 1994 election cycle, the American Hospital Association, which claims to represent forty-nine hundred hospitals and their four million employees, gave $1 million to its favorite congressional campaigners on both sides of the aisle. Independent donations from other hospitals and their PACs, mostly for-profits, pushed the total above $2 million. And none of that counts the hundreds of thousands of dollars in personal contributions from hospital officers and trustees.

THE MONEY CHANGERS

Once the placid, white-shoe representative of doctors and hospitals, the insurance industry has been torn apart by America's health care revolution. Every insurer is trying to protect its revenues and pound down the cost of health services in a market where low prices are gaining an edge over high quality. None wants government-imposed caps on its premiums. But these are about the only things on which large and small insurers can agree in the chaotic world of health care in the 1990s.

Rising demand for managed care from large government and corporate purchasers has given the big boys of insurance a mighty advantage over small-fry insurers. The big guys generally favor two changes to improve their position: incentives to create large purchasers of managed care who would need their administrative capability, and prohibitions against denying coverage to customers with preexisting medical conditions, such as heart disease or diabetes.

Such changes threaten the financial viability of many small insurers that rely on their young, healthy customers to preserve thin profit margins.

The gusty winds of change have blown the Health Insurance

Association of America apart. Once the premier representative of all health insurers, the HIAA lost the big companies during 1992 and 1993, when their economic interests no longer jibed with those of their smaller siblings. Both big and small insurers, however, agreed to stay in the American Council of Life Insurance, a shotgun marriage that has neutralized the organization on most health care issues.

Five of the largest commercial health insurers—Aetna Life and Casualty, Cigna, MetLife, Prudential Insurance Company of America, and The Travelers—disassociated themselves from HIAA, because changes in America's health care system offer them the chance to grab much of the market share from the small insurers. They lust for the big bureaucracies in any system of universal coverage, which would vastly expand their administrative operations, and to acquire large networks of providers, which would give them a corner on the big-employer market.

The five companies formed their own Alliance for Managed Competition, covering about a third of the nation's 180 million privately insured. To promote their interests on Capitol Hill, they hired well-connected lobbyists like Robert Leonard, former chief counsel and staff director for the House Ways and Means Committee, and former House Republican Vin Weber of Minnesota. They formed their own PACs and contributed $1 million to key senators and representatives in 1993 and 1994.

Meanwhile, smaller health insurers, which also cover a third of the country's privately insured, took control of HIAA and joined with the Independent Insurance Agents of America to warn that a move to "managed competition" would, in practice, squelch competition by favoring huge bureaucracies and putting many small carriers and thousands of agents out of business.

The small insurers also dipped into the well of congressional influence by hiring former ranking Republican House Ways and Means Committee member Bill Gradison. Even without the big insurers, HIAA is, as its former president Carl Schramm noted, "a very wealthy and robust organization [that] will remain very powerful." The reason? Political contributions to members of Congress and the $14 million advertising campaign in 1993 and 1994, which focused on key congressional districts and starred Harry and Louise under the cover of "Coalition for Health Insurance Choices."

All told, in addition to various advertising campaigns and fees paid to Washington lobbyists, insurance industry PACs and individual donors laid $10 million on members of Congress in the 1994 election cycle.

THE PHARMACEUTICAL INDUSTRY

Seeking to eliminate the threat of anything resembling price controls, the pharmaceutical industry contributed $6 million to congressional campaigns from 1991 to 1994.

Using its deft marketing skills in 1993, the industry bet $7 million on a "Good Medicine" campaign to sell its message that any effort to curb prices would curtail research into drugs that save lives, reduce suffering, and eliminate the need for expensive medical procedures. In 1994, the Pharmaceutical Manufacturers Association budgeted another $13 million for television and print advertising, and in May of that year further honed its pitch by adding the golden word *research* to its name—and the Pharmaceutical Research and Manufacturers of America was christened.

The industry has hired plenty of experienced congressional hands: Thomas Downey, a former House Ways and Means Committee member; Washington lobbyist Jody Powell, who had been President Jimmy Carter's press secretary; House Speaker Tom Foley's top assistant and the Senate Finance Committee's minority chief of staff.

The pharmaceutical industry is the CIA of medical lobbyists, expert at using secret agents and cover, often bankrolling specialists in particular diseases to promote FDA approval of drugs in their fields. In 1989, the industry helped finance efforts to fire up senior citizens against the prescription drug benefit that Congress had enacted in the Medicare Catastrophic Coverage Act; it saw the law as a step into the chamber of horrors of price controls.

In 1990, with Medicaid buying $5 billion worth of drugs—close to 15 percent of all prescriptions—Arkansas Democrat Senator David Pryor pushed legislation to get lower prices for the government. The PMA retained Clinton pal Vernon Jordan to help rouse minority groups to oppose Pryor, using the ploy that the legislation could force states to buy inferior drugs and lead to second-class medicine for poor African Americans. The industry was able to gut the bill that eventually passed.

In 1993, pharmaceutical companies financed the Coalition for Equal Access to Medicines, enlisting minorities and representatives of the poor to oppose congressional efforts to have Medicaid establish a formulary of pharmaceuticals, which would force companies to compete for eligibility for reimbursement. Such effective lobbying, combined with millions of dollars in political contributions, has made the pharmaceutical industry one of the most formidable lobbyists in Washington.

THE UNIONS

The bureaucratic behemoths of Clinton's thwarted plan were the state purchasing alliances, charged with buying most health care and monitoring every provider. The American Federation of State, County, and Municipal Employees, the nation's most powerful and effective union, saw these alliances as the biggest bureaucracy since the disintegration of the Soviet Union and a once-in-a-generation chance to shift most of the nation's insurance function into an arena where they know how to organize workers. But unions representing hospital employees wanted no part of legislation that pressured administrators to cut hospital payrolls.

Having negotiated health benefits for their members since the 1940s, most unions wanted their members exempt from any reform that mandated a minimum-benefit package less generous than what they were getting.

Even before announcement of the Clinton plan in late 1993, workers with broader coverage than the administration had proposed were maneuvering to protect their position. Federal employees, who had richer benefits at less cost to them than what the Clinton package offered, and members of large unions such as the United Auto Workers and Communication Workers of America, which had negotiated first-dollar coverage and no premium copayments in their health benefits, scrambled to get out from under the administration's plan.

In 1994, the American Federation of Labor–Congress of Industrial Organizations spent more than $10 million—triple what it had invested the year before in its unsuccessful attempt to defeat the North American Free Trade Agreement—to promote health care legislation to its liking—and for an advertising campaign to remind the public that the generous benefits that Congress receives could be a guidepost for federal lawmakers tempted to tinker with union-negotiated benefits.

THE LAWYERS

At a June 1993 meeting, leaders of the American Trial Lawyers of America (ATLA) warned their Iowa contingent that for any Clinton health care proposal to have a chance to pass into law, it would have to "appear" that trial lawyers were taking a hit just like the doctors. But, according to the minutes of the meeting obtained by *The Wall Street Journal,* they assured their worried members, "Trust us on this one."

Months later, in announcing his proposal, Clinton warned that sacrifices would be required of everyone, including lawyers, whose fees would be capped at one-third of any damage award. Although some lawyers made protest noises, they were chuckling on their way to the courthouse. The administration bill left the litigation-infested malpractice system intact and placed no limit on damages that could be awarded for pain and suffering. Robert Berenson, who co-chaired the administration's working group on malpractice, later wondered aloud what role the lawyers' $500,000 in donations to Clinton's presidential campaign played in White House reluctance to suggest meaningful changes.

ATLA, with a membership of sixty thousand, spends more money per member on political contributions than any other major lobbying group, including the American Medical Association. In the 1992 and 1994 campaign cycles, the trial lawyers' group passed $4 million to its favorite congressional candidates. "These guys have it all programmed," says Robert Joost, a lawyer who worked for ATLA in the 1960s. "Democracy doesn't have a chance."

CIGARETTES, WHISKEY, AND WILD, WILD LOBBYING

> *Faced with the prospect of a $2.00 increase in the cigarette tax, the tobacco industry plied senators and congressman with junkets to pleasant places like Palm Springs and Boca Raton, and passed more than $800,000 to members on three key House committees. Ellen Miller from the Center for Responsive Politics in Washington, D.C., spotted the clear correlation between money that the tobacco industry gave and the results they got. Members of the House Education and Labor Committee received $104,000 and recommended a 75¢-a-pack increase. Members of the House Ways and Means Committee received $329,000 and recommended a 45¢ increase.*
> —Nightline, *ABC Network, August 8, 1994.*

The frontal attack on health promotion and disease prevention comes from the political contributions of the tobacco and alcohol industries. The tobacco lobby has locked the Congress in its PAC prison for years. By incontestable studies and the judgment of every surgeon general since 1964, cigarettes are the top crippler and killer in the United States. Yet attempts to impose higher taxes have repeatedly been defeated or trimmed back.

Two 1994 studies exposed the relationship between campaign money from tobacco interests and the failure of legislators to support bills to raise cigarette taxes, educate the public about the dangers of smoking, and prevent the sale of cigarettes to children. One found that $2.4 million paid by tobacco interests to members of Congress had a greater influence on their voting behavior than their party affiliation and even whether they came from tobacco-producing states did. The other found that California legislators voted contrary to the wishes of their constituents in order to appease tobacco interests that had lined their pockets with $1.2 million in campaign contributions.

Holding down tax increases on cigarettes and smokeless tobacco is critical to the future of the tobacco industry. So it's not surprising that the tobacco interests pour millions of dollars into congressional campaigns, political party war chests, and state legislatures. Solely through its PAC, Philip Morris donated more than $2 million to members of Congress from 1983 through 1994. In 1990, a director of Washington relations for Philip Morris boasted in an internal memo of using influence with the White House to prevent attacks on smoking by the nation's surgeon general. The same executive later served as a White House aide for President Bush. The single largest source of direct contributions to President Bush's reelection campaign—$106,950—came from U.S. Tobacco, the leading manufacturer of smokeless tobacco products.

In the 1992 and 1994 election cycles, the beer and liquor industry used $3 million in political contributions to defeat a proposed tax increase on alcohol, even though more than eighteen million Americans suffer from alcohol abuse and addiction, resulting in billions of dollars of taxpayer health care expenditures for them, their families, and victims of their assaults and drunken driving.

Fortunately, alcohol and tobacco money doesn't always carry the day. In 1985, New York City Mayor Ed Koch asked me to chair a commission to develop a law to provide smoke-free space. Our group wanted to require that public places be smoke-free, restaurants provide smoke-free space, and smoking be prohibited in taxis. When I told Koch where we were headed, I said I realized it was hopeless because of indications that the tobacco interests would spend $5 million to kill the bill in the City Council.

"Nonsense," Koch said. "You propose the toughest law that makes sense. I'll get it passed."

I expressed skepticism about his nonchalance.

"This is New York," Koch said.

"But they'll take the money," I responded.

"Of course they'll take the money," Koch agreed. "Then they'll vote for your bill."

City Council members did take the money. Then they voted unanimously for the bill.

Members of Congress can decide to show the same independence. In 1994, Representative Charles Rangel, a reformed smoker who had opposed cigarette taxes during his twenty-four years in Congress because, he claimed, they would fall hard on his Harlem constituents, pledged his support for a "substantial" tax hike on cigarettes to help pay for health care reform. Explaining his reversal despite $34,000 in campaign contributions from cigarette makers over the previous decade, Rangel snapped, "I never had a contract" with them.

MUGGING REFORM

Thanks in good measure to its dependence on financial contributions from private contributors—particularly providers of health care services and products—the Congress rejected health care reform proposals in 1994 and has repeatedly mugged the executive branch when it stepped out to operate Medicaid and Medicare as efficiently as private sector payers manage private insurers and health care providers.

Medicaid and Medicare have been held back or slowed down in taking actions private employers and insurers use to restrain costs: seeking competitive bids for laboratory tests, claims administration, and radiology; requiring second opinions, which can reduce elective surgery; insisting that patients pay more if they go outside a list of efficient doctors or hospitals; and limiting payments to that of the lowest-priced generic drug.

They have been slow to buy cardiac bypass surgery for a fixed price from hospitals that perform a high volume of the procedure. Medicare could save money and lives by limiting its heart and cancer patients to high-volume hospitals, but members of Congress are more concerned with protecting the low-volume hospitals in their districts.

Large companies have used techniques such as these to bring their rate of increase in health spending down to only two-thirds of the federal government's. In federal programs, these tactics are frequently blocked in the fine-print restrictions of legislation written to appease health industry lobbyists.

Congress after Congress has rebuffed most efforts to restrain health care costs. Congress repeatedly increased payments to hospitals well beyond the Reagan administration's recommendations—adding at least $500 million a year to the budget during those years—even though hospitals kept open a quarter-million empty beds, a huge excess load that drives up costs. Congress rejected President Nixon's attempts to hold down costs, defeated President Carter's hospital-cost-containment bill, and ignored President Johnson's plea to change the reimbursement methods for hospitals and doctors.

In 1988, when Congress enacted a prescription drug benefit as part of its short-lived catastrophic care package, it legislated a fee to the pharmacy or mail-order supplier of $4.50 a prescription— even though mail-order suppliers were then charging corporate health care plan clients only fifty cents to fill a prescription and process a claim.

Why?

The most energetic lobby behind the new drug benefit and $4.50 dispensing fee was the American Association of Retired Persons, which runs one of the country's largest mail-order drug-dispensing business (1993 revenues: $400 million) and whose thirty-four million members represent one of the most daunting voting blocs in the nation.

Comprehensive health care reform, involving almost one-sixth of the American economy, is not a one-shot proposition, as was the enactment of Medicare and Medicaid (though even these programs for the old and poor have been amended repeatedly). Health care reform, like tax reform, is a continuing battle, with billions of dollars at stake each legislative year as the country lurches in fits and starts, with plenty of mistakes and detours, toward universal coverage, and as Congress and presidents struggle to contain costs.

Everybody wants their mitts in the trillion-dollar health care pot. As Senator Jay Rockefeller cracked in 1993, "There are so many health industry lobbyists up here on Capitol Hill, I think the line forms somewhere in Virginia." In 1994, one lobbying firm, Patton, Boggs & Blow, in Washington, D.C., had no fewer than two dozen health care clients. John Carson, chief lobbyist for the American Podiatric Medical Association, which contributed $500,000 in the 1994 election cycle, stated his goal concisely: "To make sure that medical and surgical care of the foot and ankle is included in any plan that is adopted."

Lobbyists use money to stir up "grassroots" support for their interests. Anheuser-Busch outfitted its trucks with signs urging Bud drinkers to dial 1-800-BEER-TAX; those who did learned how President Clinton's health plan would empty their pockets. John Motley, a key lobbyist for small businesses, boasted that in the first four months of 1994, his organization sent six hundred thousand pieces of mail to help mobilize grassroots support. In all, the lobbying on health care reform has entailed "the largest mobilization since the establishment of Social Security," said Frank Mankiewicz, a Washington influence peddler who once worked for Senator Robert Kennedy.

The enormous resources the health care industry invests in

influencing members of Congress and stirring up their constituents distorts the debate over changes in the health care system. That makes effective professional campaigns to get the facts about health care to the American people, such as the one mounted in 1994 by Drew Altman, president of The Henry J. Kaiser Family Foundation, so important.

Politics in America is no longer a profession dominated by volunteers and pocket-money budgets. To get elected, members of Congress need money for campaigning, radio, television, transportation, polling, computers, political consultants, advance men, and public relations gurus. To get reelected, most members spend about half their time in office raising campaign funds. Representatives on a two-year election tether are perpetually panting for funds. Senators admit to friends and colleagues that they spend virtually all their time during the last two years of their six-year term (and much of it before then) raising money.

The result is that PACs with deep pockets and wealthy special interests acquire veto power over any legislation that will hurt them badly, however strong the national interest in its passage. For more than a generation, private money has stymied efforts to give Americans an efficient, affordable system of quality care for all.

WHAT TO DO?

Only with significant reform will we free the Congressional 535 from the shackles of special interests that stifle our ability to shift our emphasis from sick care to health and thus threaten our ability to maintain the finest health care system in the world and open it to all our people.

If the American people want a national legislature that serves their interests, then they must put up taxpayer funds for legislators to run for office and limit what can be spent on their campaigns. And they must get off their duffs and to the polls on election day so that the high percentage of elderly who do vote does not continue to pump such a disproportionate share of public resources to sick care of senior citizens and to research for high-tech gimmicks to buy a few more days of life.

I've set out the corruption of the legislative process not out of cynicism, but out of experience derived from dealing with health care issues over thirty years. I write to remind the better angels in all the players—politicians, payers, and providers—that we patients have a lot at stake in their frenzy to protect their chips in the trillion-dollar health care pot. At its core, health care is the profession of caring, not the business of medicine. If we lose sight of this essential characteristic, we will have cut out its healing heart.

On June 19, 1977, as secretary of Health, Education, and Welfare, I addressed the American Medical Association. After outlining the major problems then in the system—underserved populations in inner cities and rural areas, rampant inefficiencies, no incentives for prevention, eighteen million people uninsured, economic incentives that encouraged doctors and hospitals to be wasteful, and runaway costs—I concluded:

> Clearly the health care industry, as presently structured, has become a problem for all of us—patients, physicians, providers of care, and public officials. Certainly we can understand why the American consumers and taxpayers—and more and more top executives of large corporations—are demanding that something be done.

In 1994, the underserved populations were larger, inefficiencies persisted, there was little incentive for disease prevention, forty million individuals were uninsured, and the system still encouraged doctors and hospitals to be wasteful. Without campaign finance reform, in 2014, the United States secretary of health will make a similar speech.

CHAPTER NINE

WHAT NEXT?

The future of American health care lies not on the floor of the U.S. House of Representatives or Senate, or in the Oval Office, or in statehouses and city halls across the nation—important as they are—but in ourselves and our families, our homes and our workplaces, our doctors and hospitals, our churches and schools, our culture and our values.

History teaches us three harsh lessons about legislative efforts to increase access and contain costs by manipulating the financing and delivery of sick care: such reforms will be much more expensive than anyone forecasts; they will not ensure that each American receives all the care he or she needs—and only that care—at high quality and reasonable cost; and those who predict individual and institutional conduct in response to such fixes will be surprised by unintended actions and consequences.

Private-sector forces—employers pressing for less expensive sick care for their workers; doctors, hospitals, nursing homes, and clinics combining to deliver full-service diagnosis and treatment more efficiently; insurers, HMOs, and other managed-care conglomerates scrambling for a place in the constellation—are transforming the sick-care system independently of any action in the Congress or state legislatures.

The system of financing and delivering sick care is undergoing extensive surgery, and the success of the operation will depend on our ability to preserve the best as we excise and reconstitute the worst. The private institutions and governments performing this surgery must use their scalpels with painstaking delicacy in order to preserve and enhance the intimacy and integrity of the doctor (and nurse)-patient relationship, which is the aorta of any effective system.

However, the cure for what ails the American way of health requires far more radical surgery than fixing the way we pay for and provide sick care. We must have the courage and skills to take on the fundamental forces that are driving the health care system: the substance abuse and addiction pandemic and its related violence, disease, and accidents; the aging of our population; the genius of our scientists, whose wizardry has outpaced our wisdom; and the ethical confusion and cultural hedonism that mark our time. The crucial key to preserving and enhancing the best of American medicine and democratizing it efficiently and wisely is human conduct, not legislative legerdemain.

THE LEGAL LIMITS:
FIXING THE SICK-CARE SYSTEM

There is no legislative silver bullet that will give all Americans affordable care. During the 1990s and the early years of the twenty-first century, a host of laws, amendments, amendments to amendments, and regulations will emerge from a contentious, evolving, rough-and-tumble mix of politics and money. Well-intentioned presidents and governors, federal and state legislators, mayors and city councils will struggle to keep pace with the discoveries of science and biology, mete out their blessings, and play hot-potato economics with each other and with private employers, unions, and individuals. They will take many actions—complex and perhaps contradictory—with many successes, lots of detours, and numerous mistakes as we learn more about ourselves, our genes, and the ingenuity of sick-care providers and payers.

Recognizing the limits of what legislation can achieve, however, does not diminish the importance of sensible laws, aimed at the right targets, mandating, encouraging, and nourishing individual and institutional conduct that will move the nation toward universal coverage at affordable cost.

The essential legislative step is reform of the campaign finance laws, including a system of public financing for congressional elections, to take the pernicious power of private money out of the political system. Without such action, well-funded interests of doctors, hospitals, pharmaceutical and medical-equipment companies, big unions, insurers, and profitable HMOs will dominate the health legislation landscape as they have since the 1960s.

Public financing will not provide a perfect tablet on which to legislate, but it would be a vast improvement over the culture of private money that has stained so many reform efforts by the U.S. House and Senate and state legislatures across the nation. Indeed, the private money spent by the providers of treatment to maintain their cash flows is in good measure responsible for the myopic congressional focus on sick care, its shortchanging of health promotion and disease prevention, and the defeat of reform efforts in 1994.

With campaign finance reform, the 1990s could be the decade in which all Americans are assured access to sick care. In 1994, of the

260 million Americans, 60 million were eligible for Medicare or Medicaid, and 160 million had insurance as a function of employment or as individual policyholders. Laws extending federal coverage to all poor people, requiring health insurance premiums to be rated on community risk, assuring coverage regardless of preexisting conditions and during periods of unemployment, guaranteeing portability from job to job, and mandating employer coverage of employees will take care of most everyone.

The foundation of affordable, comprehensive health care coverage in America is the employer mandate. Requiring employers to provide a minimum package of health benefits to their employees is a potent weapon in delivering sick care more efficiently and may even encourage employers to provide health promotion and disease prevention programs for employees as the cost-effectiveness of such programs becomes clear.

Phasing in the mandate by starting with large employers (most of which have long provided coverage well beyond any likely mandate) and gradually extending it to smaller businesses (helping them with subsidies or tax credits to ease their burden and encouraging them to form cooperatives to pool their purchasing power) makes sense, not only because of federal budget concerns with respect to any subsidy, but also because of the unpredictability of reform and its impact on the health care system.

The history of the minimum wage offers a telling precedent. In 1938 Franklin Roosevelt persuaded Congress to enact the minimum wage in the Fair Labor Standards Act. Initially the law covered only eleven million workers, a fifth of the total labor force and a third of nonsupervisory workers. Of those who were covered, only three hundred thousand—fewer than 3 percent—were then earning less than the new minimum wage of twenty-five cents an hour. Not until 1966, when Lyndon Johnson persuaded the

89th Congress to act, was the law extended to cover nearly all retail and trade employees and, for the first time, agricultural workers.

In a society as mobile as ours, where citizens frequently move from state to state, a federally defined package of minimum benefits, which employers would be free to exceed, makes good sense. Employees should be required to bear some portion of the costs to keep them interested in containing them. To temper the congressional proclivity to pile up mandated coverage when someone else is paying the bill, the law should prohibit requiring employers to provide any benefits not available in federally funded public programs such as Medicare.

The employer mandate builds on a part of the existing system that, by and large, is working well. It enlists the ingenuity of thousands of business managers to keep health care costs down. It draws a line of clear responsibility that will slow the cost-shifting game of hot-potato economics, which does little to make the system more efficient. It pushes some costs off the federal budget and puts them into everyday life, throughout our systems of commerce, as part of a fair wage and the purchasing decisions Americans make. The mandate would also stop the steady decline, since 1980, in the percentage of individuals with employer-sponsored insurance and put an end to employer reductions of health care benefits below the minimum package.

The rhetoric of impassioned opposition to an employer mandate echoes earlier battles. Before passage of the Fair Labor Standards Act in 1938, business leaders warned that it would precipitate a "tyrannical industrial dictatorship." They charged that Roosevelt's arguments for a mandated minimum wage were, like "the smoke screen of the cuttlefish," a cover for his plot to promote socialist planning of the U.S. economy. They asked how business could "find any time left to provide jobs if we are to persist in loading upon it these everlasting multiplying government mandates?"

In fact, American business adjusted, just as it did after passage of the Occupational Safety and Health Act, state laws mandating disability insurance for workers, and federal laws mandating safety standards for automobiles and access for the disabled.

American managers of business, small or large, have the agility to bargain more effectively for efficient, quality health care than does any government. They have become savvy negotiators with a range of providers: managed-care plans, fee-for-service doctors, traditional insurers, and new networks of health care providers. Uninhibited by the political constraints that Congress imposes on executive agencies to protect special interests, an increasing number of employers have shown that they can provide quality care far less expensively than federal and state governments. Cost-conscious employers are forcing doctors and hospitals to cut prices, eliminate excess capacity, and reduce unnecessary tests and procedures without sacrificing medically appropriate care. They and managed-care providers are squeezing deep discounts from pharmaceutical companies and limiting reimbursement for off-patent drugs to the lowest generic price.

Conservative opposition to the employer mandate on ideological grounds is difficult to understand, since the mandate would place the incentive to contain costs squarely in the private sector and capitalize on market forces that are light years ahead of Congress in restructuring the financing and delivery of health care in America.

Competitive churnings in the health care market, combined with political pressures to rein in costs as the president, Congress, and the states struggled to revamp health care delivery, helped slow down the pace of medical care inflation to 5.4 percent in 1993 and 4.6 percent (on an annualized basis) in the first nine months of 1994. Though still above the rate of general inflation, they were the lowest rates of increase since President Nixon's price controls were in effect in the early 1970s.

A government mandate that employers provide a package of benefits to their employees would ride on these healthy trends and give every American employer a stake in making the health care system cost-effective and responsive to the needs of its employees.

The experience of the Chrysler Corporation illustrates what an aroused business management can do. In 1981, as he was seeking to pull Chrysler back from the brink of bankruptcy, Lee Iacocca asked me to join the board and chair a new committee on health care, the first of its kind for any corporation. Our examination of Chrysler's health care spending revealed a system ripe with over-use and abuse, unnecessary procedures, and fraud. By introducing basic cost-cutting tools, such as mandatory second opinions before surgery, dental HMOs, and prescription drug coverage only for the generic price of a drug, we managed to save $58 million in health care costs in 1984, the first year our initiatives took hold.

Since then, Chrysler has introduced preferred provider arrangements for physician, lab, and vision services, a mail-order generic drug program, and, among salaried employees, increased deductibles and copayments. (Hourly union workers still enjoy first-dollar coverage of major medical expenses.) In 1988, we began a managed-care program of precertification review and case management of mental health services, which saved the corporation more than $40 million in three years, largely by reducing lengthy hospital stays. In 1994, we introduced a formulary for prescription drugs that is expected to save at least $30 million a year. From 1982 to 1993, Chrysler's health care costs have been growing an average of 7.5 percent a year—half the rate of increase for U.S. business generally.

In a healthy economy, the private sector subjected to an employer mandate will provide sick care to the vast majority of Americans. For the poor, the old, and the unemployed, the most vulnerable individuals in our society, we will always have to look to the common treasury. The taxpayers who have must pay for the poor who have not.

The most cost-effective way to accomplish this is by extending Medicare, initially to cover all needy pregnant women and children through their sixth year, and eventually to pick up all the poor and individuals during extended periods of unemployment, phasing out Medicaid along the way. Legislation reforming health care should be clean and lean, free of political junk and congressional nitpicking. It should scrap the bureaucratic barnacles of boards, commissions, premium caps, global budgets, price controls, big brother agencies, and other attempts to regulate every corner of the system.

With changes such as these, our <u>sick</u> care system will be fairer and more efficient, and will fulfill our obligation in social justice to provide quality medical treatment to every individual who needs it. But they are only first steps—and they are limited to the sick-care system.

The future of <u>health</u> care in America lies in our ability to reinvent our concept of health; look over the horizons of sick-care delivery and financing to see the entire universe of health, which includes research, health promotion, and disease prevention; face up to overarching trends in our society; and think through the ethical and moral conundrums that our exploding knowledge presents.

THE SYMPTOM SYNDROME

We must distinguish between the symptoms of ailments and their causes, and attend to the causes, recognizing that most are beyond the ken of the sick-care system.

Those who are addicted to tobacco, alcohol, and drugs, as well as those who abuse these substances, fill our emergency rooms and hospital beds. They spawn mental and physical illness not only among themselves, but among others ranging from family and friends to victims of their crimes and reckless conduct. Violence, poverty, environmental conditions such as lead poisoning and air pollution, and unsafe sex also crank up the speed of health care spending.

The medicine men and women have a role to play in combating these enemies of the nation's health, but often our best weapons are not medical. The rampant resort to guns in America's daily life is not something that doctors or nurses can change. They can only mend the wounds, refer the victims to sources of support and counseling, and call society's attention to the enormous health care costs of violence that television shows and movies portray as such casual entertainment.

In the mid-1960s, President Lyndon Johnson proposed laws to require that each gun be registered and each owner be licensed. Forty years later, the best we've done is the Brady Band-Aid, a five-day waiting period for the purchase of handguns, and a ban on some assault weapons, which are rarely involved in crimes and killing. It's time to put the Johnson proposal on the books. U.S. Senator Bill Bradley likens a federal license for every gun owner to the license required of every car driver.

Promiscuous sexual activity among teenagers is not something a doctor or nurse can stop, but it can spread AIDS and other sexually transmitted diseases and produce low-birthweight babies who require expensive medical treatment. The value vacuum in American society has led some public health officials to treat teenage sex as a physical health problem susceptible to health promotion and disease prevention programs stripped of any discussion of personal values.

But that is shoveling up behind the horse. Parents bear far more responsibility for the sexual permissiveness of our society and the health problems it creates. We have neglected the values that are foundations of morality and good health, and in their place sent a signal to teens that sex is perfectly acceptable, common, inevitable, and fun—but please take a moment to slip on a condom. In a world where rock groups sing "Me So Horny" and "Pop That Pussy"; where characters in daytime soap operas spend most of their time getting into or out of bed with each other; where vividly detailed sex is a mark of most best-selling books and blockbuster movies; where schoolchildren come home in time to watch Geraldo, Donahue, Oprah, and Montel parade guests who can glamorize every kind of kinky sexual experience—in such a world, what kind of sexual conduct do we expect from our teenagers?

The link between poverty and poor health is doorjamb tight. It cannot be broken by universal health insurance alone. Government must do its part to provide adequate resources to communities ravaged by poverty, violence, and inadequate housing, and lacking basic education, social, recreation, and public safety services.

Even where a fountain of health care services is available, we have not been able to get lots of individuals to drink the water. Indeed, many do not even know they're thirsty. Many doctors consider noncompliance with their instructions—to take a pill four times a day, quit smoking, stay away from fats, exercise an injured limb—their most daunting patient problem. Social workers have enormous difficulty getting poor pregnant women to take advantage of available prenatal care. The most affluent teens often eat the worst food. Busy businessmen fail to get periodic physical exams. Women don't go for Pap smears and mammograms even when they are fully covered by insurance.

We need to become as good at getting people to make timely use of available health care services as we are at getting them to buy sneakers and compact disks, watch movies, eat french fries, and wear Swatch watches. If we invested in health care marketing research the level of funds, energy, and brainpower we put into selling Coca-Cola and pizza, our sick-care bill would plummet. We can't change human nature, but we can do a better job at selling common sense and individual responsibility. We can shift our emphasis from the symptoms of disease and trauma to their causes.

THE WIDE WORLD OF HEALTH PROMOTION AND DISEASE PREVENTION

The single best hope for reining in costs, curbing pressures to ration, and extending the years of independent, healthy living lies in ourselves and our behavior. Our blithe romance with the wonders of treatment has led us to neglect disease prevention and health promotion, guaranteeing a steady grind of sick patients demanding ever more dazzling and expensive medical miracles.

Take tobacco. The highway to a tobacco-free America has many points of access, well beyond direct appeals to our citizens not to smoke or chew.

Cigarettes and smokeless tobacco should be taxed to the point where they are too expensive to be purchased by children. Vending machines should be outlawed. Sales to those under eighteen should be prohibited with stiff penalties, including closing down stores for repeated offenses, just as liquor licenses are suspended for bars that repeatedly sell to minors. Advertising should be restricted to the maximum extent consistent with the First Amendment and expenses for cigarette and smokeless tobacco advertising should not be tax deductible.

Tobacco advertising should be prohibited at all sporting events because such events tend to attract young audiences. Sixteen major league baseball parks ban tobacco advertising (and twenty ban smoking). Sale and advertising of tobacco products should be prohibited within ten blocks of any school. Teaching the dangers of smoking should be required in health education programs in elementary and high schools and in colleges, just as math and other subjects have course requirements.

Now that the dangers of secondhand smoke are clear, smoking should be banned in all enclosed public places: offices and factories, malls and restaurants, trains and planes. The owners of enclosed spaces used by the public—from airplanes to restaurants—should be held accountable for illnesses of their workers—airline attendants and waiters—due to secondhand smoke.

For illegal drugs such as cocaine, heroin, hallucinogens, and marijuana, the object is the same: Never use them.

Take alcohol. Beer and other alcoholic beverages should be treated differently because for most individuals, the object is moderation, not prohibition. The message for alcohol is more difficult to deliver, but a society that is so adroit at selling everything from Hula Hoops to Pet Rocks can figure out how to do it.

In any case, warnings should be required on all beer, wine, and liquor advertising, as Senator Strom Thurmond has suggested, and no alcoholic beverage advertising should be allowed on college campuses, in college publications, within ten blocks of any schools (a ban many cities are considering) or during television and radio broadcasts of college athletic events. States and localities should reduce the number of licenses granted to sell liquor in poor neighborhoods, and people convicted of drunk driving should forfeit their driver's licenses until they have completed education and treatment programs.

Take diet. Since the earliest days of the republic, agricultural interests have force-fed Americans through federal and state laws. Thanks to dairy interests, federal law requires that school lunch programs offer children milk at each meal and, until 1991, directed that anyone in the Navy receive a ration of butter each day. With our vastly increased knowledge of what constitutes healthy diet, laws relating to military rations and school lunch and breakfast programs should require that meals be low in fat and high in fiber and protein. The opportunities in the private sector are enormous; corporate cafeterias, college meal plans, airlines, and Amtrak can all serve healthful food.

For the elderly and those whose senior years are approaching, we must deliver the message that healthy habits such as a sound diet and regular exercise can offer years of additional independence and vibrant living. For each of us, young or old, black or white, poor or rich, the message of personal responsibility should be reinforced with financial incentives so that good health is not only fashionable, but also profitable. After all, we are fallible human beings, easily tempted, and we need all the carrots and sticks available to encourage us to pursue healthy life-styles.

THE RESEARCH BUDGET:
WINDOW ON TOMORROW'S HEALTH CARE

We must increase our investment in basic research and maintain our level of commitment to biomedical science, pharmaceuticals, and high technology, but a far larger share of our research dollars should be used to reduce and eliminate the problems that put people into the sick-care system and situations of dependency. That means a substantial investment in how and why individuals get hooked on tobacco, alcohol, and legal and illegal drugs, how to prevent experimentation that leads to addiction and abuse, and how to treat effectively those who get hooked.

Such research is especially important with respect to preteens and teens, who are so vulnerable and form so many habits that produce illness and disability in later life. If we could prevent our teens from becoming addicted to nicotine, we could save billions of dollars and untold human misery in later years—virtually no one starts smoking after the age of twenty-one—and we could go a long way toward reducing drug abuse, because the risk of twelve- to seventeen-year-olds using marijuana, heroin, or cocaine drops if they don't smoke cigarettes.

A major increase in research about aging—a "project independence" for senior citizens—is essential. Most individuals do not live much beyond eighty years. But many more are reaching eighty and millions are inching beyond this benchmark. For the elderly, the secret to a system of decent, affordable care is to maintain their independence as long as possible. Far more inquiry is needed into the conditions that render them dependent, notably Alzheimer's and other types of dementia, incontinence, fragile bones, and the basic mechanics of aging. As we eliminate, shorten, or reduce the impact of such ailments, we not only enhance the lives of the elderly, but also reduce the cost of their care.

THE DANGERS OF DISCOVERY

The most challenging task may be to deal with the confounding ethical and moral issues that medical science serves up almost daily.

Our scientific geniuses are not far from offering us ways to enhance and decrease all sorts of genetic odds. Ideally they will be able to enhance our resistance to cancer and cardiovascular disease and decrease proclivities to substance abuse and addiction, perhaps even violence.

They will almost certainly be able to manipulate genes to enhance scientific ability, athletic prowess, and physical beauty.

But do we have the ethical, moral, and legal geniuses to prevent genetic clinics from becoming little shops of horrors? As *The New Republic* reported, one sperm bank, California Cryobank, has been recruiting "brainy sperm" from Harvard University and the Massachusetts Institute of Technology, asking prospective donors whether they were of Jewish origin ("our Jewish clients want to know"), whether their family had a history of baldness, whether they were of "small, medium, or large" bone structure, and what the donor's academic achievements, such as SAT verbal and math scores, were.

Should we put the gene gurus to work if policy wonks in government conclude that we will need more neurologists or nuclear physicists in the next generation? Or that we need financial and economic manipulators to compete in the new global environment? Or greater linguistic capability to communicate better?

If we want to reduce crime, should we involuntarily sterilize perpetrators of certain crimes so they can't pass on their violent genes? Three strikes and you're sterile?

If we want to do better in the winter or summer Olympics, should we use our capability to manipulate genes to produce better skiers and swimmers? Taller basketball players? Should owners of professional teams rent wombs for heavier linemen and hockey goalies with better peripheral vision in the next generation?

If a mother will kill to have a daughter be the top cheerleader, or a competitor will bash an opponent's leg to win a skating championship, why wouldn't a woman want to manipulate the genes of her fetus to produce the next Miss America or gold medalist?

The issues surrounding the end of life are just as confounding. Are there any limits to organ transplants? Is everyone entitled? Can twenty-first-century supersurgeons switch organs around any way they want?

If painkillers accelerate death—as morphine suppresses the capacity of the cardiovascular system—should physicians pump more of them into terminally ill patients to reduce the length of hospital stays or the number of days private duty nurses are needed at home? If that seems farfetched, walk into a nursing home where patients are routinely drugged into a stupor in order to reduce the size of the staff needed to attend them.

Our mothers used to say there are things we're better off not knowing. But in our aggressive pursuit of knowledge and our insatiable insistence that we use everything we discover, that nostrum has become obsolete. If we cannot temper our rush to explore the unexplored, then we should learn from the lesson of Prometheus, who stole fire from the gods and was chained to a rock for his impertinence, that we, who are stealing the secrets of living cells, may get tangled in the chains of our own cleverness.

In another age, these ethical and moral questions would have stumped an Aristotle or Aquinas. But it is our age that must face them.

We confront them in a uniquely pluralistic society. America abounds with widely disparate religious beliefs: Catholics (split among themselves on many of these issues and often at variance with their pope), Jews (culturally united, but even more widely split as to religious beliefs among Reform, Conservative, and Orthodox), Muslims (our fastest-growing religion), Mormons, Christian Scientists, and fundamentalist and liberal Protestants ranging from the everything-is-sinful television preachers to the anything-goes Universalist church—to say nothing of aggressive secularists and atheists.

And we face them in a society dominated by relativism. One idea is as good as another. All views are entitled to equal weight. Any opinion on a problem is entitled to as much respect as any other. The gray of moral agnosticism paints over the once-familiar black and white of right and wrong.

In a free society, it is important to hear out varying viewpoints. But it is also essential to work to resolve these moral and ethical issues—realizing that few resolutions of such disquieting questions are written in biblical stone.

To that end, all sorts of forums should be open for their discussion: from the floors of Congress and chambers of the Supreme Court, to ethics advisory committees that can guide cabinet officers and governors, to hospital and corporate boardrooms. Many of these topics are not comfortable, much less familiar, for leaders of large institutions like Fortune 500 companies and managed-care networks intent on lowering prices to beat the competition. Nevertheless they are too close to the social bone marrow to leave to the politicians and physicians. The future of American health care, and perhaps the civility of our society and its capacity for compassion, depend on openly discussing them all and resolving as many as we can.

To appreciate the wrenching impact of our obsession to prolong life and produce flawless children, it must be seen in the contexts of the dawn of the four-generation society, the breakdown of the family, and the self-centered insistence of Americans that they have complete control over their own bodies and reproduction. In the increasingly common four-generation family, elderly grandparents, aging parents, young-adult children, and baby grandchildren create a tall order of expensive health needs. As parents wait till the last reproductive minute, they want a child as perfect as modern medicine can deliver.

High divorce rates and a mobile population add pressures to medicate and warehouse the elderly in nursing homes run by an industry racing toward $100 billion a year. With mounting bills to care for the sick and dependent elderly, the pressure to get rid of them is fomenting once-unthinkable thoughts—and acts—of euthanasia. What would have been guilty pleas to murder or manslaughter just a few years ago have become contested cases of "assisted suicide."

While these forces strain society's resources and test its moral fiber, the medical research community neglects the questions whose answers could reduce the increasing years of dependence among the elderly.

The continuing life of the contentious and cantankerous abortion debate will be remembered as a warmup compared to what is coming over euthanasia, the use of gene research, the future of organ transplants, and eugenics. Fetuses can't speak. But old people not only speak: In our democracy, they vote—and in higher turnouts than any other age group.

We cannot afford to postpone any longer wide-open public discussions of euthanasia and eugenics, however nasty they may become. Whose life is it—the patient's? God's? Who draws the lines between suicide, murder, and natural death? The oncologist? The patient? The spouse? The family doctor? The judge? A majority vote of the children? Can parents abort or discard an imperfect child? Who defines imperfection? Is it a matter solely between the doctor and the patient? Who is the patient? The fetus? The mother? The father? All of the above?

If we all don't get into these ethical waters, the currents will be driven by the nation's uninhibited infatuation with discovery and the premium our capitalist system puts on profits.

THE TECHNOLOGICAL IMPERATIVE

A technological imperative rules the American way of health: if a technology exists, it will be used widely with little consideration for its cost and effectiveness. Robert Reischauer, director of the Congressional Budget Office, hit the nail on the head: "In the health care world, invention is the mother of necessity. Once we discover something, we decide we need it."

Prenatal diagnosis technologies that researchers and doctors originally intended for high-risk pregnancies (where the mother is more than thirty-four years old or has a history of serious genetic abnormalities) are now routinely used by younger women and their doctors, despite the risk that performing the test may induce spontaneous abortion of what would otherwise be a normal pregnancy.

One young mother explained why, at age twenty-five, she decided to have an amniocentesis (a $1,000 to $2,500 prenatal test that can detect fetal abnormalities): "The technology exists. Why not take advantage of it?" Another said, "I didn't care if I wasn't in a high-risk group. . . . It was my right, and I wanted it done." Yet another simply feared the prospect of having an imperfect baby: "I didn't feel the trauma of losing a pregnancy was the same as the trauma of having an abnormal baby."

In the persistent parade of innovations that we call progress, new technologies have blurred the line between life and death and given doctors a remarkable ability to draw the line where they wish. Too often the power to postpone death is exercised without regard for how sickness, pain, and the indignities of the technologies themselves demean and even destroy personhood and deny the individual the right to a humane death. As the baby boom generation approaches its golden years, the magic of the medical mandrakes could detonate an explosion in sick-care spending to sustain the most marginal lives.

America's technological imperative promotes the rapid spread of innovative tools. Hospitals are constantly jumping over one another, like disks on a checkerboard, to be invested with the latest technological crown. A cease-fire is needed in this struggle, which has accelerated the medical equipment arms race with cost far beyond benefit to most Americans.

The nation needs a Medical Technology Nonproliferation Treaty. Under its terms, major institutions would share their expertise and technology, rather than needlessly duplicate them. From Oregon Health Sciences University Hospital and its surrounding community hospitals in Portland, to New York Hospital's network throughout the city's metropolitan area and the marriage of Brigham and Women's and Massachusetts General hospitals in Boston, temples of medicine across the nation have begun to consolidate their technological assets. These can be first steps in using medical miracles wisely and efficiently.

The next step is to ask, in a rigorous and systematic way, what purposes are served by each advance in medical technology. We must seek how best to use these advances to serve human needs, weighing the risks and benefits, the human and economic costs and blessings. These questions should continue to be asked long after technology is in place.

In the headlong rush for medical miracles, Americans have not explored these issues deeply enough. It is by exploring them, carefully and prayerfully, that we will move toward a society where the meaning of our lives matches the marvelous products of our labor. In this way, we can hammer out a technological morality for American medicine.

THE CULTURAL REVOLUTION

All of the above will help, but the high-five potential is in a cultural revolution to change the way American individuals and institutions view health.

Nowhere is a cultural revolution more urgent than in the American way of death, for it is here that the American way of health is in greatest danger of losing its human touch. The marvelous machines, potent procedures, and powerful pills have saved and extended the lives of thousands of patients who, years ago, would have had no hope of survival. But these wonders can also have a grotesque side, as distraught families and accommodating physicians perpetuate the lives of terminally ill patients, often for months, even years, with savage chemotherapy; with repeated, painful surgical procedures; and at the end with connections to intravenous needles and humming machines.

In a speech in Rome, Pope John Paul II reminded some two thousand Italian doctors,

> Technological development, characteristic of our time, is suffering from a fundamental ambivalence: While on the one hand it enables man to take in hand his own destiny, it exposes him on the other hand to the temptation of going beyond the limits of a reasonable dominion over nature, jeopardizing the very survival and integrity of the human person. . . . More often than is thought, in the very sphere of care for the sick person, his personal right to psychophysical integrity can be harmed with the exercise of what is actually violence: in the diagnostic investigation by means of complex procedures which are not infrequently traumatizing, in surgical treatment which now goes so far as to carry out the boldest interventions of destruction and reconstruction, in the case of organ transplants, in applied medical research, in the hospital organization itself.

Medical researchers and highly specialized physicians have a particular obligation to resist the temptation to encourage individuals to subject themselves to painful, dehumanizing tests and treatments, and enlist them in roll-of-the-dice experiments, when there is little or no hope of survival.

Ruth Good of Westport, Connecticut, went just about anywhere desperately seeking a cure for the breast cancer that was ravaging her body. Researchers eagerly subjected her to painful treatments and used her to test toxic drugs, in the hopes of discovering a cure for future patients; they knew she had no chance for survival. She was not accorded the respect due an individual willing to endure suffering that might help future victims of this dread disease. Instead, her husband said, his wife was treated "like a white rat" in a research lab.

Dying patients are particularly vulnerable because of their desperation. "The terminally ill have become our favorite research subjects," admits George Annas of Boston University's Schools of Medicine and Public Health. Doctors view them as subjects with nothing to lose. But the imminent reality of death does not justify the indiscriminate deployment of experimental treatments that sharpen a patient's suffering during the final days of life. Researchers and doctors tend to justify their experiments with the terminally ill by arguing that they are offering some hope, however microscopic. But transparently tiny specks of hope are not solid enough to support the dehumanizing crush of many of their treatments.

Many doctors pride themselves on their power to deploy weapons to battle the will of a body that is trying to die. To do more is where it's at. "There's a great pressure to do *something*," says Willet Whitmore, an attending surgeon emeritus at Memorial Sloan-Kettering Cancer Center. "If you don't do anything and things work out badly, you second-guess yourself and the patient's family second-guesses you." And if the patient dies after aggressive treatment, "you say, 'Well, I did all I can.' "

Here the patient's—victim's?—relatives and friends and the nation's legal system conspire to prolong the dance of death. Relatives press doctors to keep their loved ones alive. How many times they cry, "Can't you do anything to save my wife (child, parent, brother)?" and seek out doctor after doctor until one answers their plea. How few times do loved ones ask the doctor to ease the passage from life to death? Here the self-centeredness in the survivors can be as destructive as the mad scientist in the physician: For them, the comfortable future may lie in remembering that time of grief and confusion as one when "We made sure the doctors did everything they could for Mom. We had the finest specialists try everything in the most advanced hospital in New York."

If pressure the family places on the doctors to unsheathe all the knives and plug in all the machines to fend off imminent death is formidable, at least it comes in the form of a plea. The judges and lawyers make their case to sustain the terminally ill with an order. From them, the doctor attending the near dead feels the hot torch of malpractice litigation should he fail to resort to every tool at his disposal to save the dying patient. The result is too often a chasm between the patient's true needs and the demands of social custom, scientific ambition, misguided love, and a cockeyed legal system.

The specialization of practice, however necessary to keep up with the constant spin of the medical merry-go-round of innovation and newfound knowledge, all too often encourages this drift between a doctor's interests and a patient's needs. Specialists who treat the terminally ill are at particular risk of losing touch with the human needs of their desperate patients.

In September 1993, a sixty-one-year-old man, happily preparing for a comfortable retirement in good health, was suddenly stricken by a seizure and rushed to Princeton Medical Center's emergency room. Scans revealed a brain tumor. Four years earlier, a physician had removed a skin cancer from the man's back, which led the doctors to suspect the tumor was a metastasized melanoma, an incurable and deadly cancer.

Seeking the best medical care in the country, the man went to Memorial Sloan-Kettering Cancer Center in New York, where a highly skilled neurosurgeon recommended and performed surgery to remove the tumor. Three days later, the doctor found a second tumor. Again the neurosurgeon recommended and performed surgery. Ten days later, the doctor found a third tumor. This one, however, was inoperable. The neurosurgeon told the man that he couldn't do anything more and went on vacation, leaving a confusing array of specialists and interns to examine the patient and subject him to numerous tests before discharge without preparing him or his family for what was to come.

Within three days, the patient was back in the local hospital, unable to walk unassisted or speak clearly, incontinent and staggered by the viciously rapid spread of a disease that he had once expected to conquer. He died seven days later.

The only word the family received from the neurosurgeon was his bill for more than $20,000.

The neurosurgeon is undoubtedly overwhelmed with demands for his highly skilled services, performing one delicate operation after another in an effort to save cancer victims from life-threatening tumors. That's his job. That's what we pay him to do, and there aren't enough hours in the day for him to perform all the surgery asked of him. We don't pay him to hold the patient's hand or comfort distraught relatives. All the incentives in our medical, reimbursement, and legal systems nudge him to act in every case as he did in this one. Not only is he asked to perform more surgery than he can responsibly fit into his schedule, he must also stay abreast of the exploding knowledge in his field both to maintain his preeminence and to protect himself from the plaintiff's lawyer, who might ask, "Did you read the article by Dr. X?," or "Are you familiar with the work being done by Dr. Y?" when he is sued by the surviving spouse of a patient who died on the operating table. Yet, ironically, most malpractice lawsuits start with the plaintiff's dissatisfaction with the interpersonal process by which care is delivered; the way a doctor or nurse talks on the phone, delivers a diagnosis, or handles a patient or family's grief.

In the courtroom, our legal system has lost its common sense and ethical compass. It is telling physicians, Heal but don't touch. Judges and state laws impose legal obligations that compel doctors to maintain life. Numerous court decisions have required hospitals and doctors to keep comatose patients alive for months, even years, with machinery—just because the machinery exists. Once attached to artificial breathing or blood circulation systems, it can be virtually impossible to get unplugged.

One might well ask who is being served here: the patient or the machine. Where there is virtually no hope of a return to cognitive consciousness, much less any ability to exercise free will, the creation of God is robotized. Respect for the personhood of each individual is lost in the tangle of wires and tubes. Our legal system has lost sight of the appropriate goal of medical technology: to enhance our ability to be all we can be, not to reduce human life to breathing lungs and a beating heart.

Americans have a torrid affair with innovation that in health care amounts to worship of the newest technology and treatments. Alexis de Tocqueville, the gimlet-eyed tourist from France, wrote of his encounter with this passion in the nineteenth century as the "idea upon which a whole people direct their concerns." This romance with technology and gadgets has been embraced by every generation of Americans, with only an occasional bellow of dissent by iconoclasts like Henry David Thoreau, the apostle of the simple life. By and large, however, Americans do not accept Thoreau's austere maxim that "a man is rich according to the things he can do without."

The American way of health care and death need not accept Thoreau's maxim in order to bring the pendulum back to a decent, humane way of caring and dying. I do not mean euthanasia or "assisted death," which crosses the line between murder and suicide and, as Charles Krauthammer notes, "represents the worst instincts of medicine: the desire to dispense death," but a natural end of life in which an individual accepts the inevitability of death, and physicians and family try to ease the physical pain and emotional trauma.

For those of us who believe we are creatures of God born to serve Him on this earth until He calls us to an eternal reward, it means accepting His will. For those who profess no such belief but accept only a natural earthly order, it means recognizing the dignity of a human being in that order and accepting the individual's right to leave this world holding the hand of a spouse, child, or friend, perhaps at home, but in any case not simply tied to dripping tubes, breathing respirators, and blood pumps with their flashing electronic signals, and not, just as the lungs take their last breath and the heart records its last beat, electroshocked back from the dead for a brief period of terminal misery.

The deaths in 1994 of Richard Nixon and Jacqueline Kennedy Onassis may signal a turning point. With the whole world watching, we learned that each had signed a living will, expressing a desire to forgo the use of medical machinery that postpones imminent death. In one eulogy after another, Jacqueline Kennedy Onassis was praised for her grace under pressure as a thirty-four-year-old when President John Kennedy was assassinated thirty-one years earlier. But the grace and dignity with which she died may be her finest hour—and could have even more lasting personal influence on American social custom than the courage she displayed in 1963.

In 1990, Congress passed the Patient Self-Determination Act, which mandates that all Medicare recipients be given the opportunity to develop advance medical directives, such as durable powers of attorney and living wills, to escape a death tied to tubes and pumps. In a study of a geriatrics practice in Denver, doctors asked their patients about their wishes if they had a cardiac arrest during an acute illness. Forty-one percent said that they would want to undergo cardiopulmonary resuscitation. But after learning that their chances of survival and discharge from the hospital were 10 to 17 percent, half changed their minds and said they would not want to be resuscitated.

Unfortunately, too few people consider the difficult questions surrounding death and medical care until it is too late. In one study, two out of three patients with terminal cancer had not discussed these matters with their doctors. The most common reason given: "The subject never came up."

The financial sidebar of acceptance of death with dignity will be a significant cost savings since such a high share of Medicare expenditures is consumed during the final stage of life and, for many, in the final days and weeks. Inpatient hospital charges for Medicare patients with advance medical directives are almost 70 percent less than for those without such directives. Greater use of advance directives and hospice care is estimated to offer savings of $30 billion a year in health care spending. But any such savings are merely a bonus. More important, the relief of human pain for the patient and the family is incalculable.

The cultural pendulum may be inching back with respect to medical care generally. Doctors have traditionally recommended surgery for male patients with benign prostate enlargement. But some are using an interactive video developed by Dr. John Wennberg at Dartmouth to explain to patients the risks of such surgery, which can remedy a patient's pain and discomfort but may make him impotent and incontinent without increasing his life span. At Kaiser Permanente Denver Health Plan, the rate of prostate surgery has dropped more than 50 percent since 1989, when doctors began using the video.

Judges and lawmakers can nourish this cultural shift by making it clear that physicians and hospitals need not employ every extraordinary means at their disposal to keep us breathing. Family physicians can discuss, well in advance of terminal illness, the choices that their patients can make about extraordinary medical treatments. The religious community can, as moral theologians such as Richard McCormick and Bryan Hehir are doing, help their parishioners and congregants understand the acceptability, indeed desirability, of death with dignity and loved ones present.

THE HUMAN FACTOR

The medicine men and women of America have so wowed us with their wonders that we have lost sight of the human—psychological, emotional, and spiritual—implications of their discoveries.

On January 7, 1994, thirteen-year-old Teresa Hamilton, a severe diabetic, was admitted to the hospital and soon fell into a coma. When all efforts to revive her failed and the child's brain waves were unremittingly flat, the doctors pronounced her dead. Yet the machine that was forcing air into her lungs gave the appearance, if not the reality, that life remained in her small body. "They have claimed that she is brain dead, which is the clinical way of saying she's a goner," said her father. "But they've pursued with her care."

The parents refused to let the machine be turned off. The doctors and hospital administrators "want to call it quits," said Mr. Hamilton, but, "[we] believe that Teresa's showing us every sign that she's willing to fight." Mrs. Hamilton added, "When . . . I say, 'Teresa, would you move your leg for Mommy, please,' she moves her leg, not just a little bit, but she just raises her leg right up on the bed and . . . when I walk in the room and I say 'Hi' to her, she moves her body all over. The doctors are calling it spasms, and yet they've never seen her move, but this is one of the reasons why we believe that—that she's still there."

Doctors who coolly dismissed Teresa's movements as a spasmodic reflex bearing no signs of viable life may be losing their human touch. By treating what they considered a corpse and trying to give the parents time to come to grips with the loss of their daughter, the doctors led the parents to believe that Teresa was still alive. On March 3, Teresa went home, where the hospital continued to provide medical care and mechanical life support. Two months later her heart stopped beating and she was declared dead after an EMS team was unable to revive it. Medicaid picked up most of the $350,000 in medical bills that piled up after the family's private insurance had run out.

The sonogram lets thousands of pregnant women peek at the fetus they will someday deliver into the world. How many parents and grandparents have oohed and aahed at the fuzzy black-and-white print of their fetal child or grandchild, comfortably couched and nourished in its mother's womb? But that early snapshot of life can serve up wrenching decisions to parents it informs of heart blockages, defective kidneys, the potential that the mother might give birth to a child who could be on a respirator for life, may need a liver transplant within a year, or may live disabled forever. What to do? High-risk fetal surgery? Prepare for a life devoted to a dependent child? Turn the newborn over to an institution? Have an abortion, with its potential for causing lifelong guilt and emotional distress—and for many, such as Catholics and Muslims, self-conviction of murder?

A diagnosis of terminal cancer brings with it an arsenal of options: chemotherapy, invasive surgeries, and bone marrow transplants. They can destroy life or turn people into walking zombies. But they also hold the promise, however slim, of remission. Is the possibility of a few extra weeks or months of life worth the physical torture for the patient and emotional distress for the family? What is the patient to do?

Heart, lung, kidney, and liver transplants offer a chance for survival to patients who would have died just a few years ago. But they can fail—or give the patient years of critically disabled life. Some doctors make a transplant sound like capping a bad tooth. Others make it sound like a brush with death that the patient may not survive. Who helps the patient choose?

Respirators, dialysis, heart pumps, and electroshock can revive the near dead, without guarantees about what life will be like ever after and whether the patient will live free of the machines. Is a life tied to tubes and pumps a mechanical prison or a gift of extra time on earth? Should a wife keep her husband alive, or a parent his child, or a child her parent, under those circumstances? Does the patient have the power (right) to decide what to do? Do the relatives?

Scientists who make possible decisions such as these have usually moved on to their next challenge by the time the rest of us grapple with the consequences. Doctors are trained to perform the procedures and inform the patient of the pros and cons, risks and rewards of the medical options. But they are not trained to deal with the spiritual, psychological, and emotional pressures on the patients, spouses, parents, and children who must make the decisions.

We can live with the uncertainty. We can understand mistakes. But how do we survive the conscious decisions we must make as we confront the miracles of modern medicine? Our churches and synagogues, moral theologians and ethicists, judges and lawmakers must develop moral, psychological, and legal compasses and standards to help guide us through these painful decisions and relieve and comfort the consciences of the patient and loved ones. This is a difficult task, made far more complex by the real limits to knowledge and prognosis, and the fact that medicine, even at its best, is still more art than science. But it is a task for our time, and our religious leaders, legal scholars, and ethicists have not given it enough of their time and energy.

In our free, contentious society, the medical magicians have served up many questions that have no single ready answer. We need the patience to count to ten and hope for moderate progress toward consensus among our pluralistic people, rather than pressing impatiently for immediate national solutions. This may leave many of these questions to be answered in different ways by different communities. But quick national answers to deep questions of values and morals are usually imposed from above without sufficient attention to unintended consequences, and so they solve little and generate great strife. They tend to reflect not a consensus of the many, but the biases of a few.

Our medical researchers are doing their job pushing the envelope of knowledge, and their work should continue full speed ahead, conscious of its moral ramifications. It's the rest of us—lawyers, judges, clergy, practicing physicians, patients, and families—who must do our job of thinking through the moral, ethical, and human implications of the marvels our scientific genius serves up.

NO TRUST, NO NOTHIN'

By making the business of medicine more business and less medicine and by depersonalizing treatment with the profligate use of technology, the spiral of physician subspecialization, and the intrusion of government and insurance company bureaucrats into the art and practice of medicine—at a time when touching is more important than ever—we have laid down a chaff of distrust that is choking the growth of healthy doctor-patient relationships.

Under the best of circumstances, it is difficult to get patients to tell physicians the whole truth about their personal conduct that contributes to diseases such as cancer and heart ailments. Individuals often feel guilty about the smoking, eating, drinking, and exercise habits (to say nothing of the sexual adventures) that led to their afflictions, and doctors must first gain their patients' confidence before they can get them to open up. It takes time and a sensitive, shrewd, and perceptive physician to draw from a patient this important information, which is often essential for proper, cost-effective health promotion and treatment. It is essential for patients to have confidence in the judgment of their physicians to accept advice that asks them to do hard things—no butter on bread, getting up early to jog or walk, limiting consumption of alcoholic beverages at parties, entering a treatment program for drug or alcohol abuse.

Over the 1980s and early 1990s, a number of forces—well intentioned in their concentration on cutting costs—have combined to make this physician task infinitely more difficult. Government, insurance, and managed-care mavens pay for all the tests that attend an annual physical, but raise questions about the doctor's fee and don't believe or look kindly upon the physician who says he spent an hour (or two) talking to the patient. Health insurers under pressure to hold down costs tend to hassle doctors for "excessive" use of diagnostic procedures and treatment. The malpractice system and the failure of physician self-policing feed patients' doubts about the carefulness and competence of doctors, especially those who don't *do* enough.

Lack of trust is doing serious damage in many segments of our society—in politics, law, business—but nowhere is its potential for mischief greater than in medicine, where it encourages doctors to be skeptical of patients and patients to withhold the very trust that may be key to healing them. Patients cannot be expected in the 1990s to display the beautiful, blind faith of the bleeding woman who was confident she'd be healed if only she could touch Christ's robe. And doctors are not God. But patients' trust in their doctors' judgment and compliance with their course of treatment greatly enhance the chances of a prompt cure.

The consolidation of doctors, hospitals, and other providers into networks managing big blocks of customers can puncture the privacy essential to nourishing trust between doctor and patient. The fashionable practice of second-guessing medical judgments opens a patient's records to many eyes beyond the doctor's. Electronic billing and the computerization of patient records feed worries that individual privacy is not secure.

By commercializing medicine and making patients the commodities that doctors churn in and out of a system like customers at a discount retailer, we risk decimating the trust at the heart of effective health care. Dr. David Skinner, the head of New York Hospital–Cornell Medical Center, captured the dilemma when he spoke of physician training in the 1990s: "In the past we were taught, 'Don't miss anything—leave no stone unturned, always do the extra test.' Now, we're teaching our doctors: 'Resources are limited. Your goal is to find the most direct path to diagnosing the problem—using the fewest tests.' "

Patients must know that their doctor will act on their behalf, regardless of the financial consequences; HMOs that give doctors hefty bonuses for coming in "under budget" jeopardize this trust. Doctors must know that if they practice health promotion and disease prevention, they will be reimbursed for their effort. If they practice medicine with respect for a patient's desire to die with as much dignity and as little pain as possible, doctors must know they will not be sued and forced into financial ruin.

Medicine is a personal service business. Trust is important at every level: between doctors and nurses, between general practitioners and specialists, between hospital administrators and admitting and staff physicians, between managed-care executives and insurers and the doctors they pay, between bureaucrats administering Medicare and Medicaid and the physicians serving the programs' beneficiaries. Without a resurgence of trust, ensuring affordable, quality care for all can become a bureaucratic nightmare and an impossible dream.

Trust is easy to lose and oh-so-hard to regain. That is why the radical surgery proposed in this book must be done with such care. By using a butcher knife instead of a scalpel in the past, we have done serious damage to relationships throughout our health care system.

WHOSE RIGHT TO WHAT CARE?

Is everyone entitled to all the medical care he or she wants or can afford to buy?

A man or woman wants a highly experimental treatment for cancer or AIDS. Should an employer-funded medical plan be required to pay for it? Taxpayer-funded programs like Medicare or Medicaid?

A fertility clinic in Rome announced in 1993 that it had impregnated a sixty-one-year-old woman with a donor's eggs. A fifty-nine-year-old woman gave birth to twins thanks to in vitro fertilization. Should private and government plans pay for this newfound ability to impregnate women long past menopause? Do fifty-nine- and sixty-one-year-old women have a right to have children just because the technology is there, even though they are less likely to be alive through their baby's growth to adulthood? What about a seventy-five-year-old? Should Medicare pick up the tab in the United States?

What about a transplant for a sixty-five-year-old man who wants a young man's heart because his own is weakened by fatty diet, lack of exercise, and heavy smoking?

Should government programs fund sex-change operations? What about abortions for promiscuous teenagers high on pot or cocaine, liver transplants after a life of boozing, heart and lung transplants or coronary bypass surgery for two-packs-a-day cigarette smokers, long-shot treatments for infertility, kidney dialysis for seventy-year-olds: Is everyone entitled?

What is the role of personal responsibility in entitlement to care?

British doctors refused to perform the surgery on Harry Elphick unless he gave up his twenty-five-cigarettes-a-day habit. The doctors make no apology for their decision. "If you have the money to pay for treatment, you can have it even if you smoke five hundred cigarettes a day," his widow said. "They should operate on everyone." The National Health Service doctor thinks in terms of limited resources and an individual's responsibility to take care of himself. The widow looks at it as rationing by the thickness of the patient's wallet.

There will always be rationing by the thickness of a patient's wallet or the size of a patient's fist. In every civilization, money or power, or some combination, has accommodated the privileged with the best medical care available at the time. The British and other systems of universal coverage place limits on their health care budget by letting the elderly who need hip operations or other expensive procedures stand in lines so long they die before they reach the front. But well-to-do Britons buy out of it.

The American experiment in government-administered rationing is in Oregon. Not surprisingly, it is limited to the poor. Oregon for years did not put enough money into its Medicaid program to cover all poor people. It covered only the poorest, giving them the care they needed, whatever the ailment. Then the state decided to change its method of rationing. It would give all the poor people only some care—and cut the state's Medicaid budget in the process.

Through a series of public town meetings and computer calculations, the state listed, in order of priority by costs and benefits, 696 treatments for medical conditions. In 1994, the legislature provided funds to cover the first 565 procedures. As a result, Oregon Medicaid patients who need the other 131 treatments—including those for chronic back pain, repair of spinal deformities, transplants for liver cancer, medical therapy for acute viral hepatitis, or chemotherapy, radiation, and surgery for cancers with less than a 5 percent survival rate for five years—are turned away to a life of pain or disability, or condemned to death.

We are heading down this dark road without the light of careful moral thought and concerted attempts to follow better avenues. In bowing to their panic over health care costs, proponents of rationing invariably promote it for someone else—and without trying to contain costs aggressively.

Rationing, by whatever means, is a macabre dance of despair, especially in a society that has only recently begun to invest serious energies in making its health care system cost-effective. Until our nation has turned its head to cutting costs and our people have accepted far more responsibility for their own health, a resort to government-imposed rationing should be seen as a cop-out that will visit a special savagery on the poor, another way of continuing the nation's present rationing by wallet thickness.

We have the resources to preserve the quality of our globally preeminent health care system while making its riches and miracles available to all. What we need is the focus and will to confront the tough problems: to attack rampant substance abuse and addiction, to take the profits out of poor health, to reset the research scales more toward eliminating disability than fending off death, to make timely investments in research and treatment of our children and teenagers, to encourage health promotion and disease prevention, to clean up our corrupt system of privately bankrolling politicians, to think through the ethical and moral dilemmas our medical miracles pose, and to assert our human dominion over technology.

As each of us takes scalpel in hand to help transform America's health care system, the first radical surgery to be performed—and the most delicate and demanding—is on ourselves. Health care is above all a ministry, not an industry, and we, as well as doctors and nurses, have an obligation to minister to our own health.

HIPPOCRATIC OATH

I swear by Apollo the physician, by Aesculapius, Hygeia, and Panacea, and I take to witness all the gods, all the goddesses, to keep according to my ability and my judgment the following Oath:

To consider dear to me as my parents him who taught me this art; to live in common with him and if necessary to share my goods with him; to look upon his children as my own brothers, to teach them this art if they so desire without fee or written promise; to impart to my sons and the sons of the master who taught me and the disciples who have enrolled themselves and have agreed to the rules of the profession, but to these alone, the precepts and the instruction. I will prescribe regimen for the good of my patients according to my ability and my judgment and never do harm to anyone. To please no one will I prescribe a deadly drug, nor give advice which may cause his death. Nor will I give a woman a pessary to procure abortion. But I will preserve the purity of my life and my art. I will not cut for stone, even for patients in whom the disease is manifest; I will leave this operation to be performed by practitioners (specialists in this art). In every house where I come I will enter only for the good of my patients, keeping myself far from all intentional ill-doing and all seduction, and especially from the pleasures of love with women or with men, be they free or slaves. All that may come to my knowledge in the exercise of my profession or outside of my profession or in daily commerce with men, which ought not to be spread abroad, I will keep secret and will never reveal. If I keep this oath faithfully, may I enjoy my life and practice my art, respected by all men and in all times, but if I swerve from it or violate it, may the reverse be my lot.

ACKNOWLEDGMENTS

Over the years, so many individuals and experiences have influenced my thinking about America's health care system that it's difficult to single out a few.

Karen Davis and Julie Richmond gave me my basic education in the field and, in numerous conversations and his clear and compassionate books and articles, Dick McCormick sharpened my awareness of the excruciating ethical issues modern medicine serves up to individuals and families.

Several colleagues read all or parts of this manuscript at various stages: Greg Anrig, Jr., Fred Bohen, Hale Champion, Richard Cotton, Basil Henderson, Sue Kaplan, Herb Kleber (Chapter 4), Dick McCormick (Chapters 3 and 9), and Steve Schroeder.

My wife, Hilary, not only read the manuscript; she put up with my writing and researching over two years of early mornings and weekends, as did our children, Mark, Joe, Claudia, Brooke, and Frick, when they came to visit us in Roxbury. For her insights and all their understanding, I am especially grateful.

My colleague in working on this book was Jeanne Reid. She's an unusually intelligent and devoted young professional, with a maturity of judgment far beyond her years and a marvelous sense of humor. A lot of her is in this book and it's a more thoughtful and informed piece of work because of that. She has a brilliant career in health and social policy ahead of her and the nation will benefit from her commitment.

Matt Dolan, who also assisted with the research, and Leigh Hallingby were invaluable in the tedious but critical task of fact checking, and the library staff at Dewey Ballantine was most helpful. Donna McCreadie, Mary Lou Risley, and Joseph White helped with various drafts of the manuscript, Jo Ann McCauley kept me on schedule during some trying months, and Sue Brown kept the Center on Addiction and Substance Abuse at Columbia University running smoothly.

Peter Osnos once again edited with extraordinary perception and good humor, and he was ably assisted, as was I, by Elizabeth Rapoport. Mort Janklow is not only a friend and agent, he's an enthusiastic and wise adviser.

They and lots of others helped, but I alone bear responsibility for what's between these pages.

J.A.C., Jr.

November 1994

BIBLIOGRAPHY

In addition to the following sources, I have used numerous magazine and newspaper articles, notably from *America, The Baltimore Sun, Business Week, Common Cause Magazine, Congressional Quarterly, Forbes, Fortune, Governing, The Los Angeles Times, Medical Economics, Modern Healthcare, National Journal, The New Republic, The New York Times, Newsweek, Time, USA Today, The Wall Street Journal*, and *The Washington Post*.

CHAPTER 2. THE CUSP OF CHAOS

BOOKS AND REPORTS:

American Hospital Association. *Hospital Statistics, 1993–1994*. Chicago: AHA, 1993.

American Medical Association. *Physician Characteristics and Distribution in the U.S.* Chicago: AMA, 1994.

———. *Socioeconomic Characteristics of Medical Practice*. Chicago: AMA, 1994.

Congressional Budget Office. *Economic Implications of Rising Health Care Costs*. Washington, DC: CBO, October 1992.

———. *Projections of National Health Expenditures*. Washington, DC: CBO, October 1992.

Day, Jennifer C. *Population Projections of the United States by Age, Sex, Race, and Hispanic Origin: 1992 to 2050*. Washington, DC: Bureau of the Census, Current Population Reports, 1992.

Department of Commerce. *U.S. Industrial Outlook 1994*. Washington, DC: DOC, January 1994.

General Accounting Office. *Health Insurance: Vulnerable Payers Lose Billions to Fraud and Abuse.* Washington, DC: GAO, May 1992.

————. *Prescription Drugs: Companies Typically Charge More in the United States Than in Canada.* Washington, DC: GAO, September 1992.

————. *Prescription Drugs: Companies Typically Charge More in the United States Than in the United Kingdom.* Washington, DC: GAO, January 1994.

————. *Prescription Drugs: Spending Controls in Four European Countries.* Washington, DC: GAO, May 1994.

Health Insurance Association of America. *Source Book of Health Insurance Data, 1993.* Washington, DC: HIAA, 1994.

National Center for Health Statistics. *Health United States, 1993.* Hyattsville, MD: Public Health Service, 1994.

Office of Management and Budget. *Budget of the United States Government, Fiscal Year 1994.* Washington, DC: OMB, 1993.

Office of Technology Assessment. *The Continuing Challenge of Tuberculosis.* Washington, DC: OTA, September 1993.

Physician Payment Review Commission. *Annual Report to Congress, 1994.* Washington, DC: PPRC, 1994.

Prospective Payment Assessment Commission. *Medicare and the American Health Care System: Report to the Congress.* Washington, DC: Pro-PAC, June 1994.

Service Employees International Union. *The National Nurse Survey.* Washington, DC: SEIU, 1992.

Special Committee on Aging, U.S. Senate. *Aging America: Trends and Projections.* Washington, DC: Dept. of Health and Human Services, 1991.

Subcommittee on Oversight and Investigations of the Committee on Energy and Commerce, U.S. House of Representatives. *Less Than the Sum of Its Parts: Reforms Needed in the Organization, Management, and Resources of the Food and Drug Administration's Center for Devices and Radiological Health.* Washington, DC: U.S. Government Printing Office, 1993.

ARTICLES:

Ayanian, John Z., Betsy A. Kohler, Toshi Abe, and Arnold Epstein. "The Relation Between Health Insurance Coverage and Clinical Outcomes Among Women with Breast Cancer." New England Journal of Medicine 329 (July 29, 1993), 326–331.

Barrand, Nancy, Alan Cohen, Anne Gauthier, and Deborah Rogal. "Administrative Costs in the U.S. Health Care System: The Problem or the Solution?" *Inquiry* 29 (Fall 1992), 308–320.

Bernstein, Steven J., Lee H. Hilborne, Lucian L. Leape, Mary E. Fiske, Rolla Edward Park, Caren J. Kamberg, and Robert H. Brook. "The Appro-

priateness of Use of Coronary Angiography in New York State."
JAMA 269 (February 10, 1993), 766–769.

Bernstein, Steven J., Elizabeth A. McGlynn, Albert L. Siu, Carol P. Roth, Marjorie J. Sherwood, Joan W. Keesey, Jacqueline Kosecoff, Nicholas R. Hicks, and Robert H. Brook. "The Appropriateness of Hysterectomy." *JAMA* 269 (May 12, 1993), 2398–2402.

Brook, Robert H. "Maintaining Hospital Quality." *JAMA* 270 (August 25, 1993), 985–987.

Braveman, Paula A., Susan Egerter, Trude Bennett, and Jonathan Showstack. "Differences in Hospital Resource Allocation Among Sick Newborns According to Insurance Coverage." *JAMA* 266 (December 18, 1991), 330–339.

Burner, Sally T., Daniel R. Waldo, and David R. McKusick. "National Health Expenditure Projections Through 2030." *Health Care Financing Review* 14 (Fall 1992), 1–29.

Burstin, Helen R., Stuart R. Lipsitz, and Troyen A. Brennan. "Socioeconomic Status and Risk for Substandard Medical Care." *JAMA* 268 (November 4, 1992), 2383–2387.

Burstin, Helen R., Stuart R. Lipsitz, Steven Udvarhelyi, and Troyen A. Brennan. "The Effect of Hospital Financial Characteristics on Quality of Care." *JAMA* 270 (August 18, 1993), 845–849.

Chassin, Mark R., Robert H. Brook, R. E. Park, Joan Keesey, Arlene Fink, Jacqueline Kosecoff, Katherine Kahn, Nancy Merrick, and David Solomon. "Variations in the Use of Medical and Surgical Services by the Medicare Population." *NEJM* 314 (January 30, 1986), 285–290.

Chassin, Mark R., Jacqueline Kosecoff, R. E. Park, Constance M. Winslow, Katherine L. Kahn, Nancy J. Merrick, Joan Keesey, Arlene Fink, David H. Solomon, and Robert H. Brook. "Does Inappropriate Use Explain Geographic Variations in the Use of Health Care Services?" *JAMA* 258 (November 13, 1987), 2533–2537.

Cowan, Cathy A., and Patricia A. McDonnell. "Business, Households and Governments: Health Spending, 1991." *Health Care Financing Review* 14 (Spring 1993), 227–248.

Every, Nathan R., Eric B. Larson, Paul E. Litwin, Charles Maynard, Stephen D. Fihn, Mickey S. Eisenberg, Alfred P. Hallstrom, Jenny S. Martin, and W. Douglas Weaver. "The Association Between On-Site Cardiac Catheterization Facilities and the Use of Coronary Angiography After Acute Myocardial Infarction." *NEJM* 329 (August 19, 1993), 546–551.

Farrow, Diana C., William C. Hunt, and Jonathan M. Samet. "Geographic Variation in the Treatment of Localized Breast Cancer." *NEJM* 326 (April 23, 1992), 1097–1101.

Franks, Peter, Carolyn M. Clancy, and Marthe R. Gold. "Health Insurance and Mortality." *JAMA* 270 (August 11, 1993), 737–741.

Graboys, Thomas, Beth Biegelsen, Steven Lampert, Charles Blatt, and Bernard Lown. "Results of a Second-Opinion Trial Among Patients Recommended for Coronary Angiography." *JAMA* 268 (November 11, 1992), 2537–2540.

Iglehart, John K. "The American Health Care System—Medicare." *NEJM* 327 (November 12, 1992), 1467–1472.

Kaitin, Kenneth I., Michael Manocchia, Mark Seibring, and Louis Lasagna. "The New Drug Approvals of 1990, 1991, and 1992: Trends in Drug Development." *Journal of Clinical Pharmacology* 34 (February 1994), 120–127.

Kjerulff, Kristen, Patricia Langenberg, and Gay Guzinski. "The Socioeconomic Correlates of Hysterectomies in the United States." *American Journal of Public Health* 83 (January 1993), 106–108.

Leape, Lucian L., Lee H. Hilborne, Rolla Edward Park, Steven J. Bernstein, Caren J. Kamberg, Marjorie Sherwood, and Robert H. Brook. "The Appropriateness of Use of Coronary Artery Bypass Graft Surgery in New York State." *JAMA* 269 (February 10, 1993), 753–760.

Lu-Yao, Grace L., Dale McLerran, John Wasson, and John E. Wennberg. "An Assessment of Radical Prostatectomy." *JAMA* 269 (May 26, 1993), 2633–2636.

Medicaid Access Study Group. "Access of Medicaid Recipients to Outpatient Care." *NEJM* 330 (May 19, 1994), 1426–1430.

Schieber, George J., Jean-Pierre Poullier, and Leslie M. Greenwald. "Health System Performance in OECD Countries, 1980–1992." *Health Affairs* 13 (Fall 1994), 100–112.

Shulkin, David J., Alan L. Hillman, and William M. Cooper. "Reasons for Increasing Administrative Costs in Hospitals." *Annals of Internal Medicine* 119 (July 1, 1993), 74–78.

Thorpe, Kenneth. "Inside the Black Box of Administrative Costs." *Health Affairs* 11 (Summer 1992), 41–55.

Weissman, Joel S., Constantine Gatsonis, and Arnold M. Epstein. "Rates of Avoidable Hospitalization by Insurance Status in Massachusetts and Maryland." *JAMA* 268 (November 4, 1992), 2388–2394.

Welch, W. Pete, Mark E. Miller, H. Gilbert Welch, Elliott S. Fisher, and John E. Wennberg. "Geographic Variation in Expenditures for Physician Services in the United States." *NEJM* 328 (March 4, 1993), 621–627.

Wennberg, John E., Jean L. Freeman, Roxanne M. Shelton, and Thomas A. Bubolz. "Hospital Use and Mortality Among Medicare Beneficiaries in Boston and New Haven." *NEJM* 321 (October 26, 1989), 1168–1173.

Wenneker, Mark B., Joel S. Weissman, and Arnold M. Epstein. "The Association of Payer with Utilization of Cardiac Procedures in Massachusetts: How Who Pays the Bill Affects Cardiac Care and Treatment." *JAMA* 264 (September 12, 1990), 1255–1261.

Wiener, Joshua, and Raymond Hanley. "Winners and Losers: Primary and

High-Tech Care Under Health Care Rationing." *The Brookings Review* 10 (Fall 1992), 46–49.

Winslow, Constance M., David H. Solomon, Mark R. Chassin, Jacqueline Kosecoff, Nancy J. Merrick, and Robert H. Brook. "The Appropriateness of Carotid Endarterectomy." *NEJM* 318 (March 24, 1988), 721–727.

Woolhandler, Steffie, and David U. Himmelstein. "The Deteriorating Administrative Efficiency of the U.S. Health Care System." *NEJM* 324 (May 2, 1991), 1253–1258.

Woolhandler, Steffie, David U. Himmelstein, and James P. Lewontin. "Administrative Costs in U.S. Hospitals." *NEJM* 329 (August 5, 1993), 400–403.

CHAPTER 3. RECONCEIVING HEALTH: FROM TOP TO BOTTOM

BOOKS AND REPORTS:

American Medical Association. *Factors Contributing to the Health Care Cost Problem.* Chicago: AMA, March 1993.

———. *Violence: A Compendium from JAMA, American Medical News, and the Specialty Journals of the American Medical Association.* Chicago: AMA, 1992.

Bureau of the Census, Current Population Reports. *Poverty in the United States: 1992.* Washington, DC: Dept. of Commerce, 1993.

Callahan, Daniel. *What Kind of Life: The Limits of Medical Progress.* New York: Simon and Schuster, 1990.

Center for Population Options. *Teenage Pregnancy and Too-Early Childbearing: Public Costs, Personal Consequences.* Washington, DC: Center for Population Options, 1992.

Committee on Measuring Lead in Critical Populations, National Research Council. *Measuring Lead Exposure in Infants, Children, and Other Sensitive Populations.* Washington, DC: National Academy Press, 1993.

Committee on Ways and Means, U.S. House of Representatives. *Overview of Entitlement Programs: 1994 Green Book.* Washington, DC: U.S. Government Printing Office, 1994.

National Highway Traffic Safety Administration. *Evaluation of the Effectiveness of Occupant Protection: Interim Report.* Washington, DC: NHTSA, June 1992.

National Safety Council. *Accident Facts.* Itasca, IL: NSC, 1993.

Newhouse, Joseph P., and the Insurance Experiment Group. *Free for All? Lessons from the RAND Health Insurance Experiment.* Cambridge, MA: Harvard University Press, 1993.

Office of Technology Assessment. *Benefit Design: Patient Cost-Sharing.* Washington, DC: OTA, September 1993.

———. *Life-Sustaining Technologies and the Elderly.* Washington, DC: OTA, 1987.

Public Health Service and Battelle Centers for Public Health Research and Evaluation. *For a Healthy Nation: Returns on Investment in Public Health.* Washington, DC: Dept. of Health and Human Services, 1994.

Restak, Richard M. *Receptors.* New York: Bantam Books, 1994.

Starr, Paul. *The Logic of Health Care Reform.* New York: Penguin Books, 1994.

ARTICLES:

Brown, Martin L., Larry G. Kessler, and Fred G. Rueter. "Is the Supply of Mammography Machines Outstripping Need and Demand?" *Annals of Internal Medicine* 113 (October 1, 1990), 547–552.

Chilmonczyk, Barbara A., Luis M. Salmun, Keith N. Megathlin, Louis M. Neveux, Glenn E. Palmaki, George J. Knight, Andrea J. Pulkkinen, and James E. Haddow. "Association Between Exposure to Environmental Tobacco Smoke and Exacerbations of Asthma in Children." *NEJM* 328 (June 10, 1993), 1665–1669.

Collins, James J. and Pamela M. Messerschmidt. "Epidemiology of Alcohol-Related Violence." *Alcohol Health & Research World* 17, no. 2 (1993), 93–100.

Dockery, Douglas W., Arden Pope, Xiping Xu, John D. Spengler, James H. Ware, Martha E. Fay, Benjamin G. Ferris, and Frank E. Speizer. "An Association Between Air Pollution and Mortality in Six U.S. Cities." *NEJM* 329 (December 9, 1993), 1753–1759.

Eisenberg, David M., Ronald C. Kessler, Cindy Foster, Frances E. Norlock, David R. Calkins, and Thomas L. Delbanco. "Unconventional Medicine in the United States—Prevalence, Costs and Patterns of Use." *NEJM* 328 (January 28, 1993), 246–252.

Flitcraft, Anne. "Physicians and Domestic Violence: Challenges for Prevention." *Health Affairs* 12 (Winter 1993), 154–161.

Friedman, Emily. "Money Isn't Everything: Nonfinancial Barriers to Access." *JAMA* 271 (May 18, 1994), 1535–1538.

Gaylin, Willard. "Faulty Diagnosis." *Harper's* 287 (October 1993), 57–64.

Guralnik, Jack M., Kenneth C. Land, Dan Blazer, Gerda G. Fillenbaum, and Laurence G. Branch. "Educational Status and Active Life Expectancy Among Older Blacks and Whites." *NEJM* 329 (July 8, 1993), 110–116.

Kahn, Katherine L., Marjorie L. Pearson, Ellen R. Harrison, Katherine A. Desmond, William H. Rogers, Lisa V. Rubenstein, Robert H. Brook, and Emmett B. Keeler. "Health Care for Black and Poor Hospitalized Medicare Patients." *JAMA* 271 (April 20, 1994), 1169–1174.

Kirby, Douglas, Lynn Short, Janet Colins, Deborah Rugg, Lloyd Kolbe, Marion Howard, Brent Miller, Freya Sonenstein, and Laurie S. Zabin. "School-Based Programs to Reduce Sexual Risk Behaviors: A Review of Effectiveness." *Public Health Report* 109 (May–June 1994), 339–360.

Kogan, Michael D., Milton Kotelchuck, Greg R. Alexander, and Wayne E. Johnson. "Racial Disparities in Reported Prenatal Care Advice from Health Care Providers." *American Journal of Public Health* 84 (January 1994), 82–88.

Langone, John. "The Making of a Good Doctor." *America* 170 (January 29, 1994), 407.

Max, Wendy, and Dorothy P. Rice. "Shooting in the Dark: Estimating the Cost of Firearm Injuries." *Health Affairs* 12 (Winter 1993), 171–185.

McCormick, Richard A. "Value Variables in the Health-Care Reform Debate." *America* 168 (May 29, 1993), 7–13.

McGinnis, J. Michael, and William H. Foege. "Actual Causes of Death in the United States." *JAMA* 270 (November 10, 1993), 2207–2212.

Miller, Ted R., Mark A. Cohen, and Shelli B. Rossman. "Victim Costs of Violent Crime and Resulting Injuries." *Health Affairs* 12 (Winter 1993), 187–197.

Pappas, Gregory, Susan Queen, Wilbur Hadden, and Gail Fisher. "The Increasing Disparity in Mortality Between Socioeconomic Groups in the United States, 1960–1986." *NEJM* 329 (July 8, 1993), 103–109.

Peterson, Eric D., Steven M. Wright, Jennifer Daley, and George Thibault. "Racial Variation in Cardiac Procedure Use and Survival Following Acute Myocardial Infarction in the Department of Veterans Affairs." *JAMA* 271 (April 20, 1994), 1175–1180.

Relman, Arnold S. "What Market Values Are Doing to Medicine." *Atlantic Monthly* 269 (March 1992), 99–106.

Schieber, George J., Jean-Pierre Poullier, and Leslie M. Greenwald. "Health System Performance in OECD Countries, 1980–1992." *Health Affairs* 13 (Fall 1994), 100–112.

Starfield, Barbara. "Effects of Poverty on Health Status." *Bulletin of the New York Academy of Health* 68 (January–February 1992), 17–24.

Syme, S. Leonard. "Social Determinants of Disease." In *Maxcy-Rosenau-Last Public Health and Preventive Medicine,* ed. John M. Last and Robert B. Wallace. Norwalk, CT: Appleton and Lange, 1992, 687–700.

Weiss, Kevin B., Peter J. Gergen, and Thomas A. Hodgson. "An Economic Evaluation of Asthma in the United States." *NEJM* 326 (March 26, 1992), 862–866.

Zell, Elizabeth R., Vance Dietz, John Stevenson, Stephen Cochi, and Richard H. Bruce. "Low Vaccination Levels of U.S. Preschool and School-age Children." *JAMA* 271 (March 16, 1994), 833–839.

CHAPTER 4. PUBLIC HEALTH ENEMY NUMBER ONE

BOOKS AND REPORTS:

Anno, B. Jaye. *Prison Health Care: Guidelines for the Management of an Adequate Delivery System.* Washington, DC: National Commission on Correctional Health Care, Dept. of Justice, March 1991.

Commission on Substance Abuse at Colleges and Universities. *Rethinking Rites of Passage: Substance Abuse on America's Campuses.* New York: Center on Addiction and Substance Abuse at Columbia University (CASA), June 1994.

General Accounting Office. *Bureau of Prisons Health Care: Inmates' Access to Health Care Is Limited by Lack of Clinical Staff.* Washington, DC: GAO, February 1994.

———. *Drug-Exposed Infants, A Generation at Risk.* Washington, DC: GAO, June 1990.

Gerstein, Dean R., Robert A. Johnson, Henrick J. Harwood, Douglas Fountain, Natalie Suter, and Kathryn Malloy. *Evaluating Recovery Services: The California Drug and Alcohol Treatment Assessment (CALDATA).* Sacramento, CA: California Dept. of Alcohol and Drug Programs, 1994.

Johnston, Lloyd D., Patrick M. O'Malley, and Herald G. Bachman. *National Survey Results on Drug Use from Monitoring the Future Study, 1975–1992.* 2 vols. Rockville, MD: National Institute on Drug Abuse, 1993.

Maguire, Kathleen, Ann L. Pastore, and Timothy J. Flanagan, eds. *Sourcebook of Criminal Justice Statistics, 1992.* Washington, DC: Bureau of Justice Statistics, 1993.

Mauer, Marc. *Americans Behind Bars: One Year Later.* Washington, DC: The Sentencing Project, February 1992.

Merrill, Jeffrey C., Kimberley S. Fox, and Han-Hua Chang. *The Cost of Substance Abuse to America's Health Care System: Medicaid Hospital Costs.* New York: CASA, July 1993.

———. *The Cost of Substance Abuse to America's Health Care System: Medicare Hospital Costs.* New York: CASA, May 1994.

Merrill, Jeffrey, Kimberley S. Fox, Jennifer C. Friedman, and Gerald E. Pulver. *Substance Abuse and Women on Welfare.* New York: CASA, June 1994.

National Commission on AIDS. *America Living with AIDS: Transforming Anger, Fear, and Indifference into Action.* Washington, DC: NCAIDS, 1991.

———. *HIV Disease in Correctional Facilities.* Washington, DC: NCAIDS, March 1991.

———. *The Twin Epidemics of Substance Abuse and HIV.* Washington, DC: NCAIDS, July 1991.

National Institute on Alcohol Abuse and Alcoholism. *Eighth Special Report to the U.S. Congress on Alcohol and Health, From the Secretary of Health and Human Services*. Rockville, MD: NIAAA, September 1993.

National Institute on Drug Abuse. *Drug Abuse and Drug Abuse Research, The Third Triennial Report to Congress from the Secretary, Department of Health and Human Services*. Rockville, MD: NIDA, 1991.

Novick, Emily, and Barbara Anderson. *Fetal Alcohol Syndrome and Pregnant Women Who Abuse Alcohol: An Overview of the Issue and the Federal Response*. Washington, DC: Dept. of Health and Human Services, Division of Children and Youth Policy, February 1992.

Office of Health and Environmental Assessment. *Respiratory Health Effects of Passive Smoking: Lung Cancer and Other Disorders*. Washington, DC: Environmental Protection Agency, December 1992.

Office of National Drug Control Policy. *National Drug Control Strategy*. Washington, DC: The White House, Office of National Drug Control Policy, February 1994.

Office on Smoking and Health. *The Health Benefits of Smoking Cessation*. Rockville, MD: Dept. of Health and Human Services, Office on Smoking and Health, 1990.

———. *Nicotine Addiction: The Health Consequences of Smoking. A Report of the Surgeon General*. Rockville, MD: HHS, Office on Smoking and Health, 1988.

———. *Preventing Tobacco Use Among Young People. A Report of the Surgeon General*. Rockville, MD: HHS, Office on Smoking and Health, 1994.

———. *Reducing the Health Consequences of Smoking: 25 Years of Progress. A Report of the Surgeon General*. Rockville, MD: HHS, Office on Smoking and Health, 1989.

———. *Smoking and Health. A Report of the Surgeon General*. Washington, DC: HHS, Office on Smoking and Health, 1979.

U.S. Surgeon General's Advisory Committee. *Smoking and Health*. Washington, DC: Public Health Service, 1964.

Zawitz, Marianne W., ed. *Drugs, Crime, and the Justice System*. Washington, DC: Bureau of Justice Statistics, December 1992.

ARTICLES:

Adams, Wendy L., Zhong Yuan, Joseph J. Barboriak, and Alfred Rimm. "Alcohol-Related Hospitalizations of Elderly People." *JAMA* 270 (September 8, 1993), 1222–1225.

Baldwin, W. Andrew, Brian A. Rosenfeld, Michael J. Breslow, Timothy G. Buchman, Clifford S. Deutschman, and Richard D. Moore. "Substance Abuse–Related Admissions to Adult Intensive Care." *Chest* 103 (January 1993), 21–25.

Bloch, Alan B., George M. Cauthen, Ida M. Onorato, Kenneth G. Dansbury,

Gloria D. Kelly, Cynthia R. Driver, and Dixie E. Snider. "Nationwide Survey of Drug-Resistant Tuberculosis in the United States." *JAMA* 271 (March 2, 1994), 665–671.

Hoffman, Robert S., and Lewis R. Goldfrank. "The Impact of Drug Abuse and Addiction on Society." *Emergency Medicine Clinics of North America* 8 (August 1990), 467–480.

Inciardi, James A., and Duane C. McBride. "Legalization, A High-Risk Alternative in the War on Drugs." *American Behavioral Scientist* 32 (January/February 1989), 259–289.

Kleber, Herbert D. "Our Current Approach to Drug Abuse—Progress, Problems, Proposal." *NEJM* 330 (February 5, 1994), 361–365.

Lowry, Richard, Deborah Holtzman, Benedict I. Truman, Laura Kann, Janet L. Collins, and Lloyd J. Kolbe. "Substance Use and HIV-related Sexual Behaviors Among U.S. High School Students: Are They Related?" *American Journal of Public Health* 84 (July 1994), 1116–1120.

Milk, Leslie, and Harry Jaffe. "Saturday Night." *The Washingtonian* 28 (September 1993), 78–89.

Pelletier, Andrew, George T. DiFerdinando, Abby J. Greenberg, Daniel M. Sosin, Wilbur D. Jones, Alan B. Bloch, and Charles L. Woodley. "Tuberculosis in a Correctional Facility." *Archives of Internal Medicine* 153 (December 13, 1993), 2692–2695.

Phibbs, Ciaren S., David A. Bateman, and Rachel M. Schwartz. "The Neonatal Costs of Maternal Cocaine Use." *JAMA* 266 (September 18, 1991), 1521–1527.

Pierce, John P., Lora Lee, and Elizabeth A. Gilpin. "Smoking Initiation by Adolescent Girls, 1944 Through 1988: An Association with Targeted Advertising." *JAMA* 271 (February 23, 1994), 608–611.

Rice, Dorothy P., Thomas A. Hodgson, Peter Sinsheimer, Warren Browner, and Andrea N. Kopstein. "The Economic Costs of the Health Effects of Smoking, 1984." *The Milbank Quarterly* 64, no. 4 (1986), 489–547.

Whitman, David. "The Untold Story of the LA Riot." *U.S. News & World Report* 114 (May 31, 1993), 34–59.

Yesalis, Charles E., Nancy J. Kennedy, Andrea N. Kopstein, and Michael S. Bahrke. "Anabolic-Androgenic Steroid Use in the United States." *JAMA* 270 (September 8, 1993), 1217–1221.

CHAPTER 5. TAKING THE PROFIT OUT OF POOR HEALTH

BOOKS AND REPORTS:

Behrman, Richard E. *Home Visiting*. Los Angeles: The David and Lucile Packard Foundation, Center for the Future of Children, Winter 1993.

Bell, Karen N., and Linda S. Simkin. *Caring Prescriptions: Comprehensive*

Health Care Strategies for Young Children in Poverty. New York: National Center for Children in Poverty, 1992.

Brown, Ruth E., Anne Elixhauser, John Corea, Bryan R. Kuce, and Steven Sheingold. *National Expenditures for Health Promotion and Disease Prevention Activities in the United States.* Washington, DC: Battelle, June 1991.

General Accounting Office. *Early Intervention: Federal Investment like WIC Can Produce Savings.* Washington, DC: GAO, April 1992.

———. *Emergency Departments: Unevenly Affected by Growth and Change in Patient Use.* Washington, DC: GAO, January 1993.

———. *Medicaid Prenatal Care: States Improve Access and Enhance Services, But Face New Challenges.* Washington, DC: GAO, May 1994.

———. *Preventive Health Care for Children: Experience from Selected Foreign Countries.* Washington, DC: GAO, August 1993.

Institute of Medicine. *Overcoming Barriers to Immunization.* Washington, DC: National Academy Press, 1994.

———. *Prenatal Care: Reaching Mothers, Reaching Infants.* Washington, DC: National Academy Press, 1988.

Klerman, Lorraine V. *Alive and Well? A Research and Policy Review of Health Programs for Poor Young Children.* New York: National Center for Children in Poverty, 1991.

Konner, Melvin. *Medicine at the Crossroads.* New York: Pantheon Books, 1993.

Last, John M., and Robert B. Wallace. *Public Health and Preventive Medicine.* Norwalk, CT: Appleton & Lange, 1992.

Loebs, Stephen F. *A Study of the Causes of Health Care Cost Increases in the State of Ohio and an Evaluation of Alternatives to Contain the Increases.* Columbus, OH: Ohio State University Research Foundation, 1992.

National Commission to Prevent Infant Mortality. *Troubling Trends Persist: Shortchanging America's Next Generation.* Washington, DC: NCPIM, March 1992.

National Committee for Injury Prevention and Control. *Injury Prevention: Meeting the Challenge.* New York: Oxford University Press, 1989.

National Coordinating Committee on Worksite Health Promotion. *Health Promotion Goes to Work, Programs with an Impact.* Washington, DC: Dept. of Health and Human Services, Office of Disease Prevention and Health Promotion, 1993.

Public Health Service. *Healthy People: The Surgeon General's Report on Health Promotion and Disease Prevention.* Washington, DC: Dept. of Health and Human Services, July 1979.

———. *Healthy People 2000: National Health Promotion and Disease Prevention Objectives.* Washington, DC: HHS, September 1990.

Rice, Dorothy P., Ellen J. MacKenzie, and associates. *Cost of Injury in the United States: A Report to Congress.* San Francisco: Institute for Health and Aging, University of California and Injury Prevention Center, The Johns Hopkins University, 1989.

Russell, Louise B. *Is Prevention Better Than Cure?* Washington, DC: The Brookings Institution, 1986.

U.S. Preventive Services Task Force. *Guide to Clinical Preventive Services: An Assessment of the Effectiveness of 169 Interventions.* Baltimore, MD: Williams & Wilkins, 1989.

ARTICLES:

Adler, Nancy E., Thomas Boyce, Margaret A. Chesney, Susan Folkman, and Leonard Syme. "Socioeconomic Inequalities in Health: No Easy Solution." *JAMA* 269 (June 23/30, 1993), 3140–3145.

Bly, Janet L., Robert C. Jones, and Jean E. Richardson. "Impact of Worksite Health Promotion on Health Care Costs and Utilization." *JAMA* 256 (December 19, 1986), 3235–3240.

Braveman, Paula, Trude Bennett, Charlotte Lewis, Susan Egerter, and Jonathan Showstack. "Access to Prenatal Care Following Major Medicaid Eligibility Expansions." *JAMA* 269 (March 10, 1993), 1285–1289.

Caplan, Arthur. "Sinners, Saints and Health Care: Personal Responsibility and Health Reform." *Northwest Report* 15 (April 1994), 20–23.

Carter, Michael F. "Financial Incentives for Wellness." *The Corporate Board* 13 (November/December 1992), 10–14.

Cole, Phillip, and Yaw Amoateng-Adjepong. "Cancer Prevention: Accomplishment and Prospects." *American Journal of Public Health* 84 (January 1994), 8–9.

Fialka, John J. "Demands on New Orleans's 'Big Charity' Hospital Are Symptomatic of U.S. Health-Care Problem." *The Wall Street Journal* (June 22, 1993), A16.

Fiatarone, Maria A., Evelyn F. O'Neill, Nancy Doyle Ryan, Karen M. Clements, Guido R. Solares, Miriam E. Nelson, Susan B. Roberts, Joseph J. Kehayias, Lewis A. Lipsitz, and William J. Evans. "Exercise Training and Nutrition Supplementation for Physical Frailty in Very Elderly People." *NEJM* 330 (June 23, 1994), 1769–1775.

Fielding, Jonathan E., William G. Cumberland, and Lynn Pettitt. "Immunization Status of Children of Employees in a Large Corporation." *JAMA* 271 (February 16, 1994), 525–530.

Fries, James F., C. Everett Koop, Carson E. Beadle, Paul P. Cooper, Mary Jane England, Robert Greaves, Jacque J. Sokolov, and Daniel Wright. "Reducing Health Care Costs by Reducing the Need and Demand for Medical Services." *NEJM* 329 (July 29, 1993), 321–325.

Goldman, Lee, and E. Francis Cook. "The Decline in Ischemic Heart Disease Mortality Rates: An Analysis of the Comparative Effects of Medical Intervention and Changes in Lifestyle." *Annals of Internal Medicine* 101 (December 1984), 825–836.

Haas, Jennifer S., Steven Udvarhelyi, and Arnold Epstein. "The Effect of Health Coverage for Uninsured Pregnant Women on Maternal Health and the Use of Cesarean Section." *JAMA* 270 (July 7, 1993), 61–64.

Haas, Jennifer S., Steven Udvarhelyi, Carl N. Morris, and Arnold M. Epstein. "The Effect of Providing Health Coverage to Poor Uninsured Pregnant Women in Massachusetts." *JAMA* 269 (January 6, 1993), 87–91.

Higgins, Millicent W., Paul L. Enright, Richard A. Kronmal, Marc B. Schenker, Hoda Anton-Culver, and Mary Lyles. "Smoking and Lung Function in Elderly Men and Women." *JAMA* 269 (June 2, 1993), 2741–2552.

Igra, Vivien, and Susan G. Millstein. "Current Status and Approaches to Improving Preventive Services for Adolescents." *JAMA* 269 (March 17, 1993), 1408–1412.

Katz, Steven J. and Timothy P. Hofer. "Socioeconomic Disparities in Preventive Care Persist Despite Universal Coverage." *JAMA* 272 (August 17, 1994), 530–534.

Kogan, Michael D., Greg R. Alexander, Milton Kotelchuck, and David Nagey. "Relation of the Content of Prenatal Care to the Risk of Low Birth Weight." *JAMA* 271 (May 4, 1994), 1340–1345.

Kottke, Thomas E., Renaldo N. Battista, Gordon H. Defriese, and Milo L. Brekke. "Attributes of Successful Smoking Cessation Interventions in Medical Practice: A Meta-Analysis of 39 Controlled Trials." *JAMA* 259 (May 20, 1988), 2883–2889.

Leaf, Alexander. "Preventive Medicine for Our Ailing Health Care System." *JAMA* 269 (February 3, 1993), 616–618.

Manton, Kenneth G., Larry S. Corder, and Eric Stallard. "Estimates of Change in Chronic Disability and Institutional Incidence and Prevalence Rates in the U.S. Elderly Population from the 1982, 1984 and 1989 National Long Term Care Survey." *Journal of Gerontology: Social Sciences* 48 (July 1993), 153–166.

Marwick, Charles, and Phil Gunby. "Survey Suggests Rise in Health Habit Complacency." *JAMA* 269 (April 28, 1993), 2061–2062.

Mendelson, Daniel M., and William B. Schwartz. "The Effects of Aging and Population Growth on Health Care Costs." *Health Affairs* 12 (Spring 1993), 119–125.

Miller, Anthony B. "How Do We Interpret the 'Bad News' About Cancer?" *JAMA* 271 (February 9, 1994), 468.

Pell, Sidney, and William E. Fayerweather. "Trends in the Incidence of Myocardial Infarction and in Associated Mortality and Morbidity in a

Large Employed Population, 1957–1983." *NEJM* 312 (April 18, 1985), 1005–1011.

Rawlings, James S., and Michael R. Weir. "Race- and Rank-Specific Infant Mortality in a U.S. Military Population." *American Journal of Diseases of Children* 146 (March 1992), 313–316.

Schlesinger, Mark, and Karl Kronebusch. "The Failure of Prenatal Care Policy for the Poor." *Health Affairs* 9 (Winter 1990), 91–111.

Schoendorf, Kenneth C., Carol J. R. Hogue, Joel C. Kleinman, and Diane Rowley. "Mortality Among Infants of Black as Compared with White College-Educated Parents." *NEJM* 326 (June 24, 1992), 1522–1526.

Selik, Richard M., Susan Y. Chu, and James W. Buehler. "HIV Infection as Leading Cause of Death Among Young Adults in US Cities and States." *JAMA* 269 (June 16, 1993), 2991–2994.

Taplin, Stephen H., Carolyn Anderman, Lou Grothaus, Susan Curry, and Daniel Montano. "Using Physician Correspondence and Postcard Reminders to Promote Mammography." *American Journal of Public Health* 84 (April 1994), 571–574.

Walsh, Diana Chapman, Ralph W. Hingson, Daniel M. Merrigan, Suzette M. Levenson, Gerald A. Coffman, Timothy Heeren, and Adrienne Cupples. "The Impact of a Physician's Warning on Recovery After Alcoholism Treatment." *JAMA* 267 (February 5, 1992), 663–668.

Walsh, Diana Chapman, Rima E. Rudd, Barbara A. Moeykens, and Thomas W. Moloney. "Social Marketing for Public Health." *Health Affairs* 121 (Summer 1993), 104–119.

Walter, Heather J., and Roger Vaughan. "AIDS Risk Reduction Among a Multiethnic Sample of Urban High School Students." *JAMA* 270 (August 11, 1993), 725–730.

Wilson, Douglas M., Wayne D. Taylor, Raymond J. Gilbert, Allan J. Best, Elizabeth A. Lindsay, Dennis G. Williams, and Joel Singer. "A Randomized Trial of a Family Physician Intervention for Smoking Cessation." *JAMA* 260 (September 16, 1988), 1570–1574.

CHAPTER 6. A REALITY CHECK FOR RESEARCH

BOOKS AND REPORTS:

Carnegie Corporation of New York. *Starting Points: Meeting the Needs of Our Youngest Children.* New York: Carnegie Corp., April 1994.

Committee on Assessing Genetic Risks, Institute of Medicine. *Assessing Genetic Risks: Implications for Health and Social Policy.* Washington, DC: National Academy Press, 1994.

Committee on Technological Innovation in Medicine, Institute of Medicine. *Medical Innovation at the Crossroads, Vol. 4: Adopting New Medical Technology.* Washington, DC: National Academy Press, 1994.

Hamburg, David. *Today's Children: Creating a Future for a Generation in Crisis.* New York: Times Books, 1992.

Institute of Medicine. *Disability in America: Toward a National Agenda for Prevention.* Washington, DC: National Academy Press, 1991.

————. *Extending Life, Enhancing Life: A National Research Agenda on Aging.* Washington, DC: National Academy Press, 1991.

————. *Funding Health Sciences Research: A Strategy to Restore Balance.* Washington, DC: National Academy Press, 1990.

Millstein, Susan G., Elena O. Nightingale, and Anne C. Petersen, eds. *Promoting the Health of Adolescents: New Directions for the Twentieth Century.* New York: Oxford University Press, 1993.

National Commission on Children. *Beyond Rhetoric: A New American Agenda for Children and Families.* Washington, DC: NCC, 1991.

National Institutes of Health. *Health Research Principles: Documents Relating to the Development of Draft Health Research Principles for the Department of Health, Education, and Welfare,* Vol. 1. Washington, DC: NIH, 1979.

————. *NIH Data Book 1993.* Washington, DC: NIH, September 1993.

Nuland, Sherwin B. *How We Die.* New York: Alfred A. Knopf, 1994.

Office of Technology Assessment. *Adolescent Health, Vol. 1: Summary and Policy Options.* Washington, DC: OTA, 1991.

————. *Life-sustaining Technologies and the Elderly.* Washington, DC: OTA, 1987.

————. *Losing a Million Minds: Confronting the Tragedy of Alzheimer's Disease and Other Dementia.* Washington, DC: OTA, 1987.

————. *Special Care Units for People with Alzheimer's and Other Dementias.* Washington, DC: OTA, 1987.

Pepper Commission, U.S. Bipartisan Commission on Comprehensive Health Care. *A Call for Action.* Washington, DC: U.S. Government Printing Office, 1990.

President's Cancer Panel, Special Commission on Breast Cancer. *Breast Cancer: A National Strategy, A Report to the Nation.* Bethesda, MD: National Cancer Institute, October 1993.

ARTICLES:

Allen, Marilee C., Pamela K. Donahue, and Amy E. Dusman. "The Limit of Viability—Neonatal Outcome of Infants Born at 22 to 25 Weeks' Gestation." *NEJM* 329 (November 25, 1993), 1597–1601.

Anders, George. "Hospitals Rush to Buy a $3 Million Device Few Patients Can Use." *The Wall Street Journal* (April 20, 1994), A1.

Barker, William H. "Prevention of Disability in Older Persons." In *Maxcy-Rosenau-Last Public Health and Preventive Medicine,* ed. John M. Last and Robert B. Wallace. Norwalk, CT: Appleton and Lange, 1992, 973–981.

Cleeland, Charles S., Rene Gonin, Alan K. Hatfield, John H. Edmonson, Ronald H. Blum, James A. Stewart, and Kishan J. Pandya. "Pain and Its Treatment in Outpatients with Metastatic Cancer." *NEJM* 330 (March 3, 1994), 592–596.

Evans, Denis A., Paul A. Scherr, Nancy R. Cook, Marilyn S. Albert, Harris H. Funkenstein, Laurel A. Smith, Liesi E. Hebert, Terrie T. Wetle, Laurence G. Branch, Marilyn Chown, Charles H. Hennekens, and James O. Taylor. "Estimated Prevalence of Alzheimer's Disease in the United States." *The Milbank Quarterly*, 68, no. 2 (1990), 267–290.

Fields, Bernard N. "AIDS: Time to Turn to Basic Science." *Nature* 369 (May 12, 1994), 95–96.

Grimes, David A. "Technology Follies: The Uncritical Acceptance of Medical Innovation." *JAMA* 269 (June 16, 1993), 3030–3033.

Healy, Bernadine. "Shattuck Lecture—NIH and the Bodies Politic." *NEJM* 330 (May 26, 1994), 1493–1498.

Hunnewell, Susannah. "The Medical-Industrial Complex." *Harvard Magazine* 96 (January–February 1994), 34–37.

Jones, Howard W., and James P. Toner. "The Infertile Couple." *NEJM* 329 (December 2, 1993), 1710–1715.

Legorreta, Antonio P., Jeffrey H. Silber, George N. Costantino, Richard W. Kobylinski, and Steven L. Zatz. "Increased Cholecystectomy Rate After the Introduction of Laparoscopic Cholecystectomy." *JAMA* 270 (September 22/29, 1993), 1429–1432.

Morell, Virginia. "Evidence Found for a Possible 'Aggression' Gene." *Science* 260 (June 18, 1993), 1722.

Ray, Wayne A., and Marie R. Griffin. "Evaluating Drugs After Their Approval for Clinical Use." *NEJM* 329 (December 30, 1993), 2029–2032.

Ray, Wayne A., Jo A. Taylor, Keith G. Meader, Michael J. Lichtenstein, Marie R. Griffin, Randy Fought, Margaret Adams, and Dan Blazer. "Reducing Antipsychotic Drug Use in Nursing Homes." *Archives of Internal Medicine* 153 (March 22, 1993), 713–721.

Rice, Dorothy P., Patrick J. Fox, Wendy Max, Pamela A. Webber, David A. Lindeman, Walter W. Hauck, and Ernestine Segura. "The Economic Burden of Alzheimer's Disease Care." *Health Affairs* 1212 (Summer 1993), 164–176.

Rosenthal, Elisabeth. "Hardest Medical Choices Shift to Patients." *The New York Times* (January 27, 1994), A1.

Royte, Elizabeth. "The Stork Market." *Lear's* 6 (December 1993), 52–87.

Schapira, David A., James Studnicki, Douglas D. Bradham, Peter Wolff, and Anne Jarrett. "Intensive Care, Survival and Expense of Treating Critically Ill Cancer Patients." *JAMA* 269 (February 10, 1993), 783–786.

Schroeder, Steven A. "A Comparison of Western European and U.S. University Hospitals: A Case Report from Leuven, West Berlin, Leiden, London, and San Francisco." *JAMA* 252 (July 13, 1984), 240–246.

Shorr, Ronald I., Randy L. Fought, and Wayne A. Ray. "Changes in Antipsychotic Drug Use in Nursing Homes During Implementation of the OBRA-87 Regulations." *JAMA* 271 (February 2, 1994), 358–362.

Solomon, Mildred Z., Lydia O'Donnell, Bruce Jennings, Vivian Guilfoy, Susan Wolf, Kathleen Nolan, Rebecca Jackson, Dieter Koch-Weser, and Strachan Donnelley. "Decisions near the End of Life: Professional Views on Life-Sustaining Treatments." *American Journal of Public Health* 83 (January 1993), 14–23.

Steiner, Claudia A., Eric B. Bass, Mark A. Talamini, Henry A. Pitt, and Earl Steinberg. "Surgical Rates and Operative Mortality for Open and Laparoscopic Cholecystectomy in Maryland." *NEJM* 330 (February 10, 1994), 403–408.

Stoddard, Jeffrey J., Robert F. St. Peter, and Paul W. Newacheck. "Health Insurance Status and Ambulatory Care for Children." *NEJM* 330 (May 19, 1994), 1421–1425.

Wilfond, Benjamin S., and Kathleen Nolan. "National Policy Development for the Clinical Application of Genetic Diagnostic Technologies: Lessons from Cystic Fibrosis." *JAMA* 270 (December 22/29, 1993), 2948–2954.

CHAPTER 7. BUSTING THE MEDICAL MONOPOLIES

BOOKS AND REPORTS:

American Nurses' Association. *Nurse Practitioner and Certified Nurse-Midwives, A Meta-Analysis of Studies on Nurses in Primary Care Roles.* Washington, DC: American Nursing Publishing, 1993.

Council on Graduate Medical Education. *Improving Access to Health Care Through Physician Workforce Reform: Directions for the 21st Century.* Washington, DC: Dept. of Health and Human Services, Health Resources and Services Administration, October 1992.

Flexner, Abraham. *Medical Education in the United States and Canada, A Report to the Carnegie Foundation for the Advancement of Teaching.* 1910; rpt. Bethesda, MD: Science and Health Publications, 1950.

General Accounting Office. *Medicare: Referring Physicians' Ownership of Laboratories and Imaging Centers.* Washington, DC: GAO, June 1989.

Henderson, Tim, and Teresa Chovan. *Removing Practice Barriers of Nonphysician Providers, Efforts by States to Improve Access to Primary Care.* Washington, DC: George Washington University, Intergovernmental Health Policy Project, February 1994.

Mezey, Mathy D., and Diane O. McGivern, eds. *Nurses, Nurse Practitioners, Evolution to Advanced Practice.* New York: Springer Publishing Company, 1993.

Office of the Inspector General. *Enhancing the Utilization of Nonphysician Health Care Providers.* Washington, DC: Dept. of Health and Human Services, May 1993.

Office of Technology Assessment. *Defensive Medicine and Medical Malpractice*. Washington, DC: OTA, July 1994.

————. *Impact of Legal Reforms on Medical Malpractice Costs*. Washington, DC: OTA, September 1993.

————. *Nurse Practitioners, Physician Assistants, and Certified Nurse-Midwives: A Policy Analysis*. Washington, DC: OTA, December 1986.

Pew Health Professions Commission. *Nurse Practitioners—Doubling the Graduates by the Year 2000*. San Francisco: University of California at San Francisco Center for the Health Professions, 1994.

Rubin, Robert J., and Daniel N. Mendelson. *Estimating the Costs of Defensive Medicine*. Fairfax, VA: Lewin-VHI, Inc., January 27, 1993.

Rutkow, Ira M. *Surgery: An Illustrated History*. St. Louis, MO: Mosby-Year Book Inc., 1994.

Starr, Paul. *The Social Transformation of American Medicine*. New York: Basic Books, 1982.

VanTuinen, Ingrid, Phyllis McCarthy, Sidney Wolfe, and Alana Bame. *Comparing State Medical Boards*. Washington, DC: Public Citizen's Health Research Group, January 1993.

Weiler, Paul C. *Medical Malpractice on Trial*. Cambridge, MA: Harvard University Press, 1991.

Weiler, Paul C., Howard H. Hiatt, Joseph P. Newhouse, William G. Johnson, Troyen A. Brennan, and Lucian L. Leape. *A Measure of Malpractice: Medical Injury, Malpractice Litigation, and Patient Compensation*. Cambridge, MA: Harvard University Press, 1993.

ARTICLES:

Brook, Robert H. "Practice Guidelines and Practicing Medicine: Are They Compatible?" *JAMA* 262 (December 1, 1989), 3027–3030.

Burda, David. "JCAHO Hits a Wall with Plan on Indicators," *Modern Healthcare* 24 (March 14, 1994), 30–40.

Chren, Mary-Margaret, and C. Seth Landerfeld. "Physicians' Behavior and Their Interactions with Drug Companies, A Controlled Study of Physicians Who Requested Additions to a Hospital Drug Formulary." *JAMA* 271 (March 2, 1994), 684–689.

Cooper, Richard A. "Seeking a Balanced Physician Workforce for the 21st Century." *JAMA* 272 (September 7, 1994), 680–687.

Grabowski, Henry. "Medicaid Patients' Access to New Drugs." *Health Affairs* 7 (Winter 1988), 102–114.

Greenfield, Sheldon, Eugene C. Nelson, Michael Zubkoff, Willard Manning, William Rogers, Richard L. Kravitz, Adam Keller, Alvin Tarlov, and John E. Ware, Jr. "Variations in Resource Utilization Among Medical Specialties and Systems of Care." *JAMA* 267 (March 25, 1992), 1624–1630.

Iglehart, John K. "Efforts to Address the Problem of Physician Self-Referral." *NEJM* 325 (December 19, 1991), 1820–1824.

———. "Health Care Reform and Graduate Medical Education." *NEJM* 330 (April 21, 1994), 1167–1171.

Jones, P. Eugene, and James F. Cawley. "Physician Assistants and Health System Reform." *JAMA* 271 (April 27, 1994), 1266–1272.

Kassirer, Jerome P. "What Role for Nurse Practitioners in Primary Care?" *NEJM* 330 (January 20, 1994), 204–205.

Keeler, Emmett B., Lisa V. Rubenstein, Katherine L. Kahn, David Draper, Ellen R. Harrison, Michael J. McGinty, William H. Rogers, and Robert H. Brook. "Hospital Characteristics and Quality of Care." *JAMA* 268 (October 7, 1992), 1709–1714.

Leape, Lucian L., Ann G. Lawthers, Troyen A. Brennan, and William G. Johnson. "Preventing Medical Injury." *Quality Review Bulletin* 19 (May 1993), 144–149.

Localio, A. Russell, Ann G. Lawthers, Joan M. Bengtson, Liesi E. Hebert, Susan L. Weaver, Troyen A. Brennan, and J. Richard Landis. "Relationship Between Malpractice Claims and Cesarean Delivery." *JAMA* 269 (January 20, 1993), 366–373.

Mitchell, Jean M., and Jonathan H. Sunshine. "Consequences of Physicians' Ownership of Health Care Facilities—Joint Ventures in Radiation Therapy." *NEJM* 327 (November 19, 1992), 1497–1501.

Morrissey, John. "The JCAHO's Agenda for Expansion." *Modern Healthcare* 24 (March 28, 1994), 34–40.

Mundinger, Mary O. "Advanced-Practice Nursing—Good Medicine for Physicians?" *NEJM* 330 (January 20, 1994), 211–214.

Ortega, Bob. "State Medical Boards Let Doctors Who Move Escape Any Discipline." *The Wall Street Journal* (November 11, 1992), A1.

Pearson, Linda J. "Annual Update of How Each State Stands on Legislative Issues Affecting Advanced Nursing Practice." *The Nurse Practitioner* 19 (January 1994), 11–53.

Roberts, James S., Jack G. Coale, and Robert R. Redman. "A History of the Joint Commission on Accreditation of Hospitals." *JAMA* 258 (August 21, 1987), 936–940.

Rooks, Judith P., Norman L. Weatherly, Eunice K. M. Ernst, Susan Stapleton, David Rosen, and Allan Rosenfield. "Outcomes of Care in Birth Centers, the National Birth Center Study." *NEJM* 321 (December 28, 1989), 1804–1811.

Safriet, Barbara J. "Health Care Dollars and Regulatory Sense: The Role of Advanced Practice Nursing." *Yale Journal on Regulation* 9 (Summer 1992), 417–488.

Schroeder, Steven A. "Reform and the Physician Work Force." *Domestic Affairs* 2 (Winter 1993/1994), 105–131.

Schroeder, Steven A., and Lewis G. Sandy. "Specialty Distribution of U.S. Physicians—The Invisible Driver of Health Care Costs." *NEJM* 328 (April 1, 1993), 961–963.

Swedlow, Alex, Gregory Johnson, Neil Smithline, and Arnold Milstein. "Increased Costs and Rates of Use in the California Workers' Compensation System as a Result of Self-Referral by Physicians." *NEJM* 327 (November 19, 1992), 1502–1506.

Wennberg, John E., David C. Goodman, Robert F. Nease, and Robert B. Keller. "Finding Equilibrium in U.S. Physician Supply." *Health Affairs* 12 (Summer 1993), 89–103.

TESTIMONY:

Statement of Troyen A. Brennan, Professor of Law and Public Health, Department of Health Policy and Management, Harvard School of Public Health. "Medical Malpractice and Health Care Reform," before the House Subcommittee on Health and the Environment, Committee on Energy and Commerce, November 10, 1993.

Statement of Janet L. Shikles, Director, Health Financing and Policy Issues, Human Resources Division, General Accounting Office. "Medicare, Physicians Who Invest in Imaging Center Refer More Patients for More Costly Services," before the House Subcommittee on Health, Committee on Ways and Means, April 20, 1993.

Statement of Lawrence H. Thompson, Assistant Comptroller General, Human Resources Division, General Accounting Office. "Medical Malpractice, Experience with Efforts to Address Problems," before the House Subcommittee on Health, Committee on Ways and Means, May 20, 1993.

CHAPTER 8. FREE THE CONGRESSIONAL 535

BOOKS AND REPORTS:

Center for Public Integrity. *Well-Healed: Inside Lobbying for Health Care Reform*. Washington, DC: CPI, 1994.

Center for Responsive Politics. *Money and Politics: PACs on PACs, the View from the Inside*. Washington, DC: CRP, 1988.

Citizens Fund. *Unhealthy Money*, parts VII–X. Washington, DC: Citizens Fund, 1993–94.

Cohen, William S. *Tax Dollars Aiding and Abetting Addiction: Social Security Disability and SSI Cash Benefits to Drug Addicts and Alcoholics*. Washington, DC: Minority Staff of the Senate Special Committee on Aging, February 7, 1994.

Common Cause. *Hazardous to Your Health: A Member-by-Member Scorecard of Medical-Industry PAC Contributions to Current Members of Congress, January 1, 1983–May 31, 1993*. Washington, DC: Common Cause, September 1993.

Employee Benefit Research Institute. *Sources of Health Insurance and Characteristics of the Uninsured*. Washington, DC: EBRI, January 1994.

Federal Election Commission. *PAC Activity Rebounds in 1991–92 Election Cycle*. Washington, DC: FEC, April 29, 1993.

Makinson, Larry. *The Price of Admission: Campaign Spending in the 1992 Elections*. Washington, DC: Center for Responsive Politics, 1993.

Makinson, Larry, and Joshua Goldstein. *Open Secrets: The Encyclopedia of Congressional Money and Politics*. Washington, DC: Congressional Quarterly, Inc., 1992.

Samuels, Bruce, Clifford Douglas, Sidney Wolfe, and Phillip Wilbur. *Tobacco Money, Tobacco People, Tobacco Policies*. Washington, DC: Public Citizen's Health Research Group and the Advocacy Institute, August 1992.

Watzman, Nancy. *Government Service for Sale: How the Revolving Door Has Been Spinning*. Washington, DC: Public Citizen's Congress Watch, September 1993.

Wolfe, Sidney, Clifford Douglas, Phillip Wilbur, Michael Kirshenbaum, Phyllis McCarthy, Alana Bame, and Durrie McKnew. *The Congressional Addiction to Tobacco: How the Tobacco Lobby Suffocates Federal Health Policy*. Washington, DC: Public Citizen's Health Research Group and the Advocacy Institute, October 1992.

ARTICLES:

Glantz, Stanton A. and Michael E. Begay. "Tobacco Industry Campaign Contributions Are Affecting Tobacco Control Policymaking in California." *JAMA* 272 (October 19, 1994), 1176–1182.

Levit, Katharine R., Gary L. Olin, and Suzanne W. Letsch. "Americans' Health Insurance Coverage, 1980–91." *Health Care Financing Review* 14 (Fall 1992), 31–57.

Moore, Stephen, Sidney M. Wolfe, Deborah Lindes, and Clifford E. Douglas. "Epidemiology of Failed Tobacco Control Legislation." *JAMA* 272 (October 19, 1994), 1171–1175.

Schmitt, Richard B. "Trial Lawyers Glide Past Critics With Aid of Potent Trade Group." *The Wall Street Journal* (February 17, 1994), A1.

Warner, Kenneth E. "Profits of Doom." *American Journal of Public Health* 83 (September 1993), 1211–1213.

CHAPTER 9. WHAT NEXT?

BOOKS AND REPORTS:

Office of Technology Assessment. *Biomedical Ethics in U.S. Public Policy—Background Paper.* Washington, DC: OTA, June 1993.

Oregon Health Services Commission. *Prioritization of Health Services: A Report to the Governor and Legislature.* Portland, OR: Oregon Dept. of Human Resources, OHSC, 1993.

ARTICLES:

Beckman, Howard B., Kathryn M. Markakis, Anthony L. Suchman, and Richard M. Frankel. "The Doctor-Patient Relationship and Malpractice." *Archives of Internal Medicine* 154 (June 27, 1994), 1365–1370.

Bell, Nora K. "Ethics Committees: Providing Moral Guidance in the Hospital." *Trustee: The Magazine for Hospital Governing Boards* 46 (April 1993), 6–8.

Brook, Robert H., Caren J. Kamberg, Allison Mayer-Oakes, Mark H. Beers, Kristina Raube, and Andrea Steiner. "Appropriateness of Acute Medical Care for the Elderly: An Analysis of the Literature." *Health Policy* 14 (1990), 225–242.

Chambers, Christopher, James J. Diamond, Robert Peritel, and Lori A. Lasch. "Relationship of Advance Directives to Hospital Charges in a Medicare Population." *Archives of Internal Medicine* 154 (March 14, 1994), 541–547.

Emanuel, Ezekiel J., and Linda L. Emanuel. "The Economics of Dying: The Illusion of Cost Savings at the End of Life." *NEJM* 330 (February 24, 1994), 540–544.

Fein, Esther B. "Fetal Test Focuses the Health-Care Debate." *The New York Times* (January 5, 1994), A1.

Franks, Peter, Carolyn M. Clancy, and Paul A. Nutting. "Gatekeeping Revisited: Protecting Patients from Overtreatment." *NEJM* 327 (August 6, 1992), 424–429.

Greco, Peter J., Kevin A. Schulman, Risa Lavizzo-Mourey, and John Hansen-Flaschen. "The Patient Self-Determination Act and the Future of Advance Directives." *Annals of Internal Medicine* 115 (October 15, 1991), 639–643.

Jayes, Robert L., Jack E. Zimmerman, Douglas P. Wagner, Elizabeth A. Draper, and William A. Knaus. "Do-Not-Resuscitate Orders in Intensive Care Units." *JAMA* 270 (November 10, 1993), 2213–2217.

Kolata, Gina. "When the Dying Enroll in Studies: A Debate Over False Hopes." *The New York Times* (January 29, 1994), A6.

Lee, David K. P., Andrew J. Swinburne, Anthony J. Fedullo, and Gary W.

Wahl. "Withdrawing Care: Experience in a Medical Intensive Care Unit." *JAMA* 271 (May 4, 1994), 1358–1361.

Murphy, Donald J., David Burrows, Sara Santilli, Anne W. Kemp, Scott Tenner, Barbara Kreling, and Joan Teno. "The Influence of the Probability of Survival on Patients' Preferences Regarding Cardiopulmonary Resuscitation." *NEJM* 330 (February 24, 1994), 545–549.

Rodrick, Stephen. "Upward Motility." *The New Republic* 210 (May 16, 1994), 9–10.

Rubin, Susan M., William M. Strull, Michael F. Fialkow, Sarah J. Weiss, and Bernard Lo. "Increasing the Completion of the Durable Power of Attorney for Health Care." *JAMA* 271 (January 19, 1994), 209–212.

Virmani, Jaya, Lawrence J. Schneiderman, and Robert M. Kaplan. "Relationship of Advance Directives to Physician-Patient Communication." *Archives of Internal Medicine* 154 (April 25, 1994), 909–913.

Wennberg, John E., Albert G. Mulley, Daniel Hanley, Robert P. Timothy, Floyd J. Fowler, Jr., Noralou P. Roos, Michael J. Barry, Kim McPherson, E. Robert Greenberg, David Soule, Thomas Bubolz, Elliott Fisher, and David Malenka. "An Assessment of Prostatectomy for Benign Urinary Tract Obstruction." *JAMA* 259 (May 27, 1988), 3027–3030.

Wilfond, Benjamin S., and Kathleen Nolan. "National Policy Development for the Clinical Application of Genetic Diagnostic Technologies." *JAMA* 270 (December 22/29, 1993), 2948–2954.

About the Author

Joseph A. Califano, Jr. was born on May 15, 1931, in Brooklyn, New York, where he grew up. He received his Bachelor of Arts degree from the College of the Holy Cross in 1952 and his LL.B. from Harvard Law School in 1955. After service in the Navy and three years with Governor Thomas Dewey's Wall Street law firm, he joined the Kennedy administration and served in the Pentagon as Secretary of Defense Robert McNamara's special assistant and top troubleshooter.

President Lyndon Johnson named Mr. Califano his special assistant for domestic affairs in 1965 and he served in that post until the president left office in January 1969. During his years on the White House staff, Mr. Califano worked on the Medicare and Medicaid programs and helped shape more than two dozen bills related to health care. *The New York Times* called him "Deputy President for Domestic Affairs." At the end of his term, President Johnson wrote to Mr. Califano, "You were the captain I wanted and you steered the course well."

From 1969 to 1977, Mr. Califano practiced law in Washington, D.C., and served as attorney for *The Washington Post* and its reporters Bob Woodward and Carl Bernstein, *Newsweek,* and others during the Watergate years.

From 1977 to 1979, Mr. Califano was secretary of Health, Education and Welfare and became the first voice to alert the nation to the explosion of health care costs and teenage pregnancy, mounted an aggressive antismoking campaign, began computer policing of Medicare and Medicaid to eliminate fraud and abuse, and issued the first Surgeon General's Report on Health Promotion and Disease Prevention.

From 1979 to 1992, Mr. Califano practiced law in Washington, D.C. In 1992, he founded the Center on Addiction and Substance Abuse at Columbia University and he serves as the Center's chairman and president. He is adjunct professor of health policy and management at Columbia University's Medical School and School of Public Health and a member of the governing council of the Institute of Medicine of the National Academy of Sciences. He is an expert in health care policy and consults and lectures about America's health care system. He serves on the boards of several corporations and nonprofit institutions with interests in health care.

Mr. Califano is the author of eight previous books (two with Howard Simons, former managing editor of *The Washington Post*) and has written articles for *The New York Times, The Washington Post, Reader's Digest, The New Republic,* and other publications. He is married to Hilary Paley Byers and lives in Roxbury, Connecticut. He has three children, Mark, Joseph III, and Claudia, and two stepchildren, Brooke Byers Goldman and John F. Byers IV.